The Open University

The frozen planet

Mark Brandon and David Robinson

This publication forms part of the Open University module S175 *The frozen planet*. Details of this and other Open University modules can be obtained from the Student Registration and Enquiry Service, The Open University, PO Box 197, Milton Keynes MK7 6BJ, United Kingdom (tel. +44 (0)845 300 60 90; email general-enquiries@open.ac.uk).

Alternatively, you may visit the Open University website at www.open.ac.uk where you can learn more about the wide range of modules and packs offered at all levels by The Open University.

To purchase a selection of Open University materials visit www.ouw.co.uk, or contact Open University Worldwide, Walton Hall, Milton Keynes MK7 6AA, United Kingdom for a brochure (tel. +44 (0)1908 858793; fax +44 (0)1908 858787; email ouw-customer-services@open.ac.uk).

The Open University, Walton Hall, Milton Keynes MK7 6AA

First published 2011

Edited and designed by The Open University.

Typeset by The Open University

Printed in the United Kingdom by Latimer Trend and Company Ltd, Plymouth.

ISBN 978 1 8487 3692 4

1.1

Contents

Preface   1

1   The frozen planet   3
     1.1   Introduction   3
     1.2   The temperature in the polar regions   4
     1.3   A flat map of a spherical world   10
     1.4   The energy balance   14
     1.5   Energy from the Sun   18
     1.6   Defining the Arctic and Antarctic   23
     1.7   Conclusions   29
     1.8   Summary of Chapter 1   29

2   Frozen in time   31
     2.1   Introduction   31
     2.2   Deep time and planet Earth   31
     2.3   The climate history of the planet   39
     2.4   From the last glacial maximum to the present day   57
     2.5   Conclusions   60
     2.6   Summary of Chapter 2   61

3   The drive to the poles   63
     3.1   Introduction   63
     3.2   The first polar peoples   64
     3.3   European contact: the rush for resources   66
     3.4   Science has always been a motivation   72
     3.5   The modern era of polar research   78
     3.6   A modern Antarctic field trip   80
     3.7   Remote science in the modern age   84
     3.8   Conclusions   88
     3.9   Summary of Chapter 3   89

4   The poles and global climate   91
     4.1   Introduction   91
     4.2   The winds and the waves   91
     4.3   The frozen seas   97
     4.4   Small-scale processes, big results: the effect of sea ice on the
            ocean   105
     4.5   The frozen climate of the frozen planet   111
     4.6   Conclusions   120
     4.7   Summary of Chapter 4   120

5   Life in the polar regions   123
     5.1   Introduction   123
     5.2   Endothermic animals   126
     5.3   Marine ectotherms   138
     5.4   Adaptations of plants   141

	5.5	Conclusions	146
	5.6	Summary of Chapter 5	146
6		Habitats and ecosystems	147
	6.1	Introduction	147
	6.2	Defining an ecosystem	147
	6.3	The biomes of the frozen planet	153
	6.4	Conclusions	165
	6.5	Summary of Chapter 6	166
7		Polar oceans and food chains	167
	7.1	Introduction	167
	7.2	Seawater and marine biology	167
	7.3	The ingredients for primary production: light, mixing and nutrients	170
	7.4	The sea ice and biological production	181
	7.5	The oceanic food chain	182
	7.6	Oases in the winter pack ice – polynyas	186
	7.7	Conclusions	189
	7.8	Summary of Chapter 7	190
8		The management of the polar regions	191
	8.1	Introduction	191
	8.2	The Antarctic: activities and impacts	191
	8.3	The Arctic: activities and impacts	198
	8.4	Climate change	200
	8.5	Laws and protocols – managing the threats to the polar regions	206
	8.6	The polar regions and the issues ahead	213
	8.7	Conclusions	214
	8.8	Summary of Chapter 8	214
9		The future for the frozen planet	217
	9.1	Introduction	217
	9.2	The climate of the next 100 years	217
	9.3	The future of Arctic ice over the next 100 years	220
	9.4	The future of Antarctic ice over the next 100 years	222
	9.5	Global sea-level rise over the next 100 years	222
	9.6	Thermohaline disruption	224
	9.7	The future of polar wildlife	224
	9.8	Preserving the 'frozen planet'	225
	9.9	Summary of Chapter 9	227
Answers and comments			229
References			241
Acknowledgements			242
Module team			246
Index			247

Preface

Welcome to S175 *The frozen planet*, a cross-disciplinary module on the science of the polar regions. Written by academics with expertise in different areas of the wide-ranging subject matter, the module explores the biology and ecology of the polar regions, the global climate, the influence of humans on the environment and the history, management and future of the polar regions. Some of the team have spent several years living and working in the Arctic and Antarctic (one has even walked to the South Pole!) and are polar experts. Other team members are expert in different aspects of science – together the contrasting voices represent the true polar spirit of working together within a team.

You should think of this study book as your main focus point for the module. As you work through the study materials, it is important to study 'actively'. This means taking your time and thinking about what you are reading, and checking your understanding by completing the activities and questions.

The study book will indicate when to undertake in-text activities to help you to understand concepts and develop and practise particular skills. It will also tell you when to go to the S175 website to complete online activities (indicated by ▤) and when to complete a practical activity (indicated by ⬠). Ideally you should do each activity as you come to it, or as soon as possible thereafter. You are given an indication of how long the activity should take; this is an estimate and you may find you take more or less time than suggested.

In this study book, there are two styles of question: the first type (indicated by ■) is immediately followed by its answer (indicated by □) and can be thought of as a 'pause for thought' question, designed to encourage you to stop and think. The other type of question is numbered (e.g. Question 2.1) and is designed to test your understanding of different topics. With these questions you should always try to write out your answer in full before comparing them with those at the end of the book.

Throughout the study book, you will be provided with advice about how to study actively and will see examples of different ways of doing this.

I   The frozen planet

I.I   Introduction

The parts of our planet that are covered with ice – the so-called frozen planet – have captured human imagination for thousands of years. Restricted to high mountains and towards the poles, they have low human populations but have been the focus of interest from nations, explorers, business people and scientists. In this module the discussion will concentrate on the largest component of the frozen planet, which is closest to the poles: the Arctic to the north and the Antarctic to the south. It was the Ancient Greeks who gave us their names. They were aware of and had perhaps even visited the Arctic, which they called *Arktos*. They imagined there must be a similar but opposite cold southern landmass to balance the world so they coined the name '*Ant Arktos*', which has developed into the Antarctic. Superficially the two polar regions are very different but they also have many similarities (Figure 1.1).

(a)   (b)

Figure 1.1   Two views of the frozen planet with both showing ice- and snow-covered polar landscapes. (a) An Arctic landscape. (b) An Antarctic landscape.

In this module you will investigate and discover the processes that have shaped the polar world and its wildlife. In this first section there are two activities involving material from popular nature documentaries. You are advised to complete both of them before moving on to the subsequent sections. The first activity investigates your current knowledge of the polar regions.

Activity 1.1   Your personal view of the frozen planet

The estimated time for this activity is 15 minutes.

The aim of this activity is for you to write down your initial thoughts about the polar regions without doing any research. So please jot down your responses to the following questions, answering first for the Arctic, and then the Antarctic.

(a) What three images or impressions come to mind?

(b) What three words, phrases or names do you first think of?

(c) What is the last news story you remember about each region?

(d) Who owns it?

Once you have noted down your thoughts, take a look at the notes on this activity in the Comments section at the back of the book.

The defining feature of the polar environment is the cold so it would not be surprising if in your answers to Activity 1.1 you had mentioned it. Then there is the wildlife, the history of exploration, the isolation, the beauty and so on. Fundamentally the polar regions are most likely *all* of the things you mentioned in your answer to Activity 1.1 but they are not geographically isolated. In this module you will discover why the poles are cold, and investigate key features of the frozen planet including its history, its climate, the biological habitats and food webs, its governance and finally its future. You will discover that processes operating at the poles affect all of us and consequently their future is our future.

Activity 1.2   The poles: the most beautiful places on our planet

The estimated time for this activity is 60 minutes.

It is hard to do justice to the extremes and beauty of the polar environment with words. In this activity you will watch video clips from some popular nature documentaries to give an overview of the polar system. Within the clips the narrator makes many statements about the regions and you will revisit these statements throughout the module.

The detailed notes for this activity are in the 'Activities' section of the S175 website.

1.2   The temperature in the polar regions

One of the defining features of the frozen planet is the incredible cold. The polar climate will be covered in detail in Chapter 4, but for now you will investigate the climate by comparing and contrasting temperatures from two different locations in the polar regions. Figure 1.2 shows the average (mean) atmospheric surface temperature from two research stations, one in the Southern Hemisphere at the South Pole, and one in the Northern Hemisphere at a Canadian town called Alert on the edge of the Arctic Ocean.

The mean monthly atmospheric surface temperature is the average of the temperature data collected at that location during each calendar month.

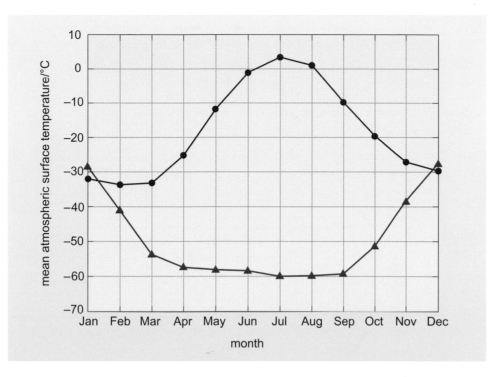

Figure 1.2   The mean monthly atmospheric surface temperatures recorded at research stations based at the South Pole, Antarctica, and at a Canadian town, called Alert, on the edge of the Arctic Ocean.

Looking at the two lines in Figure 1.2, the temperatures are reasonably close in the months of January and December but between these two months the lines diverge significantly until in July there is a difference of over 60 °C between them.

■   Which of the two lines in Figure 1.2 represents the mean atmospheric surface temperature from Alert and which line represents the temperature at the South Pole?

☐   Alert station is in the Northern Hemisphere which should have the warmest temperatures in June, July and August – so the black line (circles) represents measurements from Alert. Therefore, the red line (triangles) represents the temperature recorded at the South Pole.

Box 1.1 explains the different features of graphs and describes how averages or means are calculated.

Box 1.1   Graphs, averages and means

Graphs are diagrams that show the relationship between two different quantities. The quantities and their values are displayed on two reference lines, called the axes, that are at right angles to one another and the axes are marked to show the range of possible values of the quantities. For example, in Figure 1.2 the axes are temperature and month. In graphs, the relationship is shown by a straight line or a curve of plotted points (the points may or may not be shown), so Figure 1.2 shows the relationship between mean atmospheric surface temperature and time given by the months of the year; in other words, how atmospheric surface temperature varies over the annual cycle. With this information, one can now find corresponding values for the two quantities that are plotted. As with all scientific diagrams, graphs follow a set of clear conventions, which are highlighted in Figure 1.3.

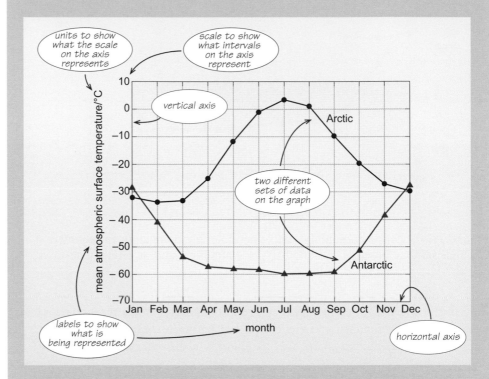

Figure 1.3   A version of Figure 1.2 with labels showing particular terms common to graphs.

The two quantities being described, mean atmospheric surface temperature and month, are represented by the vertical and horizontal axes, respectively. Each axis is labelled clearly to indicate what units are used, and has a marked scale. In this example, the vertical axis represents mean atmospheric surface temperature with units of degrees Celsius represented by °C; the scale ranges from −70 °C to +10 °C. The horizontal axis shows the months of the year. There are two lines plotted on the axes that represent the values for mean atmospheric surface temperature for two locations: one in the Northern Hemisphere and one in the Southern Hemisphere, for specific months. The circles and triangles on the lines represent the actual mean temperature at that month, and the lines join the data points to show how the mean temperature changes between them. For example, to find the atmospheric surface temperature in degrees Celsius corresponding to February in Antarctica, start by finding the point on the horizontal axis representing February, and draw a line vertically upwards until it meets the plotted line for Antarctica. Then draw a line horizontally from that intersection to meet the vertical axis and read off the corresponding temperature in degrees Celsius. *Draw these lines directly onto Figure 1.2, using the grid lines of the graph to help you.* You should find that the temperature in February in Antarctica is about −40 °C.

To work out a representative value for the temperature for each month, an average is used to give an idea of a 'typical' or expected value. There are different ways of expressing an average value but the most common is the mean (which is often referred to as the average, as done here). The average (or mean) is obtained by adding up all the values of a set of data and dividing by the number of items in the data set. In the example here, the temperatures in three successive Junes for the black line (Alert) in Figure 1.2 were 1.0 °C, 1.2 °C and 0.9 °C. The mean temperature is the total divided by the number of measurements, which is written = (1.0 + 1.2 + 0.9) / 3 = 1.0 °C. By looking at that mean of three years' data you should be able to determine a more typical value for the temperature. The data points on both lines in Figures 1.2 and 1.3 represent the mean of over 50 years of temperature data.

Having established which line represents which location, one can immediately see that the range (i.e. the difference between the minimum and maximum values on the graph) in temperature at Alert is ~35 °C with winter temperatures being about −30 °C and summer temperatures being about +5 °C.

The ~ symbol means approximately.

■   What are the corresponding summer and winter temperatures and range at the South Pole?

□   The summer temperatures in January are about −30 °C whilst winter temperatures are a staggering −60 °C. The range is approximately 30 °C.

At the South Pole, the difference between summer and winter temperatures is a little less than in the Arctic – but the regions do differ in one other important way.

■   How do the rates of change in temperature from month to month compare at the two sites?

□   In the Arctic there is a gradual rise to a maximum temperature in July, followed by a gradual fall to winter. In contrast, at the South Pole the temperature is actually reasonably constant at ~−60 °C for the months from April to September, with a relatively shorter period of cooling and warming.

Question 1.1

In London, the mean minimum atmospheric surface temperature is ~7 °C for January and the mean maximum atmospheric surface temperature for August is ~22 °C. What is the range of temperature in London between January and August and how does this compare with the two sites shown in Figure 1.2?

You will find answers to questions at the back of the book.

London is of course a long way from the poles but comparing the climate of a European city with the polar regions begs some serious questions: why does it get so cold in the polar regions? Why is the difference between the winter minimum temperatures and the summer maximum temperatures so great? Before you can answer those questions, you need to first spend a little time looking at how the polar regions are mapped (Box 1.2).

Throughout this book important key points are displayed as shown here.

The annual range in temperature in both polar regions is approximately 30 °C and their winter temperatures are below −30 °C. In the Arctic there is a smooth cycle between summer and winter, whereas in the Antarctic temperature falls to a minimum and then stays relatively constant.

Box 1.2 Mapping locations on planet Earth – the latitude and longitude system

The terms latitude and longitude are used to identify the position of particular places on the Earth. On most maps you can see vertical and horizontal lines to divide up regions. Lines that run from east to west in the maps are called lines of latitude, and the lines that run north to south are called lines of longitude. You can see this in Figure 1.4, where the vertical red lines are the lines of longitude, and the horizontal blue lines are the lines of latitude.

If you take a roughly spherical fruit such as an apple and hold it so that the stalk is at the top (equivalent to the North Pole), draw six equally spaced horizontal lines equivalent to some of the blue latitude lines in Figure 1.4, then slice along these lines, you can see that each slice will have the same width of skin because the blue latitude lines are equal distances apart. On the Earth, the distance between the middle (the Equator at 0° latitude) and the very 'top' (the North Pole at 90° latitude) is divided up into 90 lines called degrees of latitude, which are approximately 110 km apart. These 90° of latitude are the Northern Hemisphere and any latitude north of the Equator is labelled 'N' after the value. From the Equator to the South Pole there are also 90° of latitude and this is the Southern Hemisphere, which are labelled 'S' after the value. Throughout this module the term 'high latitudes' is used to denote latitudes greater than ~66° N or ~66° S, conversely latitudes in the range ~30° N to ~30° S are referred to as low latitudes.

If you take another apple and draw lines on it to match the red longitude lines in Figure 1.4, then cut the fruit along them, this time you will end up with wedges. If you think about the wedges and the skin width, the width of skin is greatest in the middle of the fruit (the Equator on Earth), whilst at both ends the width of the skin is reduced to zero. You can see this clearly in the view of the Earth from the North Pole in Figure 1.5.

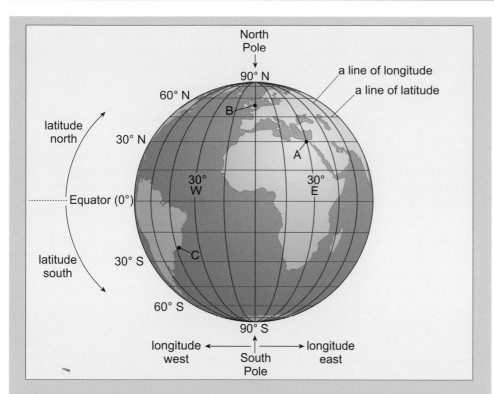

Figure 1.4   The lines of longitude and latitude on planet Earth as viewed from above the Equator. The point labelled 'A' marks the location of Cairo, point 'B' the location of London and point 'C' the location of Rio de Janeiro.

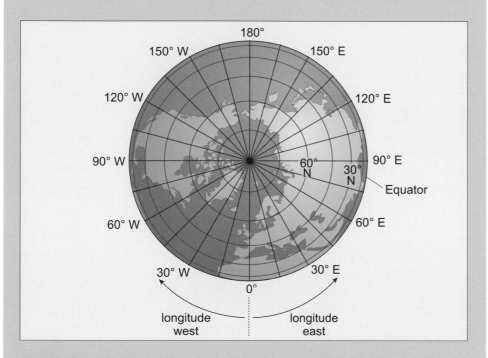

Figure 1.5   The lines of longitude (in red) and latitude (in blue) on planet Earth as viewed from above the North Pole.

At 0° longitude you can write either 0° E or 0° W.

In Figure 1.4 you can see that the blue lines of latitude are always the same distance apart, whereas Figure 1.5 shows the distance between the red lines of longitude decreases towards the North (and also the South) Pole, where they actually meet. The Earth is divided into 360 of these lines, called degrees of longitude, and at the Equator the distance between each line is 110 km, just like the distance between degrees of latitude. However, the further one goes from the Equator, the shorter the distance between the lines of longitude becomes. In London, the distance between each line of longitude is about 70 km, and even if it were possible it would take a very long time to walk all 360 degrees of longitude from London and back again around the world. At the North Pole and South Pole you could do it in just seconds. For historical reasons, the 0° longitude line runs through Greenwich in London and, looking down from the North Pole in the direction of Greenwich, in a clockwise direction the degrees of longitude range from 0° to 180° (by convention this is the Western Hemisphere labelled 'W'), and in an anticlockwise direction they range from 0° to 180° (the Eastern Hemisphere labelled 'E'). If I gave you my location in degrees latitude and longitude you could see exactly where I was on Earth – for example, I am writing this from approximately 51.57° N 0° E, which is in London, England and 51.57 degrees of latitude north of the Equator, and in line with Greenwich.

Question 1.2

Take a moment to estimate the approximate latitude and longitude of the following points on Figure 1.4: A, Cairo; B, London; and C, Rio de Janeiro.

The use of latitude and longitude was rare, except amongst sailors and the armed forces, until relatively recently. But this is changing, as ever more people are using electronic equipment such as mobile phones and in-car navigation, which routinely use satellites in a system called GPS (Global Positioning System) to determine location very accurately.

The distance between each degree of latitude is always the same wherever it is on the planet, whilst one degree of longitude varies depending on the latitude at which it is measured.

1.3   A flat map of a spherical world

A geographical map is a two-dimensional representation of the actual physical topography of a geographical region, and whilst almost everyone is familiar with, for example, a road map, mapping is a complex subject. The making of maps is called cartography and fundamentally it is about the relationship between data (the information you wish to display and convey) and space. This is both the geographic space being represented and the space available on a sheet of paper or display screen. The data are represented by points (to show location) and lines (to show connections or borders), by symbols (to convey features), and finally by names and colour and/or shading (to represent areas).

Of course, the names of places, like London, or contour lines representing height, don't physically appear on the ground where they are shown on maps!

One of the challenges facing cartographers as they try to express both data and space at the largest scales (i.e. the whole Earth or large sections of it) is the classic problem of representing features on the curved surface of a spherical Earth (or globe, see Figure 1.4) on a plane (or flat) surface.

Activity 1.3   Shapes on a peeled orange

The estimated time for this activity is 10 minutes.

Take an orange and draw the outline of two shapes on its peel with a felt pen. On one side draw a circle and on the other a square, making sure your shapes cover at least a third of the surface of the orange. Now peel the orange, trying to leave the skin in one piece. Take your peel, and put some cuts in it at the edges with a knife or scissors so that it will lie completely flat on a table.

Can you still see your shapes with exactly the same outline as when you drew them?

In your answer to Activity 1.3, whether you could see your shapes in the same way you drew them depends on where you made the cuts. But it is possible to make a flat drawing of the surface of the orange with your shapes on to show them as you actually drew them. This is called a map projection. All projections involve some sort of compromise because it is just not possible to keep everything completely accurate when shifting from three dimensions to two. An example of a projection of map data is shown in Figure 1.6a, which is the Earth in what is called the Lambert equal-area azimuthal projection. It is round like Figure 1.4 and you should be able to recognise some of the land shapes in this map.

■   Is it possible for you to hold an orange or apple in such way that you can see both poles as shown in Figure 1.6a?

☐   No! You can only see the top or the bottom at one time.

Figure 1.6a is clearly distorted so that both poles are visible.

■   What are the most distorted countries shown in Figure 1.6a?

☐   Australia is completely unrecognisable along with the Pacific coast of Russia and North America.

In Figure 1.6a, the amount of distortion changes with distance from the centre of the map at 0° N 0° E. To demonstrate this, there are a number of circles overlain on the picture. Each one of the circles encloses an equal surface area of the Earth. If you think back to your orange, imagine covering it with regularly spaced round stickers about 1 cm across. Each sticker would cover the same surface area of the orange. But in the projection in Figure 1.6a the size of the circles is varying – they are larger the further away they are from the centre of the map.

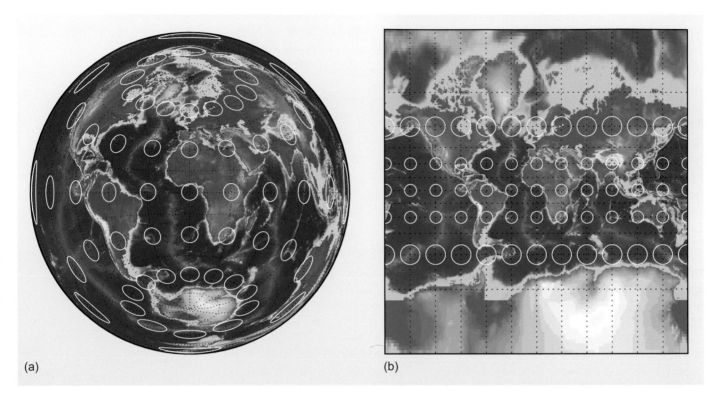

(a)   (b)

Figure 1.6   Two projections of the Earth. (a) The Lambert equal-area azimuthal projection. (b) The Mercator projection. The circles enclose an equal area of surface of the Earth.

■   If the circles appear larger but are actually the same size, what is happening to the surface area that they cover?

☐   The surface area is being distorted on the map so that it appears larger.

If there was no distortion in the projection, then all of the circles would be the same size all over the map.

A commonly used map projection is the Mercator projection (Figure 1.6b) and on it the lines of longitude and latitude cross at right angles. This picture also has the same circles as Figure 1.6a which cover an equal area.

■   How do the circles change size relative to the Equator in the Mercator projection?

☐   The circles are equal in size along lines of latitude near the Equator but increase in size with distance from the Equator.

Clearly the Mercator projection is distorting land away from the 0° latitude line.

■   Based on the size of the circles, how are Greenland and Antarctica distorted by the Mercator projection relative to their actual size?

□   Because the circles are larger towards the poles, the Mercator projection shows Greenland and Antarctica as larger than they should be. As there is no single point for a pole, Antarctica is virtually unrecognisable.

The Mercator projection is often used for maps with a small range of latitudes so there will not be very much distortion. When there is a large range of latitude like in Figure 1.6b, it is not easy to determine the relative sizes of different regions. There are many different projections and it is important to keep in mind that *all* of them distort geographic data to a certain extent. The key is to choose a projection that distorts your geographic region of interest the least. This module is focused on the polar regions and for this reason you will frequently encounter what is called the stereographic projection (Figure 1.7a, b), which is equivalent to being above the North and South Poles and looking downwards. The stereographic projection is very good for showing the high latitudes as there is only significant distortion at large distances from the poles.

Looking at the stereographic projection starting at the pole and working outwards, the lines of equal latitude are dotted and increasing in size (as shown in Figure 1.5). In Figure 1.7, the first dotted circle is at 75° north (or south) and the second 60° north (or south). Lines of equal longitude are just like hours on a clock, and are described in Figure 1.5.

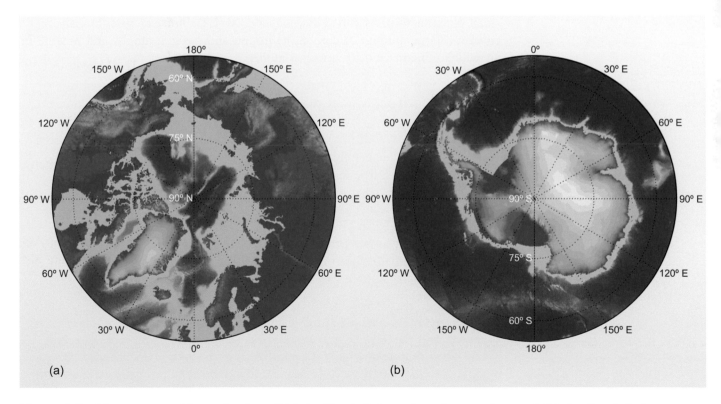

(a)   (b)

Figure 1.7   The stereographic projection of (a) the North Pole and northern regions and (b) the South Pole, Antarctica and the surrounding ocean.

Activity 1.4   Locating unfamiliar places

The estimated time for this activity is 30 minutes.

To people who live in more temperate parts of the world, some locations in the polar regions may be unfamiliar. In this activity you will use an online map to find the location of some places discussed in this chapter, and learn to locate regions in general.

The detailed notes for this activity are in the 'Activities' section of the S175 website.

1.4   The energy balance

In Section 1.2 it was noted that temperature differences between the higher and lower latitudes are large, but before continuing, it is necessary to define what is actually meant by temperature. Your experience will be from the sensations of warmth and coldness, but what is temperature from a scientific perspective? The temperature of a material is actually an indication of its energy, and to understand the relationship between temperature and energy, one needs to know the make-up of the material. All substances are made of small constituent parts called atoms (see Box 1.3). For example, humans contain a large amount of carbon, hydrogen and oxygen atoms, and breathe in air which contains mostly nitrogen atoms.

Box 1.3   The chemical elements

Every object on Earth is made of chemical elements. Most elements were created in the nuclear furnaces of exploding stars in the early Universe, so you and the Earth around us are made literally from stardust. There are 109 named elements, of which 92 occur naturally on Earth. Many will be familiar, such as carbon and oxygen. Of the known elements, up to 30 are believed to be essential to the survival of living organisms. Each element can be represented by a chemical symbol of one or two letters, a shorthand form of its current name or, sometimes, its Latin name. The smallest recognisable part of a chemical element is called an atom.

Some common examples of elements are shown in the table. C stands for carbon and Ca for calcium, Fe refers to *ferrum*, the Latin name for iron, and Na to *natrium*, which is Latin for sodium. Few elements exist as single atoms and so they are usually found combined together either with other atoms of the same element, or with atoms of other elements to make compounds. There is an enormous range of possible combinations of different elements and therefore an enormous number of chemical compounds. The smallest amount, or building block, of any substance –

compound or element – comprising two or more atoms, is called a molecule.

Element	Symbol
carbon	C
hydrogen	H
oxygen	O
nitrogen	N
calcium	Ca
phosphorus	P
sulfur	S
sodium	Na
iron	Fe

The symbols of the elements are put together to give the formula of a compound. For example, hydrogen and oxygen combine to make water, which has the formula H_2O. The number 2 indicates that two atoms of hydrogen combine with one atom of oxygen to make one molecule of water. The subscript number refers to the element it follows, so for H_2O the 2 refers to hydrogen and not oxygen. In contrast, a number before the formula refers to the number of individual molecules. For example, $3H_2O$ indicates three molecules of water, but these three molecules contain six atoms of hydrogen and three atoms of oxygen in total.

1.4.1 What is energy?

Energy is a word in common use but with a variety of everyday meanings. It does however have a precise scientific meaning and is an important concept.

■ Think of two or three phrases in which you include the word 'energy' in an everyday sense.

☐ Possible examples are: 'Where do children get their energy from?', 'I haven't got the energy to get up' or 'Sweets are full of energy'.

None of the everyday uses of the word 'energy' is very precise but they all encapsulate the notion that energy enables activity to take place. This is also at the heart of the scientific notion of energy.

Energy is a physical property possessed by a substance and it is a measure of its capability to 'make things happen'. In order for things to happen, some of the energy within the substance must be transferred to another object and a common consequence of the transfer of energy to an object is to cause its temperature to rise. For example, if I use energy to rub my hands very hard 10 times, they will be warmer when I have finished. Another example is when you burn fuel under a pan of water: energy is transferred from the flame to the water and, as a result, the temperature of the water increases. The heat is increasing the random motion of its constituent atoms or molecules and so the temperature of a substance is a measure of how much energy of motion – so-called kinetic energy – the atoms or molecules within it have. A high temperature corresponds to a high rate of internal motion and high kinetic energy of the substance's particles.

There is some heat energy flow from the interior of the Earth to the surface, but the amount is small compared with the solar contribution.

The ultimate source of almost all the energy reaching the Earth's surface is the Sun. The incoming energy is transmitted across space by solar radiation (the Sun's rays), and when it reaches the Earth it is transferred to its surface, or to your skin which, as you will know from experience, warms up. How much the Earth or your body heats up is, as described below, down to the energy balance.

1.4.2   The importance of albedo and heat capacity

Different materials reflect differing amounts of radiation away from them and the property that measures the amount of reflection (often expressed as a percentage) is called the albedo. When solar energy reaches the Earth's surface, a certain amount of it is reflected straight back out into space and only the portion that is not reflected heats up what it falls on. The result is that on a warm sunny day if you put your hand on a black car and then on a white car, you will notice that the black car feels warmer. (Perhaps you could try this the next time it is sunny.) The reason the black car is warmer is because it has a lower albedo than the white car, and so less energy is reflected away from it, so it heats up more. Table 1.1 shows the albedo of some typical surfaces on the Earth. For example, the surface of the ocean has an albedo of 3%, which means that $100\% - 3\% = 97\%$ or almost all of the incoming energy from the Sun actually heats the water.

Be careful of car alarms!

Table 1.1   The albedo of typical features on Earth.

Surface	Albedo (%)
ocean surface	3
conifer forest in summer	9
grassy fields	25
sea ice	40
desert sand	40
fresh snow	80–90

■   Using Table 1.1 how much solar energy would be available to heat up the snow surface?

☐   Fresh snow has an albedo of 80–90%. Assuming it is 80%, this means that only $100\% - 80\% = 20\%$ is available to heat up the snow surface.

Figure 1.8 shows an example of this.

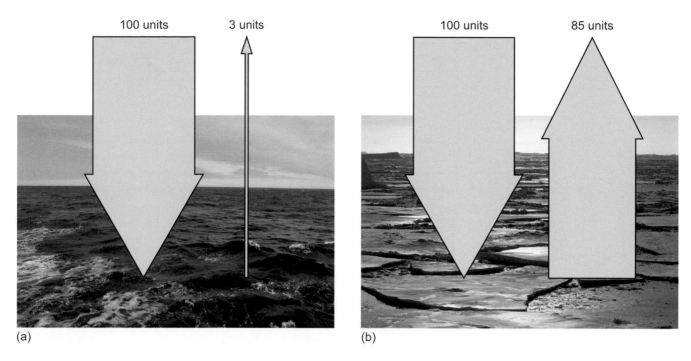

(a)   (b)

Figure 1.8   An example of the effect of the albedo on the amount of energy absorbed. (a) A sea surface absorbs virtually all of the incident energy. (b) The amount of energy absorbed for a typical snow-covered sea ice surface with water in gaps between the ice floes.

Question 1.3

If the same amount of energy reaches a desert and a conifer forest in summer, what proportion of the energy is available to heat up the material? If snow then falls to cover the conifer forest, what will be the proportion of energy available to heat up the forest?

Once the albedo has reflected away part of the incident energy, there is one more effect to consider: different materials heat up by different amounts for the same amount of energy that they receive, as determined by their specific heat capacity. This is a measure of how much energy it takes to raise the temperature of 1 kg of a particular substance by 1 °C. A lower specific heat capacity means that it takes less energy to heat up something, and vice versa. Although the term may be unfamiliar, the concept most likely is not.

Activity 1.5   The effect of specific heat capacity

The estimated time for this activity is 15 minutes.

For this activity you will conduct a thought experiment – that is, one where you only think about what will actually happen.

Imagine a hot sunny day. On a table outside in the sunlight there is a glass containing 1 kg of water (i.e. 1 litre), a 1 kg piece of cork and a 1 kg piece of iron. Ignoring albedo effects and assuming that all three items absorb the same amount of energy from the Sun, put the three objects into order determined by

You can actually do the experiment, but you may have difficulties getting 1 kg of each substance.

how hot each will become after 1 hour. (Ignore all sources of heat except that directly received from the Sun.)

Taking into account the combined effects of the albedo and specific heat capacity, even two adjacent areas, such as a beach and the sea lapping on it, will heat up by different amounts on a sunny day. If you compare a tropical sea with the high albedo icy pictures shown in Figure 1.1, you can start to get an understanding of the temperature records shown in Figure 1.2. There is one more important feature to understand before putting the Arctic and the Antarctic into context; that is, how the energy from the Sun is distributed over the Earth.

A fraction of the solar energy received by an object is reflected away depending on its albedo. The amount an object then heats up is determined by its specific heat capacity. In the range of albedos the ocean surface has a very low value of 3%, whereas fresh snow has an albedo of 80–90%.

1.5   Energy from the Sun

Although the Earth as a whole intercepts more or less the same amount of solar radiation from day to day, the amount received at any single point on the Earth's surface varies dramatically because the Earth rotates on its axis once every 24 hours. From the point of view of a person standing anywhere on the Earth's surface, the Sun appears to rise, travel across the sky and set. As a result, the angle at which solar radiation hits the Earth's surface at any one point is constantly changing. On a summer's day it is cool at dawn, but very hot by the afternoon, before again cooling at the evening. The location on the Earth is also important. If the Earth presented a flat circle towards the Sun, then the energy would be equally shared over the area of the circle (Figure 1.9a). But of course the Earth is not flat – it is a sphere.

■   Looking at Figure 1.9b, why would the solar energy received at the surface be different at low latitudes compared with high latitudes?

□   At high latitudes the light will travel through more of the atmosphere and when it reaches the surface it will be received over a larger area. So overall, the intensity will be reduced.

At higher latitudes the energy is reduced because its path through the atmosphere is longer and it is spread over a larger area. As a consequence, the equatorial regions will *always* be warmer than the polar regions simply because they receive more solar energy over the same area, but this is before the higher albedo of ice-covered land is taken into account (Section 1.4.2). You will see in Chapter 4 that this uneven heating of the Earth's surface drives the weather and ultimately the global climate system.

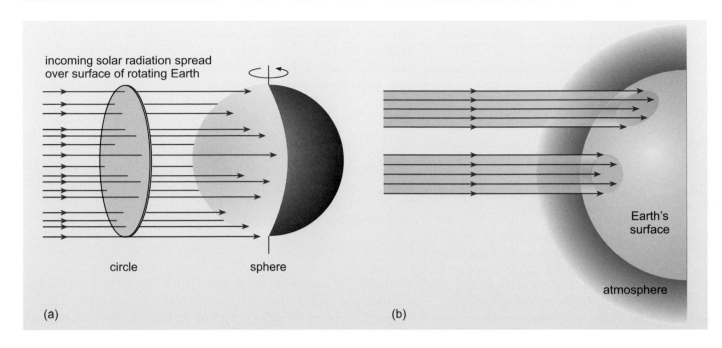

Figure 1.9   (a) The amount of energy that passes through a circle is spread over a sphere. (b) A schematic diagram showing why there is a difference in the amount of solar radiation reaching the Earth at different latitudes.

1.5.1   The seasons

There is one final point to discuss related to the cycles of energy and that you most likely noted when you looked at Figure 1.2. When it is warm in the Northern Hemisphere (the black line on Figure 1.2), it is clearly cold in the Southern Hemisphere (the red line). This is because of the seasons, and anyone living away from the equatorial regions of the Earth has experienced their effect. Figure 1.10 shows the hypothetical situation in which the Earth's axis of rotation is at right angles to the plane of its orbit.

- ■ Imagine the Earth in Figure 1.10 with the 0° longitude line just at the boundary between the black and the green. If you rotate the Earth by one complete cycle, how long will the day be at the Equator compared with high latitude?

- □ Night and day would always be the same length (i.e. 12 hours each) everywhere around the globe, except at the poles, which would have perpetual twilight.

But no planet in the Solar System has an axis of rotation that is aligned as shown in Figure 1.10.

- ■ What would be the implication on the day length if in Figure 1.10 the axis of rotation was not vertical?

- □ The length of time each latitude on the Earth was facing the Sun would be different.

If you have difficulty thinking about this you can again use an orange and a felt pen to mark out a location at high latitude and the Equator.

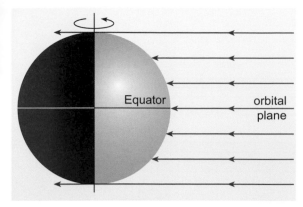

Figure 1.10 Hypothetical situation in which the Earth's axis of rotation is at right angles to the plane of its orbit around the Sun. (Note that at the poles the Sun's rays graze the Earth's surface.) The black region on the left is night, and the green region is daytime.

The axis of rotation of the Earth is currently at an angle of 23.4° to the vertical (see Figure 1.11) and, over the course of a year, the direction the axis points to changes relative to the Sun. Following on from the questions you have just answered, you can see that there will be implications for the day length at different latitudes and times of the year. At midday the Sun is overhead at the Equator only twice a year at what are called the equinoxes. These equinoxes fall on 21 March and 21 September. At other times the latitude at which the midday Sun is overhead moves between 23.4° N, which is called the Tropic of Cancer, and 23.4° S, which is called the Tropic of Capricorn, and back again (Figure 1.11b).

Figure 1.11a shows the passage of the seasons for the Northern Hemisphere. Along the Tropic of Cancer, the midday Sun is overhead and maximum solar radiation is received, during what is called the spring equinox. The longest day in the Northern Hemisphere is on 21 June, which is called the summer solstice. After this date the days begin to shorten. At the autumn equinox on 21 September both day and night are of equal length, but day length continues to shorten until the winter solstice on 21 December, which is the shortest day of the year. After this, days lengthen until the spring equinox on 21 March where again the day and night are of equal length.

This figure may appear complex but don't be concerned if you have difficulty with it at first. The activities on the S175 website should help and you can revisit this figure after studying them.

Figure 1.11   (a) The four seasons of the Northern Hemisphere in relation to the Earth's orbit around the Sun. The Earth's axis is tilted at approximately 23.4° to a line at right angles to the plane of its orbit around the Sun. (b) The angle of tilt of the Earth's axis (at present 23.4°) determines the latitude of the tropics (where the Sun is overhead at one of the solstices) and of the Arctic and Antarctic Circles (66.6°, which is 90° minus 23.4°). (c) The passage of the seasons shown in terms of the position of the midday Sun in relation to the Earth: (1) the midday Sun overhead at the Tropic of Cancer, i.e. the northern summer solstice (cf. b); (3) the midday Sun overhead at the Tropic of Capricorn, i.e. the southern summer solstice; (2) and (4) at the equinoxes, by contrast, the Sun is overhead at the Equator, and the Northern and Southern Hemispheres are illuminated equally; days and nights are the same duration at all latitudes except at the poles, which are grazed by the Sun's rays for 24 hours.

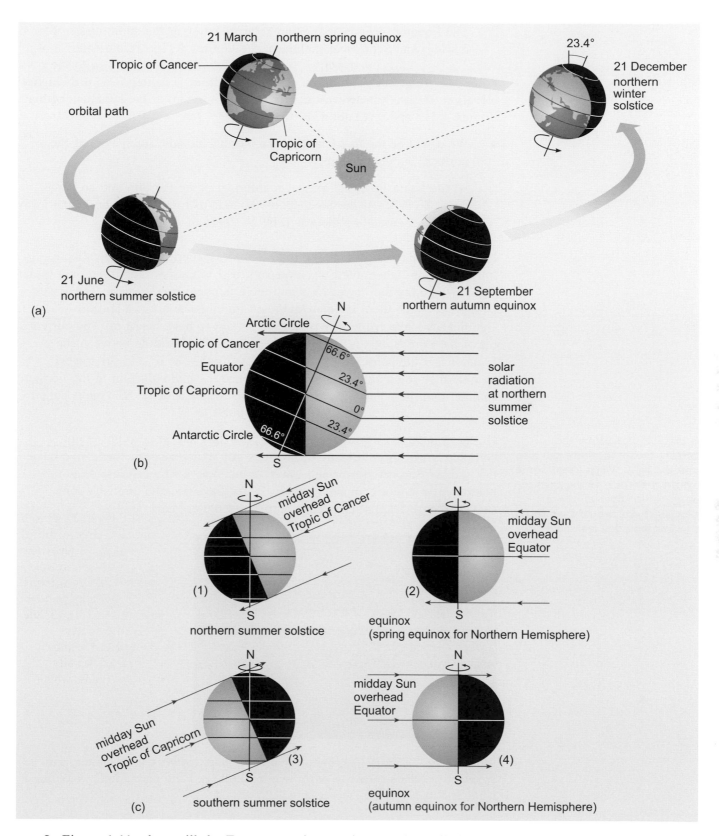

(a)

(b)

(1) northern summer solstice

(2) equinox
(spring equinox for Northern Hemisphere)

(3) southern summer solstice

(4) equinox
(autumn equinox for Northern Hemisphere)

(c)

■   In Figure 1.11 when will the Equator receive maximum solar radiation at
the surface? (*Hint*: when is the Sun overhead at midday?)

☐   The Equator receives maximum solar radiation at the equinoxes in March (spring) and September (autumn): see Figures 1.11c (2) and (4).

Poleward of the tropics, the Sun is never overhead, although it is at its highest elevation (the angle between the Sun and the horizon) at the summer solstice (Figure 1.11b and c (1) and (3)).

■   What will be the day length at the North Pole and South Pole at the northern summer solstice?

☐   At the North Pole, the axis of rotation is facing the Sun and so it will never be dark. At the South Pole, the axis of rotation will be facing away from the Sun and so there will be 24 hours of darkness.

In their respective summers, the high latitudes experience the so-called 'midnight Sun' where the Sun never sets, and in their winters there is a 'polar night' where the Sun never rises and there is complete darkness. The lowest latitude at which there is polar night and midnight Sun has a special significance and a name which you are certain to have heard of. The current tilt of the Earth's axis is 23.4° and there are 90° of latitude between the Equator and the poles (Box 1.2). So 90° − 23.4° = 66.6° and the lowest latitude that you would be able to experience the midnight Sun in the northern summer and the polar night in the northern winter is 66.6° N. This is called the Arctic Circle. The Antarctic Circle is at 66.6° S.

As the Sun dips below the horizon, the atmosphere can also bend the light, which keeps some daylight present – to experience complete darkness of a true polar night one would have to be at higher latitudes than 66.6°.

On the ground the distinction between polar day and polar night is not completely obvious. Just like the winters you experience on successive days, the midday Sun gets lower and lower in the sky. As it gets close to the horizon, if it is not completely overcast, the days become one very long sunset (Figure 1.12) with intense purple and red colours.

Figure 1.12   Approaching the polar night at high latitudes the days turn into an apparently endless sunset or dawn with beautiful red and purple light colouring the land. This is a view of the ocean as it freezes at 74° S.

To demonstrate your understanding of the sections you have read so far, now answer Question 1.4.

Question 1.4

Figure 1.2 showed that the polar regions have extremely cold winters and show a large difference in temperature between summer and winter. Fill in the blanks in the following summary, based on the information in Sections 1.4 and 1.5, using the words from the list at the end of the summary, some of which you may need to use more than once and some of which may not be needed.

It gets so cold in the polar regions because energy from the Sun has to pass through more of the _____ and so proportionally more is _____ than at _____ latitudes. Where ice-covered, the polar regions have a high _____ and so much of the energy is _____ straight back out into space. The angle of the Earth's _____ is not vertical which means that at different times of the year, the solar energy is greatly reduced, or at latitudes higher than _____ completely absent for part of the year. This also explains the divergence in the two lines seen in Figure 1.2 where when it is summer in the Northern Hemisphere it is _____ in the Southern Hemisphere and vice versa. Finally the reason there is such a huge difference between summer and winter conditions in Figure 1.2 is because both locations are at high _____ and so experience the polar _____.

Axis; absorbed; reflected; atmosphere; lower; higher; albedo; 66.6°; 23.4°; 0°; 90°; latitudes; longitudes; day; night; winter; summer.

Activity 1.6   The seasons and the polar world

The estimated time for this activity is 30 minutes.

This activity explains the principles of the Earth's orbit around the Sun (Figure 1.11) and its implications. You will watch two video clips (one filmed by the module team in the Arctic) to learn about the seasonal cycle, and the individual components that make up the polar world.

The detailed notes for this activity are in the 'Activities' section of the S175 website.

> The polar regions receive less solar energy than close to the Equator because of the shape of the planet and because the solar radiation has to pass through more atmosphere. The seasons occur because the axis of Earth's rotation is at an angle to the Sun. This angle is also responsible for the latitude of the Arctic and Antarctic Circles, and polar day and polar night.

1.6   Defining the Arctic and Antarctic

You have seen how cold the polar regions can be (Figure 1.2) but how do you define what is meant by the terms 'Arctic' and 'Antarctic'? In subsequent chapters you will see that the way this is done is extremely important for managing these areas. For example, one can hardly propose to save 'Arctic wildlife' unless you know where the Arctic begins and where for example it turns into northern Europe. Could the Arctic Circle be a useful definition for the Arctic?

■   At what latitude is the Arctic Circle?

□   The Arctic Circle is at the latitude 66.6° N.

Consider the Shetland Islands north of the British mainland. The islands are at approximately 60° N, 1° W (you can locate them on, for example, Figure 1.7a). In the Shetland Islands, the mean temperature, even in the coldest month of the year, is above ~5 °C and there are no glaciers.

■   From Figure 1.7a what latitude is the most southerly tip of Greenland?

□   The southern tip of Greenland just touches the 60° N grid line, therefore it is at ~60° N.

The southern tip of Greenland is called Cape Farewell and for seven months of the year the mean temperature is below 0 °C.

Question 1.5

On the basis of the text in Section 1.5, in no more than 100 words explain why Cape Farewell would be expected to receive roughly the same amount of solar energy as the Shetland Islands over the course of a year.

Chapter 2 will show that whilst there are no glaciers in the UK now, only a short time ago the UK was covered in ice.

The two locations in the Northern Hemisphere and at the same latitude 700 km south of the Arctic Circle have quite a different climate. Greenland, which has the largest icecap in the Northern Hemisphere, is by any definition Arctic, but the Shetland Islands are not. Clearly, a particular latitude is not adequate to define the Arctic.

One island in the Southern Hemisphere is South Georgia, which is located in the South Atlantic Ocean at 54° S, 36° W.

■   Box 1.2 gave a latitude for London, England. Would you expect South Georgia to have a similar climate to England?

□   Because South Georgia is at a similar latitude to London it would be expected to receive roughly the same amount of solar energy over the course of a year. On this basis, all other things being equal, it is not unreasonable to assume they would have a similar climate.

Figure 1.13   The island of South Georgia located in the South Atlantic Ocean at 54° S, 36° W.

Figure 1.13 shows the coastline of South Georgia and almost 60% of the island is covered by glaciers! But there are no glaciers in the UK. So choosing a latitude to define both polar regions does not seem to make sense. Another simple method could be to use the habitats of particular animals. For example, you could say that 'Antarctica is where penguins live', but there is a species of penguin found nesting on the coast of southern Africa and even a penguin species in the Galapagos Islands near the Equator! So that doesn't work either.

1.6.1   Habitats and temperatures: defining the Arctic

The difference in temperatures between Greenland and the Shetlands demonstrates that latitude – and as a consequence the amount of solar radiation received at the surface – cannot be used to define the Arctic. But what if you used temperature instead of latitude? In Africa Mount Kilimanjaro is 5895 m high and is relatively close to the Equator. Around its base is a vast diversity of trees, other plants and wildlife, but as you ascend the mountain, temperatures decrease and the diversity of plants and wildlife decrease as well. Pretty soon, if you keep climbing up, you will notice the density of trees thinning and becoming sparse, until eventually you will leave them behind. Above the line of trees (the so-called treeline), it is relatively barren compared with the base of the mountain. Keep ascending and temperatures continue to fall and eventually you will reach snow. On Kilimanjaro the temperature decreases with height – but on Earth, whilst the temperature clearly does not follow lines of latitude, it will decrease as you head towards the North Pole.

There is nothing special about Kilimanjaro – it is the same for all high mountain regions.

- If you start on the Canadian border in a forest, what do you think will happen to the number of trees as you head northwards towards the pole?

□ As you head towards the pole the temperature will decrease and, just like climbing Kilimanjaro, the number of trees will decrease until eventually they are left behind.

North of the treeline in the Northern Hemisphere is the so-called tundra, which to a person used to more temperate latitudes is really at first impression a bit bleak. At this point the mean atmospheric surface temperature in July will be approximately 10 °C. North of this it will be colder. The treeline itself represents a physical boundary beyond which trees cannot thrive because of a combination of light availability and temperature that would prevent tree growth – and so north of the treeline is often used to define the Arctic. If one circumnavigated the Northern Hemisphere and drew a line between *all* the regions where the mean atmospheric surface temperature in July was 10 °C, this line (the so-called 10 °C July isotherm) could also be used to define the Arctic. The locations of both the treeline and the 10 °C July isotherm are shown in Figure 1.14. The lines actually match rather well considering that the growth of trees is not linked to temperature alone.

You will find out about the environment of the tundra in Chapter 6.

- Can you think of one simple advantage on the ground of using the treeline to define the Arctic compared with the 10 °C July isotherm?

□ You can see the treeline and don't need any special equipment!

Question 1.6

Look at the stereographic projection in Figure 1.14 and take a moment to write down (in no more than 100 words) where the 10 °C isotherm and the treeline are close and where they are far apart, and note how they relate to the latitude of the Arctic Circle.

But both of these definitions – the treeline and the 10 °C July isotherm – are not boundaries that humans have marked, but ones that are dictated by environmental processes. In other words, they provide a natural definition.

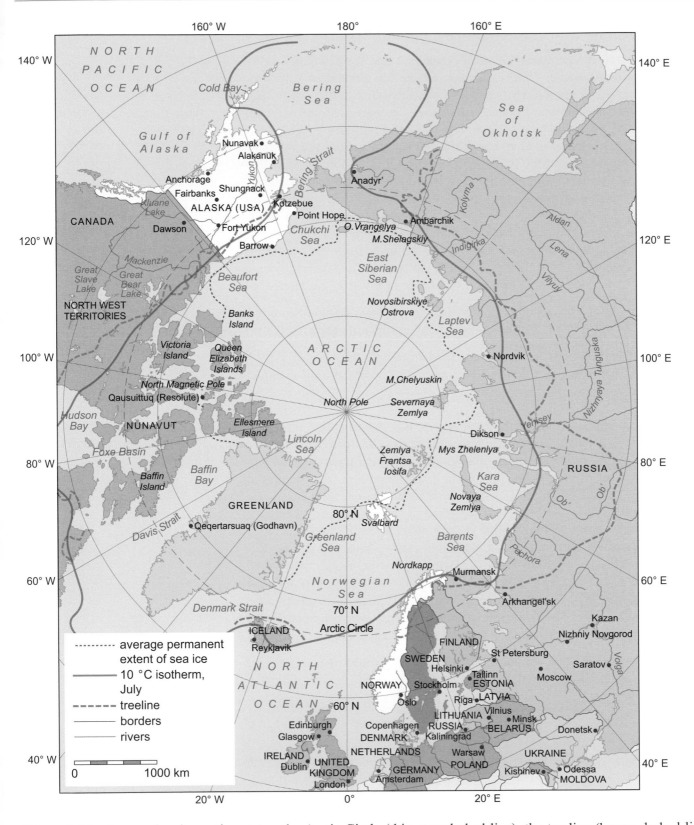

Figure 1.14 A map showing nation states, the Arctic Circle (thin grey dashed line), the treeline (brown dashed line) and the 10 °C July isotherm (pink solid line).

Another way of mapping the Arctic region is to consider who lives there and where, as shown in Figure 1.15.

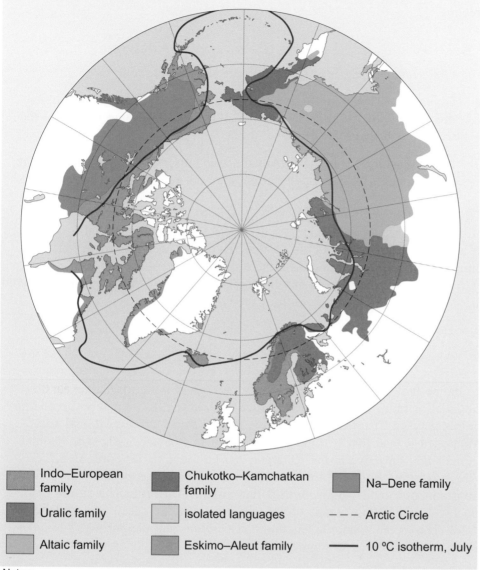

▢ Indo–European family	▢ Chukotko–Kamchatkan family	▢ Na–Dene family
▢ Uralic family	▢ isolated languages	- - - Arctic Circle
▢ Altaic family	▢ Eskimo–Aleut family	—— 10 °C isotherm, July

Notes:
Areas show colours according to the original languages of the respective indigenous people, even if they do not speak their languages today. Overlapping populations are not shown. The map does not claim to show exact boundaries between the individual language groups. Typical colonial populations, which are not traditional Arctic populations, are not shown (Danes in Greenland, Russians in the Russian Federation, non-native Canadians and Americans in North America).

Figure 1.15   Arctic peoples map showing language families. Although there are overlaps, the coloured areas are a useful quick indicator of the fact that the indigenous peoples of the Arctic are culturally diverse and do not map tidily on to the much more recently drawn political boundaries.

■   Based on the 10 °C July isotherm in Figure 1.15, how many different groups of indigenous peoples live in the Arctic?

▢   There are at least six indigenous peoples living in the Arctic.

Arctic peoples are culturally diverse and the entire region has a population of ~4 million with many different languages. Because of this the Arctic will be defined through environmental boundaries of the 10 °C July isotherm or the treeline.

1.6.2   A line in the ocean: defining the Antarctic

The final section in Chapter 1 starts with a simple question.

■   Given the distribution of land shown in, for example, Figure 1.6b, and the location of the treeline shown in Figure 1.14, do you think that the treeline will be useful for defining the Antarctic?

□   No. The majority of land in Antarctica is closer to the Equator than the treeline would be – in addition there are no trees in the ocean!

Clearly the treeline is not going to be a sensible way of defining the boundary of the Antarctic. As a continent, it is similar to Greenland in that it is covered in a very large ice cap with only a tiny fraction of the land being ice-free. Figure 1.16 shows Antarctica and the location of the Antarctic Circle at 66.6° S as a solid black line. At the beginning of this section you encountered the island of South Georgia north of the circle.

■   How much of South Georgia is covered in ice?

□   Almost 60% of the island is ice-covered.

To define the Antarctic it would clearly be a good thing to include South Georgia, as much of it is covered in ice and snow. Unfortunately there is no simple way. In Chapter 8 you will see that, in terms of international law, Antarctica is land that is south of 60° S; but in Chapter 5 you will see that animals that only live in the Antarctic can be found as far north as 52° S. Which is right? Both are, to a certain extent, but the reason the cold environment extends so far north is that around Antarctica is a strong cold clockwise-circulating ocean current which isolates the ocean and lands to the south. This is the Antarctic Circumpolar Current, and the northern boundary of it is marked in red in Figure 1.16.

The Antarctic Circumpolar Current is discussed in Chapter 4.

■   Find the location of South Georgia on Figure 1.16 at 54° S, 36° W. Which side of the red boundary is it on?

□   The island is south of the boundary.

An iceberg is a piece of glacier that has broken off and is drifting in the ocean.

South of the red boundary in Figure 1.16, Antarctic animals can range freely and icebergs can be expected at all times in the cold waters. Because it marks the division between polar and more temperate oceans, the boundary is called the Polar Front and it is so important that it will be revisited in Chapter 4. For this module the Antarctic is defined as the region south of the Polar Front.

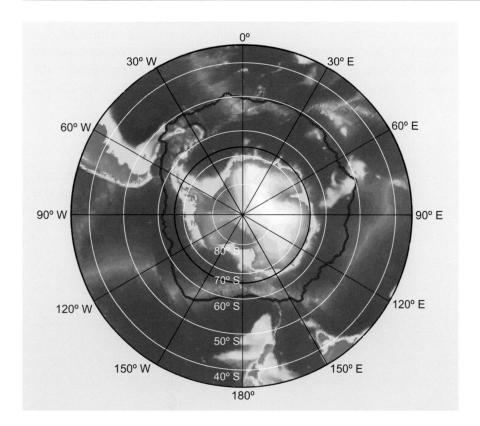

Figure 1.16 The location of the Antarctic Polar Front (red), which is a biological and physical boundary between Antarctic waters and the rest of the planet. The latitude of the Antarctic Circle (66.6° S) is shown as a solid black circle.

1.7 Conclusions

This chapter has introduced the polar climate by showing the annual cycle of mean atmospheric surface temperature at two locations. In their respective winters, both hemispheres are extremely cold and there are very large differences in temperature between winter and summer. The low temperatures are caused by reduced energy from the Sun coupled with a high albedo. It is possible to define the Arctic using both temperature and the northern limit of tree growth. But defining the Antarctic it is more problematic, and here an ocean front that separates warm and cold waters is a sensible definition. Having defined both regions, Chapter 2 follows on to discuss whether the Earth has always had this climatic environment.

1.8 Summary of Chapter 1

- The polar regions are cold because only a fraction of the solar energy received at the surface of the Earth actually heats them. The remaining energy is reflected back out into space.

- The inclination of the axis of the Earth's rotation to the Sun is responsible for the seasons, the latitude of the Arctic and Antarctic Circles and polar day and polar night.

- The Arctic is a culturally diverse region and is commonly defined by the locations of the treeline or the mean atmospheric surface temperature in July being 10 °C.
- The region south of the Polar Front is the Antarctic. South of this are cold waters, Antarctic wildlife and ice-covered lands.

2   Frozen in time

2.1   Introduction

Chapter 1 introduced the polar climate and you came across definitions for the Arctic – commonly defined as the area north of the treeline or 10 °C July isotherm (Figure 1.14) – and for the Antarctic – defined legally by the 60° S latitude circle, or perhaps more sensibly as the area south of the Polar Front in the ocean (Figure 1.16). With a planet strongly affected by ice, one can address how the planet got this way and, perhaps more significantly, whether it has always been like this.

These questions provide the underlying theme and focus of this chapter. In the following sections you will look at the age of the Earth and the climate history of the planet from its first beginnings through to today. You will see that the climate of the planet has varied greatly in the past, from no ice at all to perhaps a completely ice-covered 'snowball' Earth. The changes between the two states can be on surprisingly fast timescales and overall the changes represent the climate history of the planet.

One fact that remains is that in the most recent times, encompassing all of human existence, ice has always been a feature of planet Earth.

2.2   Deep time and planet Earth

Time is a difficult concept to understand as it is clouded by personal perception. The decades of a lifetime are nothing compared with the billions of years of deep time since the Earth has been in existence. This deep time is the time it takes for stars and planets to form and change, and is far longer than any life form has lived. How long is the deep time during which planet Earth has existed? One particularly famous estimate came from Bishop Ussher in the 17th century which stated, based on the dates given in the Christian Bible, that the Earth was formed just before nightfall on 23 October 4004 BCE! It is easy now to look at this estimate of just over 6000 years as bizarre, but it wasn't out of context with the thinking of the time. For example, Sir Isaac Newton – the great English physicist and mathematician – independently came up with a very similar age. More recently, geologists such as Charles Lyell and biologists such as Charles Darwin were amongst those who deduced that this was far too young an age. As an example, the human species has been in existence for around 7 million years. On the basis of many strands of evidence, it is now known that the Earth and our Solar System are approximately 4.5 billion years old and the Universe within which our Solar System exists is approximately 13.75 billion years old.

1 billion years = 10^9 years or 1 000 000 000 years.

The abbreviation BCE means before the common era and can be used interchangeably with BC.

■   How long after the formation of the Universe was the Earth and our Solar System formed?

□   Our Solar System was formed 13.75 – 4.5 = 9.25 billion years after the formation of the Universe.

By any measure, these are extraordinarily long periods of time. From a personal viewpoint I can see how the land around me has changed over the few decades that I have been alive. For example, a part of the coastline where I go walking has fallen into the sea and disappeared for ever, and it is clear from temperature measurements that it is warmer today at that place compared with my childhood. Those are facts: the physical environment and the climate over this short time period have changed. Surely over the 4.5 billion years of the lifetime of Earth there have been enormous changes in both the environment and the climate?

Study notes are used throughout the book to give advice on studying actively.

Keeping notes

One of the most useful study skills to acquire is a reliable method of keeping track of information, so that you can locate it again when you need it. When you are working on later chapters, you might want to check up on something you read in an earlier part of the module. You might also need to keep track of any queries you have until such time as you can return to them. You will probably want to refer back to several parts of the module in order to complete the assessment. So it is important to develop a way of managing information. For material in this book there are two main methods of doing this: making notes or highlighting the text. In this chapter you will have a chance to practise both techniques and decide whether one works better for you than the other.

In the timeline of the map you used in Activity 1.4 you can see that the first Antarctic fossils were collected by Captain Carl Larsen in 1892.

Virtually the entire Antarctic continent is currently covered in ice but the earliest scientific explorers found the few areas of ice-free coast rich in fossils. Identification of the fossil species showed that for them to have lived in what is now Antarctica, the past climate must have been much warmer – at least at the edges of the continent anyway. The real surprise came when the British explorer Ernest Shackleton led the first serious attempt to reach the South Pole in 1908. As Shackleton and his team left the coast and ventured far inland, at the final mountain range at the edge of the Antarctic plateau, Shackleton wrote:

> Wild went up the hill-side in order to have a look at the plateau. … He also brought down with him some very interesting geological specimens, some of which certainly look like coal. The quality may be poor, but I have little doubt that the stuff is coal. If that proves to be the case, the discovery will be most interesting to the scientific world.
>
> *Shackleton (1909)*

You will see in Chapter 8 that the potential for energy to be obtained from polar hydrocarbons is a significant future issue.

It was coal, and Shackleton was making an understatement. The discovery was first proof that the centre of Antarctica was once warm enough 300 million years ago to enable the growth of plants and trees that later formed coal. This Antarctic was once a tropical swamp. Early explorers also found that coal, oil and gas are present throughout much of the Arctic, and today, whilst the regions do not have the easiest access, they are productive and important. For example, the mines of Svalbard (an archipelago in the

Arctic north of Norway) provided 2.4 million tonnes of coal in 2009 to run the power stations of mainland Europe.

It is not just fossil plants that show us that the polar regions were warm. The fossilised remains of other life forms confirm this. For example, ocean-dwelling ammonites (Figure 2.1) have been found in both polar regions. The closest modern relation of the ammonite is the nautilus, a marine creature that lives in warm tropical seas such as those found off the north coast of Australia. For similar creatures to have lived at high latitudes in the past, the polar climate must once have been much warmer than it is today.

(a)

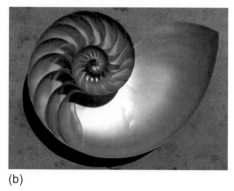
(b)

Figure 2.1   (a) A fossil of an ammonite ~250 million years old found on the Arctic island of Svalbard, and (b) a cross-section of a modern analogue – the nautilus. Both ammonite and nautilus only live in tropical seas.

Writing in the margin

As you study Section 2.1, make notes of what you see as the important points. Writing in the margin of the text or using 'Post-it' stickers is one way of keeping everything together. This is a work book and you should feel free to annotate it. Alternatively you could use a notebook or even single sheets of paper, though if your notes are loose-leaf it's a good idea to file them immediately in a ring binder, so that they don't become jumbled or get lost. Remember to mark them clearly with section/page/figure numbers, so you can relate them to the text at a later stage. Your aim is to record what you regard as important points in any format that you find helpful – full sentences, short phrases, lists or diagrams. You may also want to write down any queries you have, so that you can return to them later or maybe discuss them with a Study Adviser.

When I recently visited Stonehenge (Figure 2.2), I was looking at a site with a human history of ~10 000 years. But what was this site like 100 000 years ago? Or, given the age of the Earth, 100 million years ago? In fact 100 000 years ago this site was, as you will see below, probably snow-covered for most of the year. Much further back in time, and it is not possible to identify the area of Stonehenge because a map of Europe as it was 100 million years ago would be so different from a map of Europe today that one

Figure 2.2   The prehistoric monument of Stonehenge in Wiltshire, England. These stones were erected ~2500 BCE, but the human history of the site dates back to at least 8000 BCE.

would have difficulty recognising the shapes of the coastline. And 100 million years represents only ~2% of the Earth's history.

It is only over the last few decades that there has been an understanding of the changes that have occurred over the 4.5 billion years of the Earth's existence. A key scientific advance was made by the German scientist Alfred Wegener who first proposed the theory of continental drift. Originally, it was a hugely controversial but simple idea. For example, at a simple level the coastlines of Africa and South America match up like pieces from a giant jigsaw puzzle. Wegener and others realised it was not only the coastlines that matched up but also the species represented by fossils that are found in the different continents (Figure 2.3). With plants such as the ancient fern *Glossopteris*, it is possible that the seeds could have been distributed around the planet by the winds and the ocean currents. But Wegener realised that the fossils of identical land dinosaurs were also distributed in different continents. For example, fossils of the lizard *Lystrosaurus* have been found in Africa, India and Antarctica – regions that are now several thousand kilometres apart. With the current distribution of continents, it is hard to imagine *Lystrosaurus* making the journey by physical means. However, if the continents were once joined, then it could have simply walked.

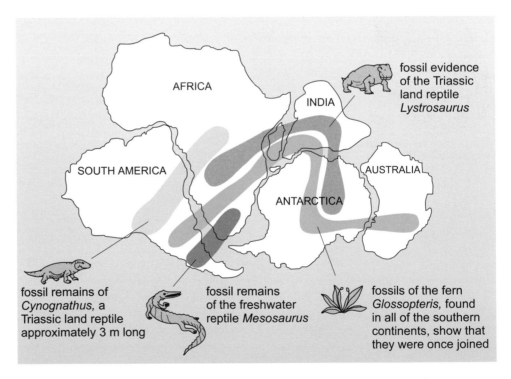

Figure 2.3   Like a giant jigsaw puzzle, the coastlines of South America, Africa, India, Antarctica and Australia match up quite well. The shaded regions show four examples of areas where fossils of the same species have been recovered. The label Triassic refers to the period in time approximately 250 million years ago when the continents were joined in this configuration.

Wegener died on an Arctic expedition in the centre of Greenland in 1930. Other scientists subsequently discovered the physical mechanisms that drive the slow and perpetual movement of the continents that he predicted. Today it is known that the continents sit on tectonic plates (Figure 2.4), which are pushed apart as new continental crust is formed through sea-floor spreading. The plates are also pulled down at subduction zones where one tectonic plate is pulled beneath another. Together these two processes and the stresses they create are responsible for earthquakes, which mainly occur around the edges of the plates. The movement of tectonic plates is in the range 1–5 cm per year (this is about the rate that human finger nails grow) although under special circumstances, plates can move over 10 cm per year. The pushing and pulling of individual plates of a few cm per year may seem incredibly slow, but the processes have been going on for hundreds of millions of years and the small annual divergence or convergence of the plates multiplied by a very long time means that there have been very large changes in the distribution of the land on our planet.

Alfred Wegener's contribution to science and polar research has now been globally recognised and the premier German polar research institute was named The Alfred Wegener Institute on its foundation in 1980.

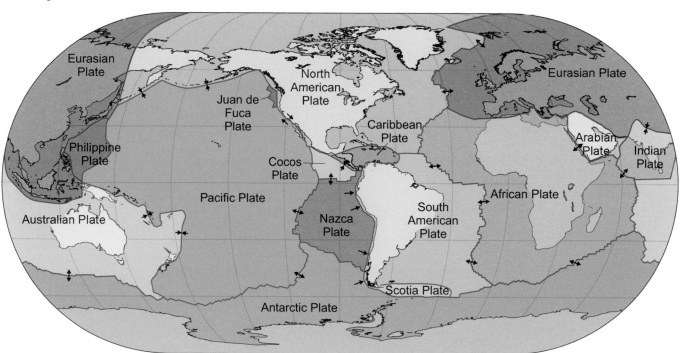

Figure 2.4   The current configuration of the tectonic plates on the Earth. Shading is different for each tectonic plate and the small black arrows show the relative directions of the plate motions caused by sea-floor spreading and subduction.

Question 2.1

The Eurasian and North American continental plates (pink and yellow in Figure 2.4) are currently moving apart at ~1 cm per year. Given that the distance of the current gap between Greenland and Norway is 1300 km, how long has it taken for the ocean between the two countries to form? (*Hint*: there are 100 cm in 1 m and 1000 m in 1 km.)

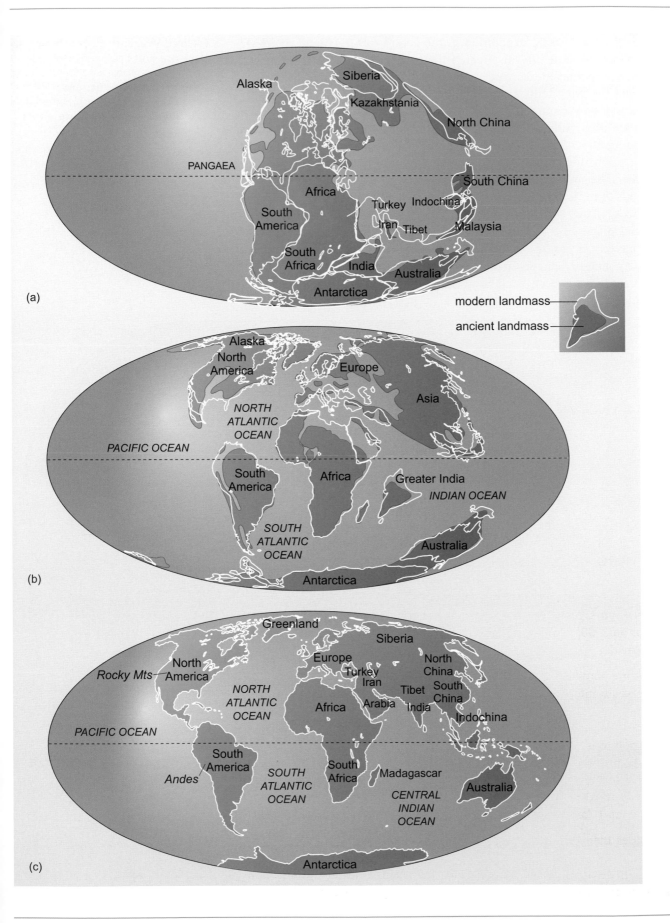

Figure 2.5   The configuration of the land on Earth at (a) 255 million years ago (in the Permian Period), (b) 65 million years ago (at the end of the Cretaceous Period) and (c) the present day. See Box 2.1 for an explanation of the geological terms.

From the rates of tectonic plate movement combined with other diverse geological evidence, past reconstructions of the distribution of land on the planet can be generated (Figure 2.5). Only a few hundred million years ago the shape of the land was unrecognisable as a giant supercontinent called Pangaea (Figure 2.5a). At this time, there was no insurmountable physical barrier to individual species of land animals and plants colonising the entire land mass. Eventually, through some unknown cause, Pangaea broke up and fragments drifted apart and after a couple of hundred million years, shapes of the continents that are recognised today became apparent. Lands that are currently in the Arctic were clearly once closer to the Equator (Figure 2.5b).

The projection of the land in Figure 2.5 is different to those encountered previously – but like those shown in Figure 1.6 it shows most of the land. Remember the projection will distort the shape of the land at the edges even more.

■   Using your knowledge of the energy balance described in Chapter 1, how would you expect the climate of the current polar regions to have differed if they were at their location in Figure 2.5a?

□   The lands were closer to the Equator so you could expect them to have been warmer than today.

In the answer to this question, the assumption has been made that the climate on the planet has remained the same whilst the processes of plate tectonics have been occurring. But this is a big assumption to make (Box 2.1).

Box 2.1   Geological time

To help understand the 4.5 billion-year history of the Earth, a timeline is shown in Figure 2.6. The abbreviation Ma stands for millions of years (1 million is 1 000 000) and all the numbers are millions of years before the present day.

Later in this chapter you will see the abbreviation ka which stands for thousands of years and the abbreviation BP which stands for 'before present'.

The timeline shown in Figure 2.6 has been divided in two ways: first at the large scale into the four geological eras, and then the three most recent eras are further subdivided into shorter periods. The naming of these eras and periods has historical connotations. The largest distinction in the timeline is that between the rocks that contain fossils in the most recent 542 million years, and those that do not. This boundary was first recognised in the 19th century and as the oldest rocks known to contain fossils then were from North Wales, this oldest fossil period was called the Cambrian (Cambria is the Latin name for Wales).

Rocks older than this are in a 4 billion-year era called the pre-Cambrian (a more appropriate but less commonly used name is the Cryptozoic – meaning 'hidden life'). The time periods that define the remaining three eras which make up the most recent 542 million years are based on substantial changes in the fossil record. The oldest of these eras is the Palaeozoic ('ancient' life), then the Mesozoic ('middle' life) and finally the most recent 65 million years which make up the Cenozoic.

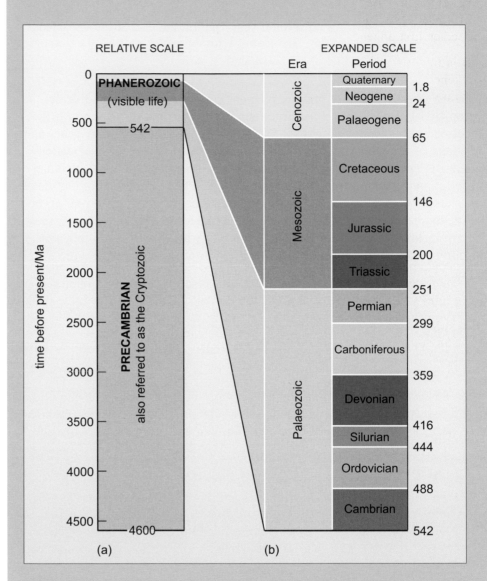

Figure 2.6   The main divisions of the geological timescale. The vertical scale of both columns is linear; the time since the emergence of the first common fossils at 542 Ma is enlarged for clarity.

These latter three eras are divided into periods. Some periods are named based on where they were first described, such as the Permian Period named after Perm in Russia; some were named after the Latin names of Welsh tribes, such as the Ordovician Period, and finally some are named after the most common rock formed during that time; for example, the Cretaceous Period is named after the Latin for chalk (*creta*).

Question 2.2

On Figure 2.6 mark the location on the timescale of the following:
(a) the ammonite in Figure 2.1a; (b) when the continents were as shown in 2.5b; (c) when coal was formed, and finally (d) when the human species first appeared.

It is important to understand that this geological timescale is, like any science, a work in progress, and almost certain to be revised in the future.

Re-reading again

Look back at the notes you have made whilst studying Section 2.2. Are there points you want to go over again? Would the notes help you to recover information at a later stage in the module? Are there any loose ends you need to follow up before you move on, perhaps by discussing them with a Study Adviser? Refining the way in which you keep track of information and ideas is an important aspect of developing your own learning strategies, so you should decide now whether you want to make adjustments to your note-taking technique before starting the next section.

2.3   The climate history of the planet

The distribution of the land on Earth has been very different in the past. Because of the different albedos of the land and sea (Section 1.4.2), the global energy balance would have also been different. Throughout geological time the concentrations of gases that make up the global atmosphere have also varied and this is important as the atmosphere is responsible for trapping some of the heat from the Sun. Today the atmosphere is ~78% nitrogen, ~21% oxygen, and the remainder is made up of what are called minor gases. Two billion years ago the atmosphere was very different and so quite different amounts of heat would be trapped. At this point, it is fair to ask how we know the composition of the atmosphere and the temperature of the planet. Today scientists have a very good idea because of global data from measurements taken by both thermometers and satellites, and they can also directly measure the gases. Unfortunately satellites only give us temperature data back to the mid-1970s, but thermometers provide a precise record going back to the mid-19th century. With one or two minor exceptions, to go back any further in time for temperature it is necessary to start using proxies (Box 2.2). Atmospheric gases, as you will see below, can be measured directly much further back in time, but for geological time you also need a proxy.

Although making up only ~1% of the atmosphere, the minor gases are hugely significant for the climate as they absorb large amounts of solar energy.

Box 2.2 Proxy data

A proxy is when scientists measure the value of one, two or even several direct quantities, and use these values to infer the values of other quantities. For example, if I measure my waistline, my weight and my height every week for a year, there would be a data set consisting of three variables measured 52 times over the course of a year. They are called variables because they are varying quantities and in this case they vary with time. Typical results would be like those shown in Figure 2.7.

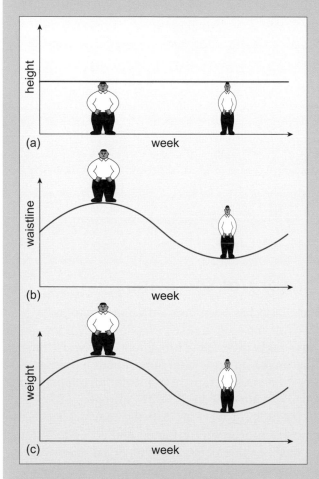

Figure 2.7 Schematic measurements of height, waistline and weight for the author throughout a year.

Because I am an adult I have stopped growing and my height does not change throughout the year. Thus in Figure 2.7a the graph is a flat line. However both my waistline and weight do vary. With my body shape, when my weight goes up most of it goes onto my waistline. So both the graph of my waistline and the graph of my weight vary in the same way. As my waistline gets bigger I get heavier. The opposite also applies – when my weight goes down my waistline reduces. Because my waistline and weight seem to vary together, the two variables are correlated; in this case, positively correlated, because when my waistline gets bigger, so does my weight. If for some strange reason my waistline got bigger and my weight decreased (not a likely scenario!), then the two variables would be negatively correlated.

Because my waistline is correlated to my weight, you can develop a relationship between the two variables; knowing one would enable you to work out the other. For example, if my waistline increased by 2 cm, I found I was 1 kg heavier. So if I just gave you the measurements of my waistline over a year, you can derive my weight over the same time period. My waistline is now a proxy for my weight. If I then told you that I tended to eat more in the winter and exercised a lot in the summer, then you could think it reasonable to actually put the months on the graphs in Figure 2.7 and my weight and waistline would then be a proxy for the time of year as well. It is important to understand that correlated variables do not tell us anything about the cause of the observation – they only tell us that they vary in a particular way. In the example above, clearly my waistline expanding is not the cause of my weight changing – it is the result of it. A clearer example of this is that the number of people in the British Armed Forces has decreased significantly since World War I, yet at the same time global atmospheric temperature has risen. Whilst these two variables are inversely correlated there is no physical mechanism for one influencing or controlling the other.

An inverse correlation is when one variable increases whilst the other decreases.

A different note-taking style

Did you persist with note-taking as you studied Section 2.2? If so, review your notes now and think about how well your system of writing things down is working. Try to experiment with a different technique in this section, by using highlighting to mark important words or ideas. You can use a 'highlighter pen' or simply underline words with a pen or pencil. You need to be selective and avoid highlighting huge chunks of text, so this method requires active reading and understanding before you wield the highlighter.

2.3.1   A very useful climate proxy: $\delta^{18}O$

The use of proxy data has revolutionised the study of past climates. The ice that makes up the world's ice sheets was originally just snow. Over hundreds of thousands of years the snow layers have built up and turned to ice, forming first glaciers, and then the great ice sheets. But still the ice is just frozen water with the chemical formula H_2O. There are two hydrogen atoms and one oxygen atom. The nucleus of an atom is made of minute particles called protons and neutrons. The number of protons determines what element the atom actually is; an atom with 1 proton is hydrogen and an atom with 8 protons is oxygen. However, the number of neutrons in the nucleus can vary. For example, oxygen atoms which always have 8 protons can have 8, 9 or 10 neutrons. Atoms with the same number of protons but different numbers of

You may find it useful to revise Box 1.3 if you are not familiar with atoms and molecules.

neutrons are called isotopes. The most abundant oxygen isotope has 8 protons and 8 neutrons and is called oxygen-16 (the 16 refers to the 8 protons + 8 neutrons), the oxygen isotope that has 8 protons and 9 neutrons is oxygen-17 (8 protons + 9 neutrons) and the oxygen isotope that has 8 protons and 10 neutrons called oxygen-18 (8 protons + 10 neutrons). Oxygen-17 is rare compared with the other two, and relative amounts of the two other isotopes (oxygen-16 and oxygen-18) are used to calculate the so-called delta O^{18} (pronounced 'delta O eighteen' and written $\delta^{18}O$) which has a very useful property: it can tell us about the past climate of the planet.

The oceans, and water in the atmosphere from which snow falls, have a proportion of oxygen-16 and oxygen-18 isotopes. But the $\delta^{18}O$ ratio of the oxygen isotopes in the water depends on the temperature of the Earth. Once it falls as snow and turns to ice, the $\delta^{18}O$ ratio does not change. In turn, the temperature of the Earth is also a proxy for the amount of ice on the planet and there is a direct positive correlation between the two.

■ If the total amount of water on the planet was constant and the amount of water locked up in ice increased, what would happen to the sea level? (Ignore any effects from plate tectonics such as land being lifted up.)

□ The global sea level would fall.

The converse is also true – when it is warmer there is less water locked up in the ice sheets and the global sea level will be much higher.

■ What happens to the $\delta^{18}O$ ratio in the water trapped as snow and ice?

□ Once fallen as snow, the $\delta^{18}O$ ratio does not change.

This means that as snow falls on an ice sheet, the successive layers of snowfall which make up the ice in a frozen ice sheet can be just like a climate time machine. If you drill down into it to extract an ice core, the $\delta^{18}O$ ratio in successive layers tells us the climate and amount of ice on the planet at the same time when the snow fell.

■ As you drill down into an ice sheet is the ice younger or older?

□ The ice will be older because the snow builds up in layers.

If you drill down into the deepest ice in Antarctica, the $\delta^{18}O$ ratio can accurately tell us the climate, the amount of ice and global sea level going back approximately 1 million years.

■ One million years is a long time, but how does it compare to the history of the planet?

□ Figure 2.6 shows that 1 million years is a tiny fraction of the 4.5 billion years the Earth has existed.

To go back further than 1 million years, the $\delta^{18}O$ ratio is still used – but from a different source. The oxygen isotopes are absorbed by creatures that live in lakes and seawater such as tiny foraminifera (Figure 2.8). This means that the $\delta^{18}O$ ratio when the foraminifera were living is locked up in their skeletons.

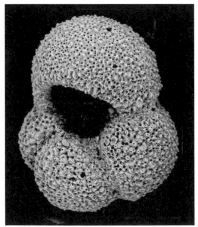

50 μm

Figure 2.8 A very small planktonic foraminiferan. This species has a skeleton consisting of four spherical chambers and has an open, arched aperture. The scale bar is 50 μm which is 50×10^{-6} m.

When they die and fall to the sea floor or lake bed they are part of the mud which makes a sedimentary layer sitting over the bedrock. In the ocean over millions of years, metres of sediment can be laid down just like the layers of snow in an ice sheet. If one drills down into the sediment, just like in the ice, we are again going back in time – but now much further, perhaps back as far as 60 Ma. To go back further than what the ocean sediment can provide, we have to look at the climate record stored in ancient sedimentary rocks and that left by geological processes such as glaciation.

By putting the pieces of evidence from $\delta^{18}O$ together, it is now understood that the climate has varied in a surprising and irregular way. There have been extremely warm periods separated by what is believed are shorter periods of intense cold (Figure 2.9). The colder periods when ice was present on the planet are called the ice ages or glacial periods.

■ Why does the line representing mean global temperature in Figure 2.9 vary in a relatively smooth way from the Proterozoic Period (~2.5 billion years ago) to the Eocene Period (about 55 Ma ago), and then in a more jagged way in more recent periods?

□ The geological scientific sampling techniques prior to the Eocene Period presumably can infer temperature changes only over long time periods. More recent techniques using sediments and cores from ice sheets can infer temperature changes on much more rapid timescales.

Question 2.3

Just like you did for Figure 2.6, mark on Figure 2.9 the location on the time axis of the following: (a) the ammonite in Figure 2.1a; (b) when the continents were as shown in Figure 2.5b; (c) when coal was formed; and finally (d) when the human species first appeared. Note whether they are relatively cold periods or relatively warm.

Question 2.4

From Figure 2.9 how many and at what time were the relatively cold periods in the earliest 4 billion years of the Earth's history?

Reading for understanding

The story of the Earth's history presented here is necessarily a simplified one; even so, some detailed information is presented. It is there to provide you with a picture of some of the richness of the Earth's history. However, you are not required to remember all the details. Treat this material as a celebration of our planet and of the skills of scientists in unravelling some of its secrets. Read it with the aim of identifying the main changes that have occurred to the Earth over its long history. With that in mind, try not to be too concerned about remembering exact dates and the names of geological periods.

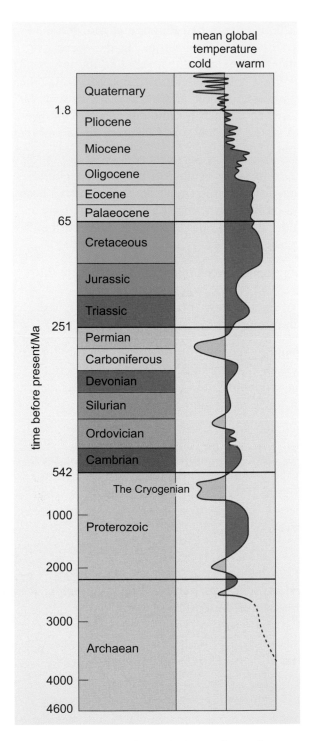

Figure 2.9 The estimated change in surface temperature of the Earth as compiled from several proxy data sources. There are periods of relative warmth separated by cold. Note that the vertical axis does not have equally spaced time intervals between 542 and the present, and the pre-Cambrian has been divided into two further periods: the oldest being the Archaean, and the younger period Proterozoic. The most recent 65 million years has been divided into shorter duration periods.

2.3.2   Snowball Earth – the Cryogenian

The long and sustained cold period shown in Figure 2.9 that makes up the ice age from approximately 1 billion to ~600 million years ago is arguably the most sustained and coldest period that has yet been determined on planet Earth. At this time, much of the land distributed over the Earth was at equatorial latitudes and yet there is significant evidence to suggest that the entire planet was covered with ice – both on land and at sea. For this reason it has been called the snowball Earth. It is a controversial theory, mainly because it was originally suggested that the entire planet was covered in ice kilometres thick; however, more recent ideas suggest that conditions were less extreme with the land being covered by thick ice, and oceans with much thinner ice. It is perhaps not a surprise that this latest version has been called the 'slushball Earth'. The consensus is that this is a much more convincing theory and because there is now global evidence for the snowball/slushball Earth it has been suggested that this period be called the Cryogenian (from the Greek *cryos* meaning 'cold' and *genesis* meaning 'birth').

■   Using Figure 2.9, which geological period is the Cryogenian in?

□   The Cryogenian is in the Proterozoic.

How could the Earth enter a period where it was entirely covered with ice? Section 1.4 described the energy balance – the greater the area covered by ice the more solar energy is reflected away.

■   What would happen to global temperatures if more solar energy was reflected away?

□   Global temperatures would fall.

Feedback loops

A cycle where what comes out depends on what goes in is called a feedback loop. In this case, large areas of ice result in falling temperatures which in turn leads to more ice. So it is called a positive feedback because an increase in what goes in (the so-called input) increases what goes out (the output).

For an as yet undetermined and extraordinary reason – perhaps a temporary dimming of the Sun through huge volumes of volcanic dust in the atmosphere – there could have been the initiation of a runaway feedback loop which resulted in the entire planet being covered with ice. This would be the onset of what could be called a genuinely frozen planet. It is not hard to imagine what such a climate state would do to any evolving life.

Once planet Earth was in such a peculiar ice-covered state it would take another extraordinary process to remove the complete ice cover. It has been hypothesised that over time – perhaps millions of years – the composition of the atmosphere changed. For example, CO_2 is released directly from

Carbon dioxide (CO_2) and methane are particularly good at trapping heat from the Sun and so they are called greenhouse gases.

volcanoes and also as a by-product from the ice-weathering of rocks. As the atmosphere changed, the global temperature would consequently increase until the ice began to melt. At this point another albedo feedback loop would take over again. First the ice would be reduced to the polar regions, and then finally it would completely disappear. Figure 2.9 shows that over the time period 542 to 65 Ma ago there were a further two cold periods, but this was followed by the Cretaceous Period where global temperatures reached their warmest since the first billion years of the Earth's existence. Next you will look at the most recent 65 million years, the Cenozoic, in more detail.

2.3.3 The Cenozoic and the great global cooling

Figure 2.9 shows that the Cenozoic Era is subdivided into further geological periods.

■ What has happened to the overall trend in global temperatures from the end of the Eocene to the present day?

□ Figure 2.9 shows the overall trend throughout this period has been relentlessly downwards.

The planet has been cooling for a long time. The initiation of the trend of temperature decrease (~80 Ma ago) most likely was due to a reduction in atmospheric CO_2 – and then other feedback processes have started to operate. Figure 2.10 shows an enlargement of the global climate history over the Cenozoic Period based on isotope proxies and the times where geological evidence suggests that the great ice sheets of the Northern Hemisphere (including Greenland) and Antarctica began to form.

■ Which continental configuration in Figure 2.5 was in existence at the beginning of the time period in Figure 2.10?

□ The horizontal axis starts at 65 Ma so it corresponds to the configuration shown in Figure 2.5b.

At this time period, Antarctica was already over the South Pole, and the Arctic lands were already at very high latitudes. As South America and Antarctica separated ~35 Ma ago, the Antarctic Circumpolar Current (ACC) formed and Antarctica became completely isolated both geologically and biologically.

You will revisit the Antarctic Circumpolar Current in both Chapters 4 and 7.

■ What happened to the temperature in Figure 2.10 as the Antarctic Circumpolar Current formed?

□ The temperature fell very rapidly at this point.

The effect of this geological change ~35 Ma ago can be clearly seen in Figure 2.10 and it was at this point that it became cold enough for snow to remain on the Antarctic land over the entire summer without melting. As snow layers built up, an albedo-driven feedback loop took over and the growth of the greatest current ice sheet on the planet – the East Antarctic Ice Sheet (EAIS) – began. For the first 25 million years of its existence the EAIS periodically grew and decayed but, for approximately the last 10 million years

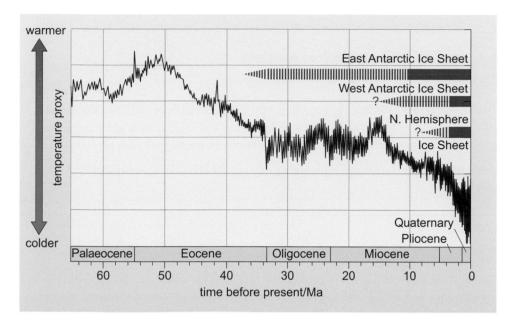

Figure 2.10   An isotope-based temperature reconstruction over the Cenozoic Period with the time periods of the formation of the great ice sheets. Where the blue bars are hatched it indicates that the ice sheet is transitory. The question marks indicate that the exact period of ice sheet formation is uncertain.

or so, it has been in constant existence covering east Antarctica with ice on average 4 km thick. Within the last 15 million years the marine West Antarctic Ice Sheet (WAIS) began first a transient existence and for the last 3 million years or so it too has been a permanent feature on our planet.

■   Using Figure 2.10, when did the Northern Hemisphere Ice Sheets form?

□   The Northern Hemisphere Ice Sheets formed ~8 Ma ago.

In the Northern Hemisphere the growth of the ice sheets including that on Greenland (the Greenland Ice Sheet (GIS)) started much more recently, most likely because it is not geographically isolated like Antarctica. But as the entire planet cooled, the growth of the GIS was inevitable through a transient existence before it became permanent for approximately the last 3 million years.

■   When did the Northern Hemisphere Ice Sheets (including the GIS) become permanent compared with the West Antarctic Ice Sheet (WAIS)?

□   Both ice sheets have been permanent for approximately the last 3 Ma.

Trapping of water as all three ice sheets grew meant that the global sea level has fallen by more than 100 m over the time period shown in Figure 2.10 and essentially the planet has been in a continual ice age for the last 10 million years or so.

Activity 2.1 Rivers of ice: glaciers

The estimated time for this activity is 60 minutes.

How do glaciers and ice sheets form? In this activity you will watch a short video clip and interact with a computer model of a glacier, allowing you to investigate how glaciers form and what controls their growth and decay.

The detailed notes for this activity are in the 'Activities' section of the S175 website.

2.3.4 The climate of the most recent three million years

Figure 2.10 shows that the rate of cooling over the most recent 10 Ma appears to have increased (the line on the graph is descending more rapidly). Could our planet be heading for another runaway feedback loop towards a snowball/slushball state?

■ What would have been the configuration of the land and continents on Earth over the last 3 Ma? (*Hint:* you saw in Section 2.2 that the drift is relatively small.)

☐ Because the movement of plates on which the continents sit is relatively small, the configuration would be approximately similar to that in Figure 2.5c.

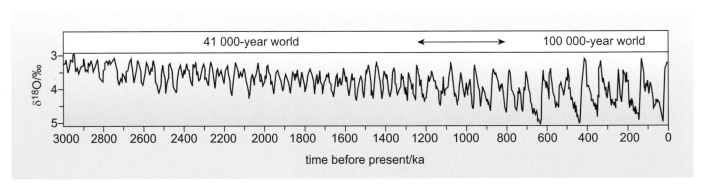

Figure 2.11   A compilation of $\delta^{18}O$ data showing the global temperature over the last 3 million years. The period of warm to cold cycling was initially 41 000 years but more recently has become slower and more pronounced at ~100 000 years. The symbol ‰ means 'per mil' and is equivalent to 1 part in 1000. Lower values of $\delta^{18}O$ on the vertical axis indicate warmer temperatures.

Figure 2.11 shows a higher resolution $\delta^{18}O$ record from the last 3 million years. The impression that this time enlargement shows compared with that of Figure 2.10 is both different and more subtle. Over the longer time period the overall temperature trend is still downward, but the global temperature jumps from warm to cold and back again relatively rapidly.

For the first 2 million years or so, this pattern of temperature change occurred approximately every 41 000 years (the so-called 41 000-year world) but ~1 million years ago the pattern slowed to one cycle approximately every 100 000 years (the 100 000-year world). Proxy data from Antarctic ice cores can show this temperature cycling data for the last million years in great detail – but with one unique addition. When the snow first settles, there is air trapped between the flakes. As the snow builds up and turns to ice, the gaps between the ice crystals become smaller and they are closed off from contact with the atmosphere (Figure 2.12). When a core of ice is drilled, not only can the $\delta^{18}O$ tell us accurately about the temperature of the Earth, but the bubbles in the ice enable us to measure the actual composition of the atmosphere close to that time.

Figure 2.12 Air bubbles trapped in a piece of Antarctic ice.

■ Using Figure 2.9, what geological period is the 100 000-year world within?

□ It is part of the geological period called the Quaternary.

Figure 2.13 shows temperature converted into a temperature difference relative to current global conditions, derived from the $\delta^{18}O$ ratio, for the most recent 800 000 years. A temperature difference of 0 °C would be the same temperature as we experience today whilst a difference of −1 °C would mean the planet was 1 °C colder than today. Also shown is the concentration of atmospheric CO_2 in units of parts per million as directly measured from the tiny bubbles trapped between the ice crystals.

Parts per million (ppm) may seem a small concentration but greenhouse gases are very effective at storing the energy from the Sun. As a consequence, these relatively low values are very important.

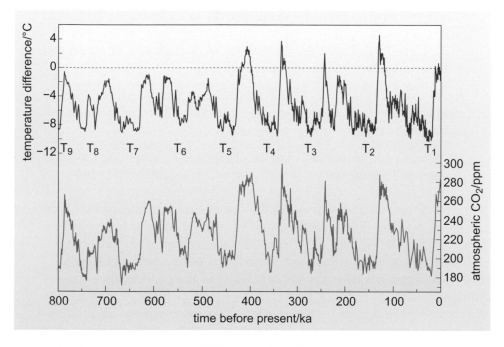

Figure 2.13 The temperature difference of the Earth and the concentration of CO_2 over the most recent 800 000 years from the European Project for Ice Coring in Antarctica (EPICA) ice core. The dashed line represents the temperature today and the labels T_1 to T_9 represent glacial periods.

- Using the temperature data in Figure 2.13, what is the maximum range of the temperature variations between a 'low' where the temperature is at a minimum and the successive temperature 'high', and how long in time does this change from minimum to maximum temperature take?

☐ There are several large cycles. One example is at approximately 350 ka BP and the temperature difference is a minimum at ~−9 °C, whilst perhaps ~20 ka later the temperature difference is a maximum at ~+4 °C. This is a range of 13 °C in 20 ka.

But how can this representation of a global mean temperature change be put into some context? If London were on average 13 °C colder than today, then the 10 °C July isotherm line which marks the Arctic (Figure 1.14) would be much further to the south. London would have a climate like that of Svalbard.

Figure 2.13 shows that in total there were nine distinct cold periods over the 800 000-year period of the ice core (labelled T_1 to T_9), and at present the planet is in a relatively warm phase. Despite that, it has a polar world with polar wildlife such as penguins and polar bears, and ice sheets storing vast quantities of water. This time period goes back more than half a million years before modern humans *Homo sapiens* ever walked the Earth. In short, Figure 2.13 shows that modern humans have, to date, *always* lived in a glacial age.

Question 2.5

Consider the most recent four cycles of cold to warm from 400 000 years BP to present and labelled T_4 to T_1 in Figure 2.13. Describe a typical cycle in general terms starting from the warmest period before T_4 and considering both the overall change in temperature and the time taken for each of the phases.

- Again using Figure 2.13, describe how the pattern of temperature change compares with the pattern of change in concentration of atmospheric carbon dioxide.

☐ There is a good match between the changes in atmospheric CO_2 and the changes in temperature.

Considering the previous five cycles the planet has spent most of the time in a cold phase, with relatively short periods of relative warmth (see answer to Question 2.5). During the cold periods the atmospheric CO_2 has been ~180 ppm, whilst during the warm periods the concentration has been ~280 ppm. There are currently no direct data of the concentration of atmospheric CO_2 going back further in time than the EPICA ice core, but there is no reason to believe that this relatively narrow range of atmospheric CO_2 was not present during the 41 000-year world as well. The concentration of atmospheric CO_2 is providing a positive feedback loop to the global temperature, with high values driving warm temperatures and vice versa. But as you will see below, there is another physical control on top of this feedback loop. Implicit in the discussion so far is that the focus has been on global climate and not weather patterns (Box 2.3).

Question 2.6

In four or five sentences, describe what you would expect to have happened to the size of the Arctic over the most recent 150 000 years.

There is ample evidence to show the climate has undergone large and rapid temperature changes over the last 3 Ma.

Box 2.3   Weather or climate?

It is easy to confuse weather, the changes that happen from day to day and week to week, with climate, which is the long-term average of the weather. For example, when I compare the weather I lived through in London in January 2009 with that of January 2010 they were very different. Both were cold – it was January after all – but in 2010 it was bitter. There were temperatures below −9 °C in central London and snow and ice covered the streets for weeks. I even went sledging a few times in my local park. But what was the mean temperature of January 2009 compared with January 2010? The UK Meteorological Office maintains a temperature series for the UK called the Central England Temperature (CET) data set which is the longest instrumental record of temperature in the world and it goes back all the way to 1772. It is an average temperature of a roughly triangular area of the UK enclosed by Lancashire, London and Bristol, and in January 2009 the CET temperature was +3.0 °C whereas in January 2010 it was +1.4 °C. Despite my memories (and photographs) there was only a difference of 1.6 °C in the average monthly temperature between the two years. Of course in 2010 it was only the beginning of the month of sustained cold – there were 9 days below 0 °C with the coldest daily average being −4.6 °C, compared with 5 days in 2009 and a coldest daily average of −3.0 °C. By taking the monthly mean, the extremes of temperature have been averaged out and overall, January 2010 was only a little colder than January 2009.

The weather is what we experience every day, whereas the average weather conditions recorded over a long time period gives the climate.

2.3.5   The glacial world

As you have just seen, the size of the polar regions has not been static, and they have been expanding and contracting, reflecting changes in the global climate. But what was the world, and the polar regions, like during the cold phases of cyclical temperature variations in Figure 2.13? As the planet cooled, the snowline moved southwards to lower latitudes and over the thousands of years of the cooling in Figure 2.13, successive layers of snow formed ice and covered previously ice-free regions. Glaciers grew and moved down from

Because the Antarctic Circumpolar Current isolated Antarctica, there were relatively much greater changes in the Northern Hemisphere.

mountains and southwards from the polar regions, and eventually new ice sheets of similar thickness to the current Antarctic ice sheet formed. Because water was stored in the vast new ice sheets, global sea level dropped significantly and the planet was in a glacial period. With the rapid warming shown by the data in Figure 2.13, the new ice sheets retreated in extent, sea level rose and the planet entered an interglacial period.

■ By comparing Figures 2.10 and 2.13, over the last 800 ka BP in an interglacial period, did the planet ever become ice-free?

☐ Figure 2.10 shows when the great ice sheets developed, and over the most recent 800 ka BP they did not disappear. The planet was not ice-free during this period.

For the entire period of the record in Figure 2.13, the planet has had permanent ice cover at high latitudes, even during the warm interglacial periods that were up to 4 °C warmer than today. Although now ice-free, the landscape at lower latitudes still shows evidence that the ice was once present, due to distinctive shapes and gouges left in the topography as the ice retreated and boulders carried and then dropped by the retreating ice (Figure 2.14). The evidence in the geological record, such as the features shown in Figure 2.14, provided the first evidence – hundreds of years before isotope data – that the climate had undergone significant changes. As our understanding of the extent of the ice and its retreat increased, it was a 20th-century Serbian geophysicist called Milutin Milanković who formulated a theory of what drove the glacial–interglacial cycling.

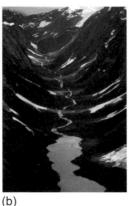

(a)   (b)   (c)

Figure 2.14 The geological evidence of past glacial periods. (a) Glacial scouring on bedrock. Stones trapped in the bottom of an advancing glacier act as a giant abrasive file grinding down the rocks below to leave scours and gouges in the bedrock that are aligned with the direction of ice flow. (b) An example of a U-shaped valley formed by an extended period of glacial erosion. (c) A so-called glacial erratic in the middle of a Yorkshire moorland which was carried by the advancing ice, and then dropped as the ice retreated.

You will almost certainly find some sections of the module harder than others. When you hit a difficult section, the most important thing is not to give up entirely. Make a serious attempt to understand the material, but if you are still struggling, then make a note of the problem and move on. You may find it all seems clearer if you come back to it later and have done the activities. Alternatively, you could discuss the problem with a Study Adviser. If you find the next section hard going then be reassured that the rest of the chapter is an easier read.

2.3.6   What drives the glacial–interglacial cycling?

There is clear cycling in the climate shown by Figures 2.11 and 2.13, with successive periods of rapid warming followed by a much slower cooling period. In Chapter 1 it was noted that the Sun's energy controlled the climate – but what would happen if this energy changed in a cyclic way? The Sun's overall energy output has varied little over the Quaternary and yet there are still climate cycles – so there must be some other cause. The Victorian scientist James Croll realised that small variations in the Earth's orbit around the Sun would change the amount of solar energy that arrived at the surface of the Earth. These ideas were developed and refined by Milanković into what is now known as the Milanković cycle and he suggested that when the solar energy is weak at high northern latitudes during summer there would be glaciation. So essentially summers were not warm enough to melt away the snow from the previous winter and over successive years the ice would grow and advance.

The orbit of any planet around the Sun is elliptical, with the Sun at one of the two foci. But because of the attraction of the Sun and of the other planets in the Solar System (in particular the giant planets Jupiter and Saturn), the shape of the ellipse – the so-called eccentricity – varies with time (Figure 2.15) in two ways. There is a weak variation with a period of ~400 000 years and a stronger variation with period at ~100 000 years. These changes affect the total amount of solar radiation reaching the surface of the Earth. At one extreme, as shown in Figure 2.15, the shape of the orbit would mean that the Earth was closest to the Sun over a period of a year (dashed line orbit) and the solar radiation would be at a maximum and when furthest (the solid line orbit) it would be at a minimum. The variation of the eccentricity over the period of the EPICA ice core is shown in Figure 2.16a. There are two further variations in the orbit that affect the amount of solar radiation reaching the Earth's surface.

An ellipse is like a slightly squashed circle which has two centres (foci) instead of one.

The first is the tilt of the N–S axis through the poles to the Sun and is called the inclination.

■   From Chapter 1 what else does this tilt of the axes cause?

☐   It is responsible for the seasons we experience on the Earth (see Section 1.5.1).

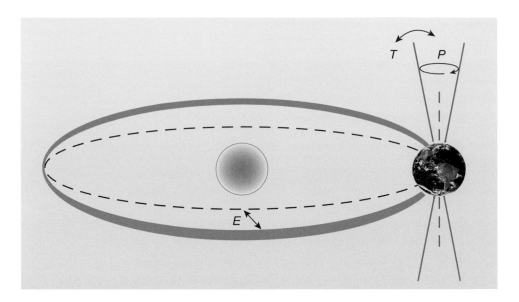

Figure 2.15 The variations in orbital cycle of the Earth around the Sun. The three key components are the eccentricity of the orbit *E*, the tilt of the axis *T*, and the precession of the axis *P*. The Earth and Sun are not drawn to relative scale.

The inclination is not fixed and it wobbles with a time period of approximately 41 000 years (Figure 2.15 labelled '*T*' and the result is in Figure 2.16b).

■ What do you think the latitude of the tropics would be if the angle of tilt increased so that it was 24.4°, rather than its current 23.4°?

□ If the angle of tilt increased to 24.4°, the tropics (over which the Sun would be directly overhead during the summer solstice) would be at 24.4° N and 24.4° S, and the Arctic and Antarctic Circles would be shifted towards the Equator (see Figure 1.11).

The greater the tilt of the axis, the larger the difference is between winter and summer. At present the tilt is decreasing so summers should be getting cooler and winters warmer – but in both cases slowly. Finally, if you look down on the North Pole, the alignment of the north–south axis slowly traces out a circle with one full circle every ~23 000 years. This is called precession (labelled '*P*' in Figure 2.15) and the result is shown in Figure 2.16c). In just over 11 000 years from now, the positions in the orbit of the northern and southern summer will be reversed as the seasons (i.e. the solstices and the equinoxes) will have moved clockwise around the orbit. In the 11 000 years following that, they will be back in their current positions.

The combined effect of the variation of eccentricity ('*E*' in Figure 2.15), tilt ('*T*' in Figure 2.15) and precession ('*P*' in Figure 2.15) on the solar radiation at the surface of the Earth at 65° N is shown in Figure 2.16d. To put this graph into context, in the UK the typical value of insolation in June is in the range 450–500 W m^{-2}.

The unit W m^{-2} is a unit of energy which means watts per square metre. In the UK in June this is typically in the range 450–500 W m^{-2}.

■ What is the maximum range of insolation at 65° N in Figure 2.16d?

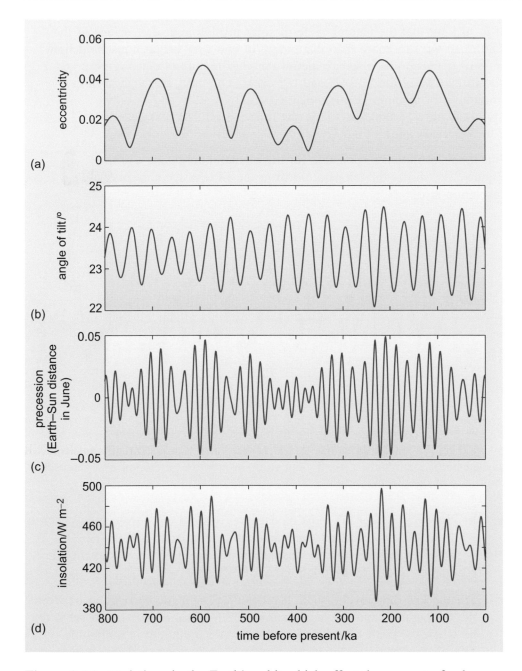

Figure 2.16 Variations in the Earth's orbit which affect the amount of solar energy incident on the surface of the Earth over the time period of the EPICA ice core. (a) The variation in the eccentricity of the orbital ellipse E in Figure 2.15. (b) The variation in the angle of tilt of the Earth's axis T in Figure 2.15. (c) The variation in precession of the Earth's axis P in Figure 2.15. (d) The variation in the solar energy reaching the surface of the Earth (the insolation) at 65° N in July as a result of the changes in (a), (b) and (c).

□   The maximum range is at about 220 ka BP where the minimum is ~390 W m^{-2} and just before when the maximum is ~490 W m^{-2}. The range is therefore ~100 W m^{-2}.

It is striking that the natural cycle of solar insolation at the surface of the Earth can vary by more than the energy in one very bright household light bulb over every single square metre! Another feature is that Figure 2.16d shows that when the 'E', 'T' and 'P' cycles coincide, the change from minimum to maximum can happen extremely rapidly and in only approximately 15 000 years (e.g. the time period 215 000 years to 230 000 years ago).

But is this variation responsible for the glacial–interglacial cycling? Figure 2.17 shows the temperature from the EPICA ice core overlaid on July insolation at 65° N.

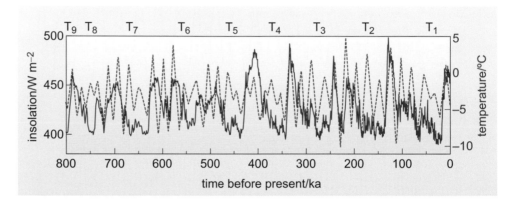

Figure 2.17 Temperature from the EPICA ice core in red (from Figure 2.13), overlaid on the insolation in July at 65° N from astronomical calculations (blue dashed line). The numbers T_1, T_2 and so on which are on the top axis represent the times of the glacial periods.

■ In Figure 2.17 over the most recent three warm cycles from today back to ~300 ka BP, how well do the glacial and interglacial periods labelled T_1, T_2 and T_3 correlate with the insolation in July at 65° N? Does the same correlation apply from 700–800 ka BP?

☐ For the last three cycles there has been a reasonable correlation between the temperature and the insolation at 65° N. Glacial periods do seem to be when the cycle of solar insolation is at a minimum in amplitude. The peak interglacial temperature also corresponds to a relative high in amplitude of the insolation. Going back further in time by 700–800 ka BP the correlation has broken down.

There is good geological evidence that Milanković cycles have been important agents of climatic variation over much of the last ~500 million years. However, as Figure 2.17 shows, the link is not as clear as one might think. In the so-called 100 000-year world (Figure 2.11) it seems reasonable to believe that variations in the eccentricity of the Earth's orbit (Figure 2.16a) are the main control on the climate. Further back in time into the 41 000-year world (Figure 2.11) it has been proposed that the more rapid ~40 000-year variations in the tilt (Figure 2.16b) are the control. It sounds logical, but currently scientists are not able to determine what changed the periods from the rapid cycling of 2.5 million years ago, to slower cycling of the most recent

400 000 years (Figure 2.11). The difficulty could simply be that the records of Figure 2.11 and 2.13 derived from $\delta^{18}O$ can infer the total ice volume on the planet. But if the Northern Hemisphere ice sheets grew whilst the Southern Hemisphere ones retreated by the same amount, then the total volume change would be zero. Amongst the other important varying factors are, as you saw in Figure 2.13, the changing composition of greenhouse gases such as CO_2, the position of the continents on the planet (Figure 2.5) and the strength and direction of ocean currents.

Overall the complexity of the climate system and interactions between the different components, including both positive and negative feedback effects, mean that it is difficult to predict the result of a variation of incoming solar radiation on the climate. Despite this, the Milanković cycles play an important role in linking the periodic variations of incoming solar radiation to the long-term glacial and interglacial periods.

> Milanković cycles are most likely very important in driving the long-term climate variation on our planet – although the lack of correlation in Figure 2.17 demonstrates that it is clearly not the only important factor.

Activity 2.2   Milanković cycles and ice cores
The estimated time for this activity is 30 minutes.

This activity will help you to understand how the Milanković cycles affect the solar radiation received at the surface of the Earth with use of animated versions of Figure 2.15 and Figure 2.16. You will also learn how scientists can use the ice sheets to inform us about them.

The detailed notes for this activity are in the 'Activities' section of the S175 website.

2.4   From the last glacial maximum to the present day

The peak of the last ice age is called the last glacial maximum (LGM), and at this time the global temperature was more than 9 °C colder than today.

■   From Figures 2.13 and 2.17, when was the LGM?

☐   The last glacial maximum was about 20 000 years ago.

Large areas of both hemispheres were covered in ice sheets kilometres thick. In North America a large ice sheet joined with the Greenland Ice Sheet, Scandinavia and much of northern Europe was covered along with a smaller sheet covering Iceland (Figure 2.18a). In the Southern Hemisphere, as well as

In Chapter 4 you will see that this freshwater may even have temporarily changed the global ocean circulation.

an extended EAIS and WAIS, part of South America was covered along with a smaller ice sheet over New Zealand (Figure 2.18b). A consequence of these vast ice sheets was that global sea level was more than 120 m lower than today and many of our shallow seas did not exist. As Figure 2.13 shows, the exit from the ice age was rapid and the water stored in the ice sheets flooded into the oceans to raise sea levels.

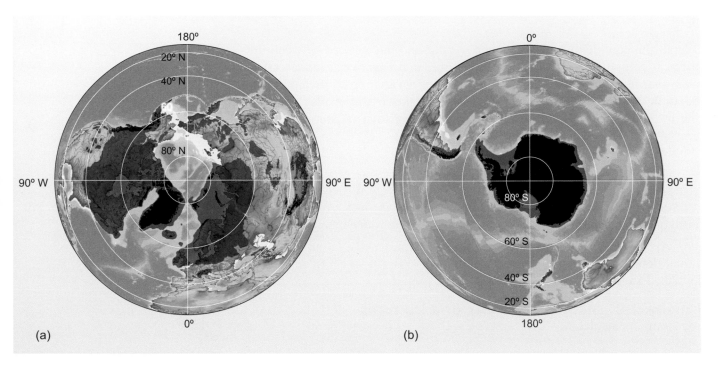

Figure 2.18 The permanent land ice cover in both hemispheres at the time of the last glacial maximum and conditions today. In both plots, the land ice cover at the LGM is shown grey, ice in the current interglacial is black. (a) The Northern Hemisphere. (b) The Southern Hemisphere.

■ Given that the large ice sheets in Figure 2.18 indicate the planet is colder, how would the amount of sea ice at the LGM compare with current conditions?

☐ In a colder world the amount of sea ice would be much greater and extend to lower latitudes.

At the LGM sea ice covered much of the sub-polar regions of the North Atlantic and in winter it even extended down to the coast of Spain. In later chapters you will address how such extreme conditions affect vegetation and wildlife.

The climate of the most recent 20 000 years is shown in Figure 2.19 along with the solar radiation (insolation) from Figure 2.16d.

■ From Figure 2.19, how much variation has there been from the present temperature over the most recent 10 000 years?

☐ The temperature has not varied by more than about 2 °C from the present temperature.

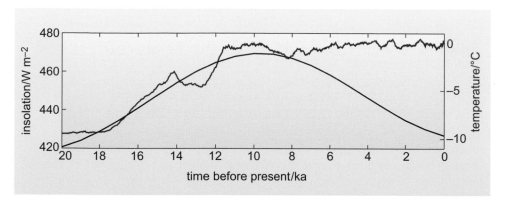

Figure 2.19 Temperature from the EPICA ice core (from Figure 2.13), in red, with the vertical axis on the right-hand side, overlaid on the insolation in July at 65° N from astronomical calculations (from Figure 2.16d), in black, with the axis on the left-hand side. Data for the last 20 000 years.

Looking back over the entire EPICA record in Figure 2.13, there is no other period where the temperatures have been so consistently stable. It is so unusual that it has been named the Holocene geological period. It is during this very stable climatic period of the Holocene that agriculture, large-scale animal domestication and civilisations have developed. Modern humans have flourished in this unusually stable climate.

■   How closely does the red temperature record match with the amount of sunlight (insolation) reaching the Earth over the timescale of Figure 2.19?

☐   In the time from about 20 000 years ago to about 8000 years ago, the temperature record and the amount of sunlight match pretty well. The insolation and temperature both rise, though the temperature curve is more irregular. From 8000 years ago to the present, the insolation falls steadily but the temperature remains roughly constant.

This relatively constant temperature is possibly a result of climate change due to human activity and it will be addressed again in Chapters 8 and 9. Figure 2.19 shows that the warming at the end of the last ice age apparently ceased about 14 000 years ago. This fall in global temperature is called the Younger Dryas (Box 2.4).

Activity 2.3   The glacial world

The estimated time for this activity is 30 minutes.

Professor Doug Benn is a leading glaciologist working in the high latitudes of the Arctic. In this activity, which contains two video clips, you will learn about how complex glacial processes can be.

The detailed notes for this activity are in the 'Activities' section of the S175 website.

Box 2.4   Climate gets cold again: the Younger Dryas and the 8.2 ka event

Approximately 14 000 years ago the temperature was within a couple of degrees of today (Figure 2.19). However, this was followed by very rapid cooling of a few degrees over only 20 years or so. The sudden change is not so apparent in Figure 2.19 because the data have been smoothed to make the overall trend clearer. What is clear is that climate cooled very rapidly in a few decades. This relatively cold period from 12 900 to 11 600 years ago affected most of the planet and is called the Younger Dryas after a pretty Arctic alpine flowering plant called the white dryas (Figure 2.20). This plant lives on mountains and at high latitudes but as the planet cooled its geographical range spread. If you focus on the period 20 000–11 600 years ago, it could have been assumed that the planet was heading for another glacial period but then the warming resumed, sea levels continued to rise as the ice sheets retreated, and the extent of the white dryas retreated. There is another dip in temperature at ~8200 years ago before the planet entered the stable climate of the Holocene. This later cooling is called the 8.2 ka event and was much shorter in duration and possibly not global in influence like the Younger Dryas. The cause of both of these events is most likely due to disruption in the global ocean currents, which will be discussed in Chapter 4.

Figure 2.20   The white dryas. The Latin name of this pretty flower is *Dryas octopetala* (dryas flower with eight petals – although as you can see from this photo it can have more petals).

2.5   Conclusions

Over the 4.5 billion years of the Earth's existence, neither the configuration of the continents, nor the climate has been stable. The cold was extreme in the Cryogenian, and warm enough for extensive global swamps in the Cretaceous. Both extremes greatly affected life on Earth. Over the most recent 65 million years the general trend of global temperature has been cooling, and over the last 800 000 years there have been nine distinct glacial periods before the stable Holocene. As you have seen, modern humans when they left Africa have always known an ice world at high latitudes. Chapter 3 will discuss the reasons why people travel and live in the polar regions.

2.6   Summary of Chapter 2

- The Earth and our Solar System have been in existence for ~4.5 billion years and neither the configuration of the continents, nor the climate has been stable. There have been times when there has been an ice-covered world (the Cryogenian) and vast swamps (the Cretaceous).

- The trend in global temperature has been downwards for the most recent 65 million years. As the great ice sheets began to grow, the planet has been in an ice age for the last ten million years or so.

- The record of the most recent 3 million years shows that whilst the overall temperature trend is still downward, global temperature apparently jumps from warm to cold and back again at different periods related to the orbit of the Earth around the Sun.

- The last glacial maximum (LGM) was approximately 20 000 years ago and temperatures were ~9 °C colder than today. Water locked up in the great ice sheets at this time meant that sea level was ~120 m lower than today.

- The present Holocene is a period of unusually stable climate compared with earlier eras and modern humans have flourished.

3   The drive to the poles

3.1   Introduction

Chapter 2 showed that modern humans have always lived in a polar world. This chapter investigates the changing frontier of our interaction with the ice.

Figure 1.15 showed that there are at least six indigenous peoples living in the Arctic. In Activity 1.1 you identified nations that you believed owned Arctic territory.

■   Are the individual peoples clearly associated with the nations you identified in Activity 1.1?

□   They do not match individual Arctic nations; for example, the Uralic family extends across Finland and Russia and the Eskimo–Aleut family extends across the United States and Canada.

You will see in this chapter how the native peoples settled in the polar regions, and investigate the contact of the early settlers with modern Europeans. Although not widely acknowledged, scientific curiosity has always been a significant motivation for people to head to high latitudes. What has become known as the Heroic Age of polar exploration was not just about planting flags. The generation of scientific knowledge and attempting to understand the planet was also a focus of their endeavours and, for them, reason for their extreme hardships. Bringing the story to current times, the chapter will discuss modern polar research with its complex network of requirements. But you will see that even these requirements are being altered by the impact of new technologies at this scientific frontier.

The Heroic Age includes the time period that Scott, Shackleton, Amundsen, Nansen and others headed for the ice.

From Chapter 2, at the last glacial maximum (LGM, Figure 2.18) the high latitudes were ice-covered and were an unpopulated wasteland.

■   In the Arctic at the LGM where would the 10 °C July isotherm have been compared with today?

□   Large ice sheets meant that the north was much colder and so the 10 °C July isotherm would be closer to the Equator compared with today.

Keeping direction

This chapter is different in character to the previous one in that its aim is broader – how and why people head to high latitudes. There is a narrative element to the text and you may feel there are a lot of facts to remember. For this reason, this is a good time to check that your system for taking notes is still effective for you. Try to focus on the overall theme and keep in mind what you have already learnt in Chapters 1 and 2 to stay on track.

3.2   The first polar peoples

Hominins are our ancestors and include *Homo sapiens*.

Hominins left Africa to spread out through Eurasia long before the domestication of animals and crop farming. Perhaps they followed animals north as they hunted, or were driven north through population expansion. At least 30 000 (and perhaps as early as 40 000) years ago, *Homo sapiens* coped well in cold environments and hunted species such as mammoths, which are extinct today (Figure 3.1).

Figure 3.1   A life-sized model of a mammoth – a prime species hunted by early humans in the Arctic. Note the small child for scale.

■   What would the climate of the Earth have been like 30 000–40 000 years ago compared with current conditions (Figure 2.13)?

□   The global temperature would have been more than 8 °C colder than today.

Question 3.1

Would the hunters have had access to the Arctic Ocean at the LGM?

Figure 2.13 shows that from 30 000 years ago, the planet had still not reached the LGM and so the hunters were still at relatively high latitudes. At the end of the LGM as the planet warmed, they followed the retreating ice northwards. Other species did not adapt so well and mammoths soon died out, although whether this was because of an inability to cope with changing climate or human overhunting remains to be determined. Hunters could reach what is now the Arctic coastline, and because the water stored in the great ice sheets meant that global sea level was much lower than today, the Arctic Ocean would have been even further north. Lands that are currently separated by seas were still joined (Figure 3.2) and in summer when snow retreated, humans and animals could walk to North America. When sea levels rose, the Arctic and Pacific Oceans were connected by the relatively shallow ~85 km wide Bering Strait, and North America and Eurasia have been separated ever since. Some of the peoples that crossed the land bridge in Figure 3.2 migrated south, but small isolated communities stayed in the Arctic lands.

It is interesting to note that whilst Eurasia was being colonised by a flow of people from south to north, it is thought that the Americas, until recent history, were colonised only through this initial migration across the land bridge. This means that *all* of the native peoples of the Americas were once from the Arctic lands. And, whilst the peoples who lived to the south have developed complex interacting societies and civilisations, the polar peoples have remained largely isolated for thousands of years.

Question 3.2

Was there an equivalent land bridge between South America and the Antarctic continent at the last glacial maximum?

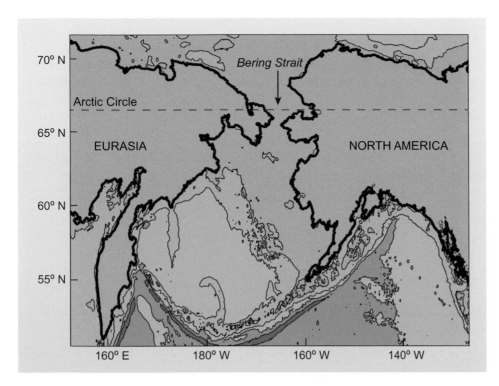

Figure 3.2 At the last glacial maximum the configuration of the land was approximately as shown in brown on this map. As the great ice sheets retreated and sea level rose, the modern coastline (heavy black) is what remained, and the two continents have been separated for thousands of years.

In later chapters you will discover that the existence of the polar peoples is precarious and the entire current population of the Arctic – the so-called Inuit – across Russia, Alaska, Canada and Greenland is most likely no more than 200 000 in total. Considering the vast area of land, it is humbling that these lands are inhabited by a population smaller than a medium-sized city. But it is an indication of how many people the landscape can support. The Inuit communities were based around hunting and gathering resources and there are only so many seals and whales that could be sustainably exploited. The small populations may be the optimum number.

Arctic people are diverse and a single name does not fit. Eskimo is from the French word *Esquimaux* and is for some offensive. A more modern and widely used name is Inuit.

■ Take a few minutes to note what resources the isolated Inuit could have used to survive.

□ They could have used animals, fish and wild plants (e.g. berries in summer) for food, and animal skins and bones for materials such as clothes, tents, needles for sewing and so on.

Because the Arctic is north of the treeline you would not expect the Inuit to have access to wood. Yet when European explorers first encountered them they were, along with the commodities noted above, commonly using wood as a material for protection (Figure 3.3), making spears and bows, and even creating art. But where could the wood have come from?

One possibility is trading – but it is hard to imagine what the polar communities could trade, with the exception of produce. What is more likely

Figure 3.3 A pair of carved wooden snow goggles from Canada from c. 1780.

Had people managed to reach the Antarctic, some of the resources listed would have been available. But the climate was harsher and there were never plants or supplies of berries.

is that the wood arrived in the Arctic through natural processes such as being carried in rivers or drifting in ocean currents from the forests to the south. You will revisit the transport of wood in Chapter 4, but it is clear that there have been sustained Arctic communities since the LGM. The peoples lived a hunter-gatherer lifestyle based on hunting, fishing and local resources, with an additional bounty provided by wood brought to the region.

Scanning ahead

Another useful study technique is 'scanning' material before starting to study it more thoroughly. Scanning involves a very quick read through, during which you ignore questions and activities, and simply try to identify the main topics and the new concepts. Include the diagrams in your scan, just to get an idea of the relative numbers of simple and complex ones. Try scanning Section 3.3 now. To make sure you don't get bogged down in detail allow no more than 20 minutes for this. Don't make notes or do any highlighting while you are scanning. When you have finished, make a quick note of any parts that you think will be straightforward and any parts that you feel will require particularly careful study. Keep these notes safely until you have finished studying the section properly.

3.3   European contact: the rush for resources

European contact with the Arctic goes back to at least the Vikings if not earlier. For example, there is a suggestion that in 4 BCE the Greek Pytheas reached a frozen sea after a few days' sailing northwards of Britain. It is more certain that in ~980 CE the Viking Eric the Red reached and explored a coast he named Greenland. As a result several farming settlements existed there until the 14th century. Why the Viking settlements in Greenland failed is still debated, but very high-resolution ice cores show the region had become substantially colder and archaeologists have shown that farming ceased.

The age of modern exploration began with an expedition led by the Englishman Martin Frobisher (Figure 3.4) who was, depending on your outlook, either an explorer or a pirate. In the late 16th century, England was at war with the Spanish and the English Queen Elizabeth I allowed private ship owners to attack and destroy enemy ships. Frobisher was one of these so-called privateers. Elizabeth and her court were aware that some believed the Arctic was both habitable and rich in natural resources but initially Frobisher was looking for a route to India and China that avoided the dangerous Spanish-controlled Drake Passage between South America and Antarctica. So began the search for the fabled North-West Passage across the top of the Americas.

Over the course of three voyages to the Arctic, Frobisher attempted to plant crops, thought he had discovered gold, and perhaps most significantly on Baffin Island:

Figure 3.4   Martin Frobisher claimed the Arctic for Queen Elizabeth I and England.

… being ashore, upon the toppe of a hill, he perceived a number of small things fleeting in the Sea a farre off, whyche hee supposed to be Porposes, or Ceales, or some kinde of strange fishe: but coming nearer, he discovered them to be men, in small boates made of leather.

McGhee (2005)

Frobisher had met the Inuit. It was entirely consistent behaviour for the Europeans of the time to deduce from their animal skin clothing and apparently primitive tools that the Inuit were of low intelligence and not worth interacting with, let alone conquering. As a consequence they were ignored, along with any claim to lands they lived on. Contemporary examples of European contact with other native civilisations such as the Aztecs demonstrate they got off lightly. Sadly for Frobisher, he shipped over 1000 tonnes of 'gold' ore back to England before it was determined to be a worthless iron compound called iron pyrite – its common name of 'fool's gold' shows he was not alone in making this mistake!

The English were not the only Europeans looking for shortcuts to rich trading lands. A contemporary of Frobisher's – the Dutchman Willem Barents – was seeking a North-East Passage to China across the top of Europe (Figure 3.5). Barents too failed to reach the trading lands, but he did find ample natural resources such as walrus, bears and arctic foxes. With both European explorers discovering resources, who owned them is important. This is called sovereignty, and although it seems quite clear-cut now that a nation can claim ownership of land, it is actually a relatively recent legal concept (Box 3.1).

(a)

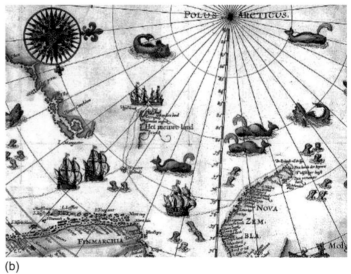

(b)

Figure 3.5   (a) Artwork from 1596 shows that the Dutchman Willem Barents and his crew were interacting with the polar wildlife in their own way. (b) A section of Barents' chart (1599) showing the Arctic coastline of the islands of Svalbard and Novaya Zemlya to the west.

■   What resources are specifically represented in Willem Barents' chart of 1599 (Figure 3.5b)?

☐ There are the heads of seals visible near the coast of the island of Novaya Zemlya and whales in the waters to the north. (There may even be 'sea monsters' at very high latitudes.)

Box 3.1   Sovereignty and the Arctic

The colours on political maps of the Arctic such as that in Figure 1.14 show ownership – or sovereignty – over lands, and they have their roots going back to the mid-17th century. Around that time, the very destructive Thirty Years' War had raged across Europe as permanent national borders began to be established, and by 1648 the so-called Peace of Westphalia came into force. This legal document enabled Europe's monarchies to agree to recognise each others' right to rule their own territories without interference from neighbouring sovereign powers and, in effect, can be considered to be the source of all modern international law. Sovereignty can be defined as an exclusive right to have control over a territory and people. States have the legitimate authority to set and raise taxes, make and enforce laws and control the police and the army within their borders.

In the populated areas of Europe this makes sense, but indigenous peoples whose land had been colonised in preceding centuries (above all by Europeans) did not fit into this system. Before colonisation the Inuit lived outside what Europeans recognised as the boundaries of political community. They had no comparable structures of government or record of their inhabitation. More significantly, they had only modest power or organisation to resist the technologies of the European colonists. For these and other reasons, indigenous peoples, whether in Australia, the Arctic or South America, were seen as living beyond the norms of European societies and presented no obstacle to a colonial claim. In the last three decades of the 20th century, indigenous peoples campaigned for new legal settlements and rights. In the Arctic this is reflected in the formation of the Inuit Circumpolar Council which consists of representatives from the United States, Canada, Greenland and Russia, with a focus on transnational issues.

Whaling and sealing as commercial industries were developing just as the great cities were demanding ever more resources, including whale oil for lighting and bone for ladies' clothes. As a result, they rapidly expanded with vast profits to be made. Unfortunately, as you will see in Chapter 8, the exploitation was soon unsustainable. From first Inuit contact through to the Victorian era, the Arctic was almost entirely viewed in terms of resources. Transnational trading companies such as the Muscovy Company (established in 1555) linked the Russian Arctic resources with the might of Europe, and the Hudson Bay Company (established in 1670) was to provide a similar service to the Arctic American. All the time, whaling expeditions by the British and Europeans headed northwards.

Northern sealers and whalers were not averse to travelling to the Southern Hemisphere for untapped sources of their prey. This means that the initial explorations to the Antarctic region were virtually all based on semi-secret commercial expeditions.

Question 3.3

Why would commercial sealing and whaling expeditions be made in secrecy?

A notable exception was the voyages of the Englishman Captain James Cook in the ships HMS *Resolution* and HMS *Adventure* to the high southern latitudes. Cook made the first recorded landing on the island of South Georgia in January 1775 and promptly claimed it for King George III. At first he thought he had discovered the fabled Terra Australis Incognita, but a circumnavigation of the island put paid to that. He was, however, astonished at the extent of ice at this relatively low-latitude sub-Antarctic island (Hough, 1994):

> Who would have thought that an island of no greater extent than this is situated between the latitude of 54° and 55° should in the very height of summer be in a manner wholly covered many fathoms deep with frozen snow.

A fathom is an old-fashioned unit of length usually used by mariners to measure depth. Today 1 fathom = 1.83 m.

Question 3.4

Looking back at Chapters 1 and 2, describe in no more than 100 words why South Georgia is covered in ice.

Overall it is fair to suggest Cook was not overwhelmed with the potential of South Georgia. He wrote:

> Not a tree or shrub was to be seen, no not even big enough to make a toothpick.

And of the potential lands further south than this island he wrote that, if anyone was to discover land:

> I make bold to declare that the world will derive no benefit from it.

But he also noted:

> Seals or Sea Bears were pretty numerous … the shores swarm'd with young cubs.

If the Royal Navy could not recognise the potential of the resources the marine mammals could provide, the sealers and whalers certainly could, and by 1825 the English explorer and sealer James Weddell calculated that 1 200 000 sealskins had been taken from this one island alone in the 50 years since its discovery! Over the next 100 years or so, although records are unclear, it is certain the sealers and whalers continued to head south and they exploited whales and seals on all the known sub-Antarctic islands, along the northern edge of the Antarctic Peninsula.

James Weddell was to become one of the legends of Antarctic exploration with the Weddell Sea named in his honour.

Activity 3.1   How profitable was it to go to the polar regions?

The estimated time for this activity is 30 minutes.

Despite the terrible hardships and a long history of ships being lost in the ice, it is clear that much of the exploration of the polar regions – particularly in the Antarctic and Greenland areas – was by whaling and sealing ships. In this activity you will work out how much money was made by a single ship on one expedition to the Arctic, and convert this to how much it would be in modern money.

The detailed notes for this activity are in the 'Activities' section of the S175 website.

3.3.1   The search for the North-West Passage

The potential of an oceanic route from the North Atlantic to the North Pacific through the Canadian Archipelago dominated polar exploration in the mid-19th century. Whilst the names of the actual explorers are still relatively well-known, one of the main personalities is not. That man was Sir John Barrow – secretary of the British Navy for almost 40 years. His enthusiasm for a shipping route meant a continual stream of naval expeditions to the Canadian north including those led by John Ross, James Clark Ross, William Parry, and perhaps the most (in)famous – Sir John Franklin.

John Franklin was 59 years of age and on his second polar expedition when in 1845 he set out in command of HMS *Erebus*, HMS *Terror* and 129 officers and men to traverse the North-West Passage (Figure 3.6). *Erebus* and *Terror* were state-of-the-art ships, well equipped and fitted out with the latest technologies such as engines and tinned food. Unfortunately, after entering the east of the archipelago, the entire expedition completely disappeared.

Figure 3.6   The North-West Passage through the archipelago to the north of Canada. The red line shows routes through the islands connecting the North Atlantic Ocean to the Pacific Ocean. The location of the magnetic North Pole (Section 3.4) is shown as a yellow star.

■   Franklin's expedition travelled close to Alert in Canada. From Figure 1.2 what winter temperatures would they have experienced?

□   You can see that they would have experienced temperatures below −30 °C for several months of the year.

The British Admiralty sent a succession of rescue expeditions north to find its men and in the process, perhaps ironically, virtually the entire archipelago was mapped. From 1850 to 1854, whilst on this search, the Irishman Sir Robert M'Clure was the first to traverse the passage; however, he abandoned his ship HMS *Investigator* and had to finish the journey by sledge (Figure 3.7).

The true horror of Franklin's fate was communicated by the Scot John Rae who (unusually for the time) actually talked to the Inuit (Figure 3.8). He wrote to the Admiralty:

Figure 3.7   M'Clure's ship HMS *Investigator* which was abandoned in June 1853. The sunken ship was rediscovered in July 2010 in relatively good condition.

> The bodies of some thirty persons were discovered on the continent, and five on an island near it …. Some of the bodies had been buried, (probably those of the first victims of famine), some were in a tent or tents, others under the boat, which had been turned over to form a shelter, and several lay scattered about in different directions. Of those found on the island one was supposed to have been an officer, as he had a telescope strapped over his shoulders, and his double-barrelled gun lay underneath him.
>
> From the mutilated state of many of the corpses and the contents of the kettles, it is evident that our wretched countrymen had been driven to the last resource – cannibalism – as a means of prolonging existence.

The Times (1854)

Rae sent his letter privately to the Admiralty, never meaning for it to be published unedited in a national newspaper. But it was, and unfortunately he was vilified for casting aspersions on the character of Franklin's men.

That their fate was awful is clear. It took until the latter part of the 20th century before archaeologists exhumed expedition members and determined that overall their fate was most likely a combination of pneumonia, tuberculosis, starvation, and lead poisoning from the 'modern' tins of food they took with them. Towards their end, there is also ample evidence that they did engage in cannibalism, although it clearly didn't help.

The North-West Passage was first navigated by ship, after three years of trying, in 1906 by the Norwegian Roald Amundsen on the *Gjøa* using the final link discovered by Rae. M'Clure's ship – the sunken HMS *Investigator* – was re-discovered in July 2010 in relatively good condition and in shallow water by Canadian archaeologists in Mercy Bay. Today, as you will see in Chapter 9, the ability to traverse the North-West Passage almost every year means it is used as

Figure 3.8   Franklin's funeral as depicted on the memorial at Waterloo Place, London.

evidence for human-driven climate change. As a result, its legal status over whether it is part of Canadian waters and so under Canadian jurisdiction, or what is called an International Strait, is the subject of much discussion.

Did the scanning work?

Now you have finished studying this section, look back at the quick notes you made after your initial scan and think about whether the scan helped you in your more detailed study of the section. For instance, was it helpful to have an idea of the 'storyline'? Were you correct in your identification of the parts that were straightforward and those that you had to work through more slowly, and was it useful to know this in advance? Decide whether you need to approach the scanning process any differently and then try scanning Section 3.4. Again, at the end write very brief notes about how you think you should apportion your study time for the section.

3.4   Science has always been a motivation

The British national priority may have been finding a route to the east across the top of North America but given the hundreds of years of experience going back to Frobisher, the commanders knew about the dreadful conditions they would encounter. Why else would they have equipped Franklin with tinned food? Surely the simple fact that as a route it was probably never going to be commercially viable must have been clear to them? It certainly was to the Arctic whalers, and more than 30 years before Franklin set out one of them wrote:

> The discovery of a North-West Passage could be of no service; for no one would have encouragement to attempt a passage, if the chance of succeeding were so small, for the sake only of the possibility of gaining a few months in an India voyage, when it could always be accomplished in the old way with so much more certainty.

> *Scoresby (1820)*

So why did the military go? William Scoresby was a successful whaler from Whitby in Yorkshire and he wrote about the Arctic at length, based on a career that started at the turn of the 19th century. Whilst the Royal Navy were throwing themselves into the terrible hardships of polar exploration, he was there for the profit. But strangely his expertise was snubbed by them. Scoresby did however have one thing in common with the military men – as a ship's captain he was profoundly aware of the difficulties presented by polar navigation. Today many mobile phones have some form of satellite navigation built in, but it takes imagination to think of how hard it is to find direction when out of sight of land. A compass needle points to the north, so it can show directions. Unfortunately, it is not really that simple. A compass needle does not point to the North Pole, which is the top end of the axis about which the Earth rotates (see Box 1.2) – it points to the magnetic North Pole

(Figure 3.6). Above the magnetic North Pole a compass needle would point vertically downwards – not to the actual (i.e. geographic) North Pole.

The magnetic field produced by a bar magnet is usually demonstrated by putting the magnet beneath a sheet of paper and sprinkling iron filings onto the paper. The filings trace out an arc between the ends of the magnet in a so-called dipole field (Figure 3.9a). The dipole comes from the fact that there are two poles on the magnet, one at either end. The Earth's magnetic field is often visualised as there being an imaginary bar magnet at the Earth's centre. However, the axis of the imaginary magnet at the Earth's core is at an angle to the north–south axis of rotation. The result is the geographic location of the North Pole is not the same as the magnetic pole (Figure 3.9b).

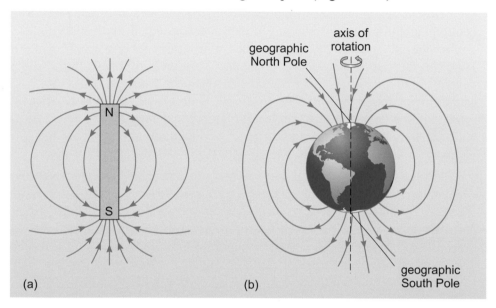

Figure 3.9   (a) A dipole magnet showing the orientation of the magnetic field lines between the magnetic poles. (b) A schematic of how the theoretical dipole is orientated relative to the axis of rotation of the Earth.

To navigate with a compass the location of the magnetic North Pole is critical. Unfortunately the inclination of the imaginary dipole magnet moves over time.

■   What would happen to the location of the magnetic North Pole as the inclination of the imaginary dipole magnet changed?

☐   The location of the magnetic North Pole would change as well.

To use a compass to navigate, one must understand both where the magnetic North Pole currently is on Earth *and* the rate of its movement. This movement is called the magnetic variation and it affects all of us. For example, in London if you wanted to head northwards based on a compass, you have to adjust your direction by more than 3° to actually head to the geographic North Pole. But this is changing at rate of ~0.15° per year.

Franklin and the other North-West Passage Arctic travellers knew about the magnetic variation. Part of their mission was to accurately locate the magnetic pole (Figure 3.6). Suddenly the exploration of the North-West Passage makes sense. Along the way they, like Scoresby, investigated other aspects of polar science such as meteorology and the wildlife. It was the same in the Antarctic and expedition members were mapping, investigating and describing the flora, fauna and physical processes that they found on their travels (Box 3.2).

Box 3.2 Stop press – cat stops science

HMS *Erebus* and HMS *Terror* had been to the Antarctic with James Clark Ross (1839–43) long before Franklin took them to their doom in the North-West Passage. Ross's expedition was hugely successful and he discovered the location of the magnetic South Pole at the southern end of the notional dipole magnet in the Earth (Figure 3.9). He also made many geographical discoveries including Ross Island on which the location of current largest base in Antarctica resides, and Mount Erebus which is the most spectacular volcano on the continent. Ross took civilian experts to describe and write about their discoveries and they produced vast scientific volumes to record their results. It is no exaggeration to say that science in the polar regions was leading global understanding. Unfortunately the official reports from Ross's expedition reveal that the pathway to knowledge is sometimes more complicated than originally envisaged:

> When the ships were in the high latitude of 77° 10' S, and long. 178½° [W], a fish was thrown up by the spray in a gale of wind, against the bows of the Terror, and frozen there. It was carefully removed … and a rough sketch was made of it by the surgeon, John Robertson, Esq., but before it could be put into spirits, a cat carried it away from his cabin, and ate it. The sketch is not sufficiently detailed [so] … we have introduced a copy of the design merely to preserve a memorial of what appears to be a novel form.

Richardson (1844)

This was a tragedy as the fish was a species new to science that had very unusual features including long fins and very pale flesh. Sixty years were to pass before a scientist on the expedition led by Adrien de Gerlache on the ship *Belgica* rediscovered and named the fish Robertson had drawn (Figure 3.10).

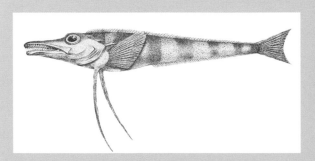

Figure 3.10 The cod icefish rediscovered and published in 1904 by Louis Dollo. The original caption in the expedition report read 'Mangé par le chat de l'équipage de la Terror' or 'Eaten by the *Terror*'s cat!'

Each degree of latitude is divided into 60 so-called minutes. So 77° 10' S is 77 degrees 10 minutes south.

Next time you look at the online map, take a moment to see where the fish was discovered and look at the timeline of notable expeditions heading both north and south.

The fish was a so-called icefish – a member of a remarkable species able to live in the very cold Antarctic waters. Animal blood is a fluid which carries nutrients around the body and it consists mainly of liquid called plasma, red and white blood cells and another cell type called platelets. In most animals, the red blood cells carry the oxygen throughout the body, but as Richardson noted, the icefish was very pale, which means it has very few red blood cells. It does, however, have unusual plasma which can carry oxygen and contains antifreeze proteins as well. Chapter 4 will show that the Southern Ocean has a high concentration of dissolved oxygen. This together with the antifreeze and the special plasma means that the pale-coloured icefish with few red blood cells can nevertheless extract enough oxygen to thrive in the cold polar waters.

In effect, Franklin, Scoresby and the others were using the polar regions to study processes of global importance because they were best studied in the poles.

■   Imagine the Earth with a dipole magnet at its core. If the dipole magnet changes orientation relative to the axis of the Earth, where will the greatest movement in the magnetic field be?

□   At the poles (Figure 3.9b).

If they happened to discover a shorter trading route to the Far East at the same time, then so much the better. Simultaneously they studied processes and entities that only occurred at the poles. If you want to study an icefish or polar bear, then obviously you have to go where they live. The same applies for physical processes such as discovering how giant icebergs are formed.

This modern approach to science in the high latitudes continues to this day, and revisiting the most famous of expeditions of the Heroic Age shows that science was invariably at their core. Sadly the scientific work they did is often neglected. For example, the Norwegian Fridtjof Nansen proved (as you will see in Chapter 4) that the sea ice drifted across the Arctic Ocean by freezing his ship *Fram* into the ice and living on it whilst it drifted from 1893 to 1896. The reputation of Robert Falcon Scott has suffered greatly in the hundred years since his death in Antarctica with various ill-informed commentators speaking at dull length on his leadership style or Edwardian social class sensibilities and so on. However, the many thousands of pages of science that came from his two expeditions are rarely mentioned. When Scott and his four colleagues died after pulling their sledge in backbreaking work for over 2500 km, the relief party recovered over 17 kg of rocks from the Trans-Antarctic Mountains from their sledge. Chapter 2 noted Shackleton observed coal in these mountains but Scott's party were bringing back *actual* fossils and, even when it must have been obvious to them that they were in trouble, they did not throw them off their sledge. These rocks remained the only samples from inland Antarctica for almost the next 50 years. And they didn't just investigate geology (Box 3.3); members of Scott's expedition built on their polar work and went on to be giants in their respective fields. For example, Frank Debenham (just 28 in 1910) became a leading geologist at

Cambridge; the meteorologist George Simpson (33 in 1910) was head of the London Meteorological Office for 18 years and Edward Nelson (26 in 1910) was a senior naturalist at the Plymouth Marine Laboratory before dying at the age of only 39.

So why isn't this scientific story more widely known? It is fair to suggest that for true historical note an expedition needs tragedy to cement it within the public sphere, and Scott's expedition was no exception. But there has been amazing research from many great polar expeditions, led for example by William Spiers Bruce, Adrien de Gerlache and the Australian Douglas Mawson, that significantly advanced understanding of the planet – but are almost forgotten today.

Box 3.3   Happiness is a penguin's egg

The doctor on Scott's Terra Nova expedition was Edward Wilson. Wilson and Scott had visited Antarctica in 1901 and discovered the astonishing fact that the emperor penguin laid and incubated its eggs during the Antarctic winter. You saw this incubation and the terrible conditions the penguins endure in Activity 1.2. On return to the UK, analysis of abandoned eggs they had collected suggested that the embryo of the emperor penguin may show an evolutionary link between reptiles and birds. Wilson made a winter journey to collect some egg samples a priority for the expedition. His journey to achieve this aim in 1911 with Apsley Cherry-Garrard and Henry Bowers was to become known as the 'Worst Journey in the World'.

It wasn't a particularly long sled journey by polar standards, but it was the first in the horrendous Antarctic winter (Figure 3.11).

Figure 3.11   Sledging in the Heroic Age of Antarctic exploration. A chalk and charcoal sketch by Dr Edward Wilson, the surgeon and naturalist and leader of the 'Worst Journey' on Scott's Terra Nova expedition.

■   From Figure 1.2, what temperatures would the three have had to cope with?

☐   From April to September the temperatures at South Pole are below −60 °C. It is reasonable to expect they endured similar conditions.

Cherry-Garrard (1922) wrote that it was more than difficult for them:

> Antarctic exploration is seldom as bad as you imagine, seldom as bad as it sounds. But this journey had beggared our language: no words could express its horror.

You saw the blizzards they had to cope with in Activity 1.2, but they were successful and did return three unbroken emperor penguin eggs. In addition they had made the first observations of how the birds could cope with the worst of the Antarctic weather. Unfortunately, when investigated by scientists at the Natural History Museum (London) the eggs did not provide the link Wilson was investigating. But the 'Worst Journey' was successful science. They had a theory – that the embryos in the eggs would show a 'link' to reptiles – and they collected eggs to investigate their theory. The result was an unequivocal answer to the initial question. The emperor penguins were not an evolutionary link between birds and reptiles. The horrors they endured were worthwhile and as Cherry-Garrard said:

> If you march your Winter Journeys you will have your reward, so long as all you want is a penguin's egg.

The Heroic Age of exploration ended in the north with Nansen's three-year drift across the Arctic Ocean, and arguably later in Antarctica with the death of Shackleton at South Georgia in 1922. A suitable epitaph for this era was provided by Apsley Cherry-Garrard, the youngest member of Scott's expedition:

> I would like to serve under Scott, Amundsen, Shackleton and Wilson – each to his part. For a joint scientific and geographical piece of organization, give me Scott; for a Winter Journey, Wilson; for a dash to the Pole and nothing else, Amundsen: and if I am in the devil of a hole and want to get out of it, give me Shackleton every time. They will all go down in polar history as leaders, these men.

Cherry-Garrard (1922)

It is also true that during this era of science and exploration, large areas of the high latitudes were claimed and so science was linked to sovereignty.

Since the end of the Heroic Age before World War II there have been expeditions to study both polar regions, but on a small scale. For example, in Greenland the British Arctic Air Route Expedition of 1930–31 led by Gino Watkins collected meteorological data from the Greenland Ice Sheet with the purpose of increasing the safety in air travel across the Atlantic Ocean. In the Antarctic, John Rymill's British Graham Land Expedition (BGLE 1934–37) investigated the geophysics of the Antarctic Peninsula. But even the 16 people of the BGLE looks a huge undertaking compared with an expedition from 1920–21 in which just the 19-year-old Thomas Bagshawe and 29-year-old Charles Lester spent the winter on the Antarctic Peninsula alone and studying penguins, while living in an upturned boat! Today Bagshawe and Lester would be called irresponsible – but their scientific work revealed important knowledge about the Antarctic climate and wildlife and stands as testament to their skill and commitment.

After World War II, polar expeditions became mainly the preserve of national governments but in the background the sealing and whaling industries continued to flourish, first based on land, and later from giant factory ships that scoured the polar seas.

> A significant motivation for the early exploration of the high latitudes was science. Sometimes they were the best place to study processes that are global in nature, and sometimes they were the only place where specific aspects of science could be studied.

Did your scanning get more effective?

Now you have finished studying this section, look back at the quick notes you made after your initial scan and think again about whether the scan helped you in your more detailed study of the section. Do you think that spending time on the scan made your study time for the material longer or shorter overall? Decide whether you are going to continue using this approach for subsequent sections and chapters.

3.5 The modern era of polar research

Before World War II, with the exception of Nansen in the Arctic and Amundsen, Shackleton and Scott's parties in the south, the central high latitudes remained untouched because of very difficult physical access.

■   Can you think of a profound difference in the geography and political environment between the Arctic and the Antarctic that could influence the way scientific research is conducted?

☐   The Arctic is surrounded by nation states with sovereignty rights. The Antarctic is remote without a single government and no established population.

Svalbard – a small island at ~79° N administered by Norway – is an exception to issues of sovereignty as it has special treaties guaranteeing continued international access.

This difference affects virtually all polar research. For example, today, without complicated negotiations with Canada it would be unlikely that the Ukraine could run a research expedition to the North-West Passage. In complete contrast, the Ukraine can (and has) operated many scientific expeditions to the Antarctic within what some consider to be British Antarctic Territory (as you will see in Chapter 8). Another control on the way polar science is conducted is provided by the way data is obtained. To a certain extent, the maps are already drawn and so the scientific unknowns have changed from what they once were. To a modern scientist who wants to understand how a particular penguin colony changes over time in relation to the environmental conditions, the most useful and appropriate way of doing it would be using a fully equipped and resourced polar research station.

But the decision to build a research station is just the beginning of a complex process. For example, in Antarctica the location is limited by the ice cover. What else would you need? A coastal location would require a ship with the capability to work within the frozen seas and a harbour for loading and unloading. If the location is a remote station on, for example, the Greenland Ice Sheet you would require air transport. Aeroplanes require fuel, airports (or at least runways) and air traffic control. If a base were to exist for several years, what sort of food, fuel and clothing supplies would be required? How much paper and how many pencils are required for a year or more? There would need to be a medical facility more substantial than a general practice surgery. Would you need a dentist? How long would you expect the people who would work on the base to be away from home? Mawson, Scott and Nansen thought nothing of spending a couple of years being completely isolated, but is that appropriate today? What accommodation would be required? Some scientists require laboratories which would need to provide the same safety levels and technical standards as those available in a university. There would have to be computer facilities, power, a kitchen and dining room, equipment stores, even a sewage facility. Finally, there would need to be an inherent maintenance operation able to resolve everyday problems such as the kitchen oven breaking.

Clearly, setting up a base is a complicated, wide-ranging and expensive operation that demands long-term commitment. It should not be a surprise to know that significant polar research programmes are run entirely by government research organisations.

Activity 3.2   Polar research stations

The estimated time for this activity is 30 minutes.

It is important that national programmes are managed cost-effectively. Given that the aim of a research station is to conduct research, in this activity you will estimate how many people you think could be involved in running a small Antarctic research station with five scientists in the field. You will also investigate actual polar research stations operated by different nations in both hemispheres.

The detailed notes for this activity are in the 'Activities' section of the S175 website.

Almost every polar researching nation has either a central research organisation, or a central logistics agency to support remote science. For Britain it is the British Antarctic Survey (BAS, Figure 3.12a), for the Germans it is the Alfred Wegener Institute for Polar and Marine Research (AWI, Figure 3.12b), and both organisations have research interests and facilities at both poles. For the Australians, the Australian Antarctic Division (AAD) plays

The US Antarctic program is so large there is military support as well.

the same role although lacking the Arctic component. For all three organisations science is the focus, coupled to a logistics component. Other nations such as Argentina and Chile have logistics run by their military, and finally there are nations like the United States which have a logistics contractor (currently Raytheon Polar Services). Just because there is a central organisation providing focus, it doesn't restrict access; for example, a British person does not have to be a member of the BAS to go to Antarctica. In addition, there is cross-collaboration between nations and I have conducted research in both polar regions using German, American and British logistics – although each one has a distinctive national 'flavour'.

(a)

(b)

Figure 3.12   Two leading European polar institutes. (a) The British Antarctic Survey in Cambridge, England, and (b) The Alfred Wegener Institute for Polar and Marine Research based in Bremerhaven, Germany.

■   Can you think of different scientific endeavours requiring similar levels of government support or degrees of isolation?

☐   There are similarities to the human space program in the way logistics have to be managed and, from a lifestyle point of view, similarities to working on a submarine.

The space program is in some ways a good analogy because the people on the ground know exactly what supplies, spares and tools the astronauts have with them. In the case given previously of a kitchen oven breaking, the people at 'home' have knowledge of what would be on the base, what the repair would require, and what would need shipping to Antarctica. Overall, running a sustained scientific research base is far more complicated than a single expedition and is a staggering feat of organisation.

Compared with working on a submarine, both have small isolated groups living in close proximity.

3.6   A modern Antarctic field trip

There is a famous apocryphal joke in polar research where the explorer Shackleton is alleged to have placed an advert in a newspaper saying: 'Men wanted for hazardous journey. Low wages, bitter cold, long hours of complete darkness. Safe return doubtful. Honour and recognition in event of success.' It is a nice story but a modern research expedition to Antarctica begins somewhat differently. To show how it happens I will describe a trip I went on in 2007 to the Antarctic to conduct oceanographic research. Whilst the details of this process will change for any particular experiment, the experiences are common to most polar research trips. It began with an idea based on how the ice sheets at the edge of the continent of Antarctica could be melting. I and others thought warm ocean currents could be responsible for the melting, so we wrote a proposal and sent it to a government research agency called the Natural Environment Research Council. The agency delegates the decision on whether any particular piece of research should be undertaken to independent international scientists who judge its excellence, achievability and whether it is good financial value. This is a highly competitive process and there is a low success rate, which ensures that the available resources are most wisely spent. The grant was successful and it took perhaps 8–9 months from proposal writing to a funding decision. It took a further two years for the work to be scheduled by the British Antarctic Survey, as they were already committed in the shorter term.

In 2006 we boxed and carefully itemised our equipment and in mid-July we sent it to the British Antarctic Survey in Cambridge, England. We then had a comprehensive medical and were measured for polar clothing. By August the clothing and freight were taken by lorry to Grimsby and loaded on a ship and sent to the Falkland Islands. In February of the *following year* we left the UK to travel to the Falkland Islands on a military flight via Ascension Island. It had taken over three years from starting out and over 15 000 km of travel before making any measurements! Once in the Falkland Islands, we boarded the research ship RRS *James Clark Ross* (Figure 3.13a) and the work began. Cargo was recovered from boxes that had been packed more than six months earlier and the ship became a mass of activity as equipment was installed and secured to solid benches so that once we sailed nothing would move. Within 48 hours we sailed and headed south to the ice, becoming an isolated team of 10 scientists and 23 crew for over 50 days (Figure 3.13b).

Within five days the ship was working in the pack ice fringing the ice shelves of Antarctica on 24-hour shift work. Depending on the science aims, we worked on the sea ice (Figure 3.14a) or made extensive oceanographic measurements (Figure 3.14b) to make the best of the work time. Working on shifts in a routine meant even the 50 days we were away was over relatively quickly. It was early April and time to head north again.

The science behind the expedition is described in Chapter 4.

■   At the start of the trip in early February, why would there be 24-hour daylight at high latitudes?

□   The South Pole is orientated towards the Sun and it is Antarctic summer. This means that at a latitude higher than the Antarctic Circle (66.6° S) there could be the midnight Sun.

At high latitudes as the Sun skims the horizon there is little warmth in the light. But because the Sun is low in the sky, there are vivid sunset colours for virtually the entire day (Figure 1.12).

(a)

(b)

Figure 3.13 (a) The Royal Research Ship *James Clark Ross*. This fully equipped research ship is able to spend up to two months working in ice with 25 scientists on board. (b) Once the ship leaves the Falkland Islands, the next land it will reach will be the sea ice and ice shelves of the Antarctic, about five days later.

(a)

(b)

Figure 3.14 Ship-based science in the Antarctic. (a) Working on the sea ice at dusk. (b) Deploying a piece of oceanographic equipment from the ship.

■ What would happen to the length of the days over the course of an Antarctic trip from February to April?

□ In the Southern Hemisphere winter would be approaching. The solstice in March would have passed (Figure 1.11c) and the days would be getting rapidly shorter.

The location and the climate at Rothera Station is shown in the online map.

When the science expedition was over, after a long detour the ship visited the largest British research base on Adelaide Island on the Antarctic Peninsula, known as Rothera Station (Figure 3.15a). Although this detour added many days to the trip, it allowed people, equipment and refuse from the base to be removed from the Antarctic. Rothera has approximately 20 personnel over the

1,2,34

Antarctic winter, although in summer the population can reach 150 before people leave for research on the Antarctic Continent in ski-equipped aircraft (Figure 3.15b) or ships. On our return to the Falklands with 45 passengers plus crew it was cramped, and the planes soon left the base to spend the Antarctic winter in the Northern Hemisphere. The remaining people were isolated for several months (Figure 3.15c) until the following spring, when the ice retreated and the ships, aircraft and people returned once more.

(a)

(b)

(c)

Figure 3.15   (a) Rothera Research Station on Adelaide Island on the Antarctic Peninsula. (b) A ski-equipped de Havilland Canada DHC-6 Twin Otter aeroplane. Four of these planes are operated from Rothera Research Station. (c) A party of scientists and support staff left to stay for the winter in Antarctica.

Question 3.5

The photograph in Figure 1.12 was taken close to the middle of the day in April. There are beautiful sunset colours. Based on what you have learnt in Chapter 1, this chapter, and on the S175 website, in less than 100 words explain why the sunset goes on so long, and if there were similar weather conditions whether you would expect to see a similar effect in a couple of days.

This 50-day science voyage dominated our lives for approximately 3.5 years, but only on return could we analyse and understand the data from the hundreds of people who were either directly or indirectly involved in collecting.

The experiences are common to other national programmes, whether drifting in the frozen pack ice of the Arctic or drilling an ice core on the summit of Antarctica. In the 21st century, field science is not based around upturned boats like Bagshawe and Lester used in 1920, and despite the commitment, organisation and expertise required, they are much more effective for it.

■ Why are so many of the transport items and people in the photographs in Section 3.6 red in colour?

□ Red is generally an unnatural colour in the polar regions and so it always stands out and any sight of it is worthy of a second look. Scientists, ships, aeroplanes and even tourists often use the colour red in order to be seen.

Question 3.6

There are 30 people in the photograph in Figure 3.15c who are going to spend the winter at Rothera. There are also two more on the base out of shot. Given that Rothera is a large base and has a lot of winter maintenance, estimate – based on your answer to Activity 3.2 – how many scientists there could be in this party.

Activity 3.3   Science at high latitudes

The estimated time for this activity is 30 minutes.

Polar scientists have personal reasons for wanting to go to the high latitudes. In this activity you will investigate the human dimension to modern work in the polar regions by watching interviews with scientists and looking at the way science at the poles can help us today.

The detailed notes for this activity are in the 'Activities' section of the S175 website.

3.7   Remote science in the modern age

A field-based expedition is often the most effective way to investigate the frozen planet, but as you have seen, the investment of time and energy is huge for a relatively small amount of time in the field. Often the process that one wishes to investigate only occurs at a particular time of the year.

■ If you wanted to collect emperor penguins' eggs like Wilson and his team (Box 3.3), which time of the year would you need to be in Antarctica?

□ You would need to be in Antarctica in the winter, which would be from May to September (Figure 1.2).

The same applies, for example, if you wanted to study a winter process such as the growth of sea ice, and the logistical problems are even more significant than usual. However, today for some areas of science you have access to data that would be unthinkable just a few decades ago.

3.7.1   Measuring the ice

You can see this decline on the online map.

Scientists only know about the recent decline of Arctic sea ice because of satellites orbiting the Earth. These in turn give firm guidance about priority areas for land expeditions. The most modern satellite is the European Space

Agency's (ESA) CryoSat mission led by a British team and dedicated to monitoring the changes in the thickness of ice floating in the polar oceans and variations in the thickness of the ice over Greenland and Antarctica (Figure 3.16).

Standard meteorological satellites can measure the amount of sea ice in both hemispheres every single day. Figure 3.17 shows data from 5 October 2010: in the Arctic the sea ice is growing, whilst in the Antarctic it is melting.

■ Looking at Figure 3.17, is the sea ice of uniform concentration poleward of the ice edge?

□ In the Arctic the concentration of sea ice is generally high, with purple colours. In the Antarctic there are many regions where the concentration is much lower, in the yellows and greens.

The lower concentrations of ice in the Antarctic could be a feature of the coming melt, as October is spring in Antarctica. Data from satellites can show the ice visually and there is a stunning complexity in the ice edge that one could only imagine before the satellite era. Whilst close up, the sea ice may look

Figure 3.16 The European Satellite CryoSat which will measure the global ice loss by human-driven climate change using a sophisticated radar system.

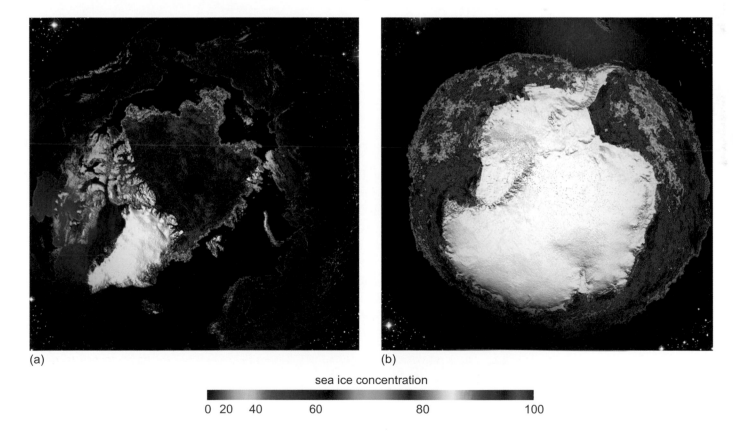

(a)　　　　　　　　　　(b)

sea ice concentration

0 20 40 60 80 100

Figure 3.17 The concentration of sea ice measured by meteorological satellites on 5 October 2010. Colours represent the amount of ocean that is covered: purples indicate total cover; yellows and greens, about half the ocean covered; and blues, very low proportion covered. (a) The Arctic, (b) the Antarctic.

like a dense sheet with no distinguishing features (e.g. Figure 1.1a or 1.8b), from space it has the whirls and swirls of cream in a cup of coffee (Figure 3.18).

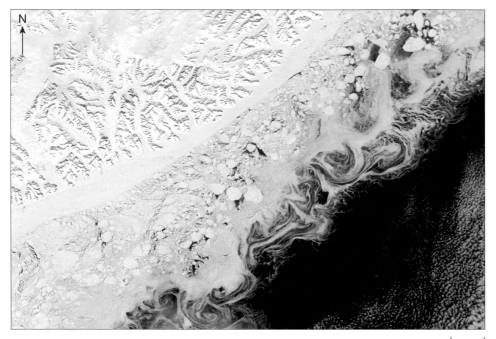

25 km

Figure 3.18 A high-resolution satellite image of the coast and sea ice of east Greenland. The ice shows swirls and flows on the scale of tens of kilometres that could only be imagined before such images were available.

3.7.2 Tracking animals

Biologists also use satellites to determine where animals roam, with sometimes surprising results. A tag on a single female polar bear revealed tracks of more than 14 500 km across an area of almost 500 000 square kilometres as the bear sought its main prey species – the seal (Figure 3.19a, b). On Antarctica, grey head albatross satellite tags show that these too forage over staggering distances, with one bird making two circumnavigations plus other trips over the South Atlantic (Figure 3.20a, b). The results of tracking different penguin species show similar wide foraging ranges. What is clear is that such wide ranges will, as you will see in Chapter 8, have profound implications for polar wildlife management.

3.7.3 Using animals to measure the ocean

Miniaturisation of electronics has enabled marine scientists to not only track seals but to use them to study the ocean as well. One has to choose the species of seal wisely as some (e.g. leopard seals) stay relatively close to one location whereas others such as elephant seals range over wide areas.

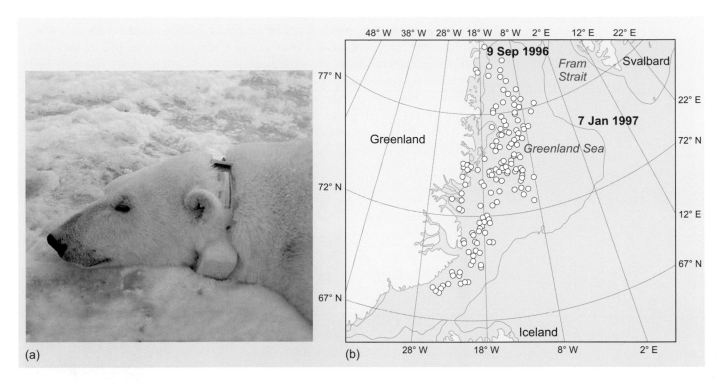

Figure 3.19   (a) A drugged polar bear with a satellite collar attached to its neck. Although it looks a tight fit, the collar is carefully designed to expand as the bear grows, whilst not falling off as it moves about. (b) The travels of a female polar bear tracked over 1415 days between 1994 and 1998; also shown are the minimum (9 September 1996) and maximum (7 January 1997) ice extent.

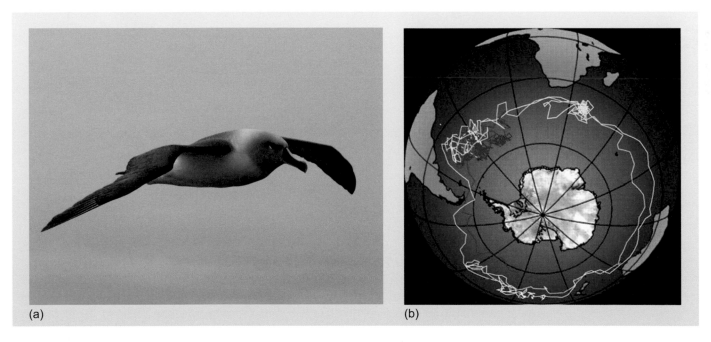

Figure 3.20   (a) A grey head albatross. (b) The travels of one male grey head albatross. Different colours represent data collected in successive years, and one of the circumnavigations shown took just 46 days.

Figure 3.21 shows the results from 58 elephant seals around Antarctica and such plots can bring a quantum leap to our understanding of the ice-covered seas. Further integration of physiological sensors, such as heart rate and body temperature sensors, means the seal biology can be investigated in combination with the physical environment. The data set in Figure 3.21 collected by tagged elephant seals is more than nine times larger than the entire Antarctic ship collected using instruments such as those in Figure 3.14b over the same time period.

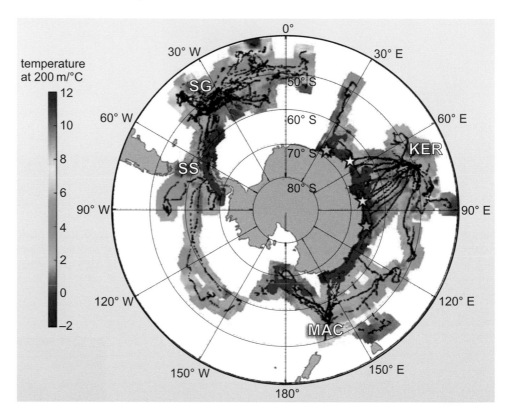

Figure 3.21 The temperature at 200 m depth in the Southern Ocean collected by elephant seals equipped with oceanographic sensors at South Georgia (SG), the South Shetland (SS), Kerguelen (KER), and Macquarie (MAC) islands. The black tracks are where seals went and red tracks indicate profiles collected within sea ice.

3.8   Conclusions

The hunter-gatherers of the Arctic were relatively isolated for thousands of years until Europeans headed north for resources including minerals and wildlife. In more recent times science has always been a driving force for the exploration – even if this has been missed and unacknowledged by media and the general public. Today the scale of the logistical issues raised by the science can only be sensibly addressed by a government-led operation, often run with military support backed up by unique technologies and techniques.

The next four chapters focus on the science of the polar world including the physical environment and the biological systems present. You will see that the reasons for exploration noted in Section 3.4 are evident throughout. Chapter 4 begins where Chapter 3 ends, with the polar oceans.

3.9   Summary of Chapter 3

• Humans have lived in the Arctic ever since they followed the ice retreat at the end of the LGM. Once there, they adopted a hunter-gatherer lifestyle.

• Early European explorers were seeking trading routes but rich animal resources drove the exploration in both hemispheres.

• The enforcement of sovereignty had no regard for any rights that may be due to indigenous peoples who lived beyond the norms of European culture.

• Science has been at the forefront of polar exploration since Victorian times.

• Science at the poles is done for two main reasons. First, it is where a process such as ice formation and decay actually happens; and secondly, it can be used to study processes such as magnetism that are of global importance but are best studied at the poles.

• In the modern era, large national organisations have developed to place scientists effectively in the field.

• Remote sensing technologies are allowing huge advances and access to measurements such as the melting of an entire continent, the tracking of wildlife over inconceivable distances, and extensive oceanographic data.

4 The poles and global climate

4.1 Introduction

You saw and heard in Activity 1.2 that Antarctica is the coldest and windiest continent on the planet with temperatures below −70 °C and that the Arctic winter is also hostile. This impression is often repeated and views such as these may have influenced your answers in Activity 1.1.

■ From Figure 1.2 what were the winter temperatures of Alert in the Arctic and the South Pole in the Antarctic?

□ The winter temperatures at Alert were just below −30 °C, whilst at the South Pole they were below −60 °C.

If you consider the energy balance described in Section 1.4 it would be strange, for example, to expect the northern tip of the Antarctic Peninsula to have the same climate as the South Pole. Because the two regions are ~3000 km apart they receive very different amounts of energy from the Sun. It is as unlikely as London having the same climate as North Africa.

The Antarctic Peninsula is often referred to as the 'banana belt' because of its moderate climate. One research base is called Copacabana Station, named after the Mexican beach, and has a palm tree as its logo!

In this chapter you will focus on the key features of the northern and southern polar climates to unravel the varied climate of the polar regions. Whilst the fundamental reason the poles are colder is because of the energy balance, here you will see that relatively small-scale processes that happen only at high latitudes are part of a linked system controlling the climate of our entire planet. Ultimately, the climate of the UK and coastal Northern Europe is moderate partially because the oceans freeze at high latitudes.

This chapter begins by asking the question: how is it known that there is a global atmospheric circulation?

Building on your understanding

In Chapter 3, you tried various techniques for making notes from the study material and you should continue to use your preferred method for keeping notes as you work through Chapter 4. You may have found that your notes contained different items, such as reminders about important ideas, comments about points you wanted to return to or to discuss with a Study Adviser, and answers to questions. As you work through this chapter, you should try to practise turning some of your notes into short summaries in your own words. This is an excellent way of demonstrating to yourself that you really do understand the material.

4.2 The winds and the waves

When scientists first drilled deep ice cores in Greenland, they identified annual layers of snow which indicated features of past climates (Section 2.3).

However, these ice cores also showed more. Amongst the layers of frozen snow were irregularly spaced dark bands which under a microscope were identified as volcanic ash.

Volcanic ash provides an independent way to date ice cores. For example, ash from a vast eruption in 1783 in Iceland is clearly visible in the Greenland ice.

■ How can volcanic ash end up trapped within an ice core layer in Greenland when the closest volcano is hundreds of miles away in Iceland?

☐ The ash must have been carried onto the ice sheet by the winds and then buried by the snow.

When snow crystals first form (a process called nucleation) the ice often grows around miniscule pieces of dust. The dark bands in the ice cores from Greenland demonstrated that when large volcanoes erupt (Figure 4.1), some of the dust they produce is eventually trapped in the ice. Because the source of dust is not close, it provides direct evidence (albeit only one of many pieces) for the global atmospheric circulation. The obvious question is how does the global atmospheric circulation arise?

Figure 4.1 The 1991 eruption of Mount Pinatubo in The Philippines. Some ash from this volcano is now trapped in the ice of Greenland and Antarctica.

On a global scale, the balance of incoming and outgoing energy is critical (Section 1.4). Air at the Equator is warmed by the increased solar input, its density is reduced and the air rises. At the poles exactly the opposite is happening – the air is cooled, becomes denser and sinks.

■ Can you think of an example of heating and cooling which changes the density of air, causing it to rise and sink?

☐ A hot air balloon traps less dense warm air and as a result it rises. When the air cools the balloon sinks.

You can see these convection currents with a tiny amount of talcum powder scattered above a radiator.

But from your own experience you know that the atmosphere is not just vertical movements of air – after all, how often do you feel a vertical wind? The atmosphere has much stronger horizontal movements. To picture how horizontal motion can arise from vertical forces, imagine a room with a radiator on one wall and an open freezer on the other (Figure 4.2). The radiator is transferring energy to the air in contact with it and as a result the air molecules become more widely spaced apart. Fewer molecules in the same volume mean that the density is reduced and the air rises in a convection current to the ceiling where it then spreads out.

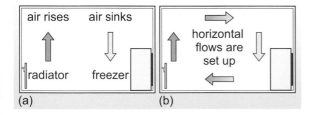

(a)   (b)

Figure 4.2 (a) A room with a radiator on one wall and an open freezer on the other will cause air to rise and sink at opposite ends; (b) horizontal flows are set up to replace this ascending and descending air.

■ What would you feel if you had bare feet and opened an upright freezer?

☐ The cold air that was within the freezer would flood over your feet as it sank to the floor.

Inside the freezer the air is cooled and the molecules are closer together. This increases the density of the air inside compared with the air outside. When you open the freezer door the air sinks and spreads across the floor. The two vertical motions – upward above the radiator and downward near the freezer – set up a horizontal circulation pattern (called a cell) across the room. The same overall process is happening on Earth. At the Equator warm air is rising, and at high latitudes it is sinking.

On Earth the pattern is more complicated. With air only rising at the Equator and sinking at the poles the circulation is not stable, and so a pattern of six cells develops – three in each hemisphere (Figure 4.3). Each cell is similar in principle to the heating and cooling in Figure 4.2, but the link between the Equator and each pole is now more complex. Winds in an east–west direction also arise due to the energy balance.

Question 4.1

What would be the typical albedo in North America at 30° N in Figure 4.3 compared with that at the same latitude in the Pacific Ocean? Which of these two locations would have the greater specific heat capacity? (*Hint*: see Section 1.4.2.)

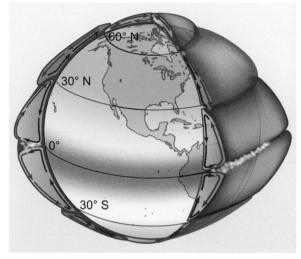

Figure 4.3 A more sophisticated model of the latitudinal atmospheric circulation with three circulation cells in each hemisphere. Where the two cells either side of the Equator meet is called the Inter-Tropical Convergence Zone (ITCZ).

Sites an equal distance from the Equator receive the same amount of solar energy, but because of different specific heat capacities and albedos the land heats up to different extents. As a result, the air above the land is warmed more than air above the ocean. Like in Figure 4.2, this differential heating leads to horizontal winds. Once in motion the moving air is deflected by the Coriolis effect. This is a force that arises due to the rotation of the planet to the east. As a result, winds in the Northern Hemisphere are deflected to the right, whilst those in the Southern Hemisphere are deflected to the left (Figure 4.4).

The winds are also deflected by the high mountains. The result is the relatively complicated mean surface wind pattern shown in Figure 4.5. The three-dimensional global winds are a composite of the schematics shown in Figure 4.3 and 4.5.

■ Why is the prevailing wind direction in Figure 4.5 different for January and July?

☐ In January it is the southern summer whilst in July it is the northern summer. At each time period, the energy balance which drives the winds is different because of the global distribution of land.

In the same way that a sailing boat is pushed by the wind (Figure 4.6), friction transfers wind energy to the sea surface. Initially it generates tiny ripples that develop to form surface waves. The waves then act as 'sails' to further transfer energy. The result is that typically the speed of the wind-driven ocean surface current is about 3% of the wind speed pushing it.

Question 4.2

If a wind is blowing at a speed of 20 m s^{-1} over the surface of the ocean, what would be the speed of a typical wind-driven ocean current?

The 3% of the wind speed that is transferred seems small, but the winds act on a very large ocean surface area. Once in motion the surface current is

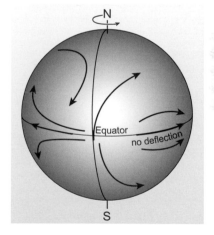

Figure 4.4 The Earth's rotation deflects winds following example paths (arrows). Note that apparent movement increases with latitude.

The unit m s^{-1} means metres per second. It is the distance the wind would travel in 1 second.

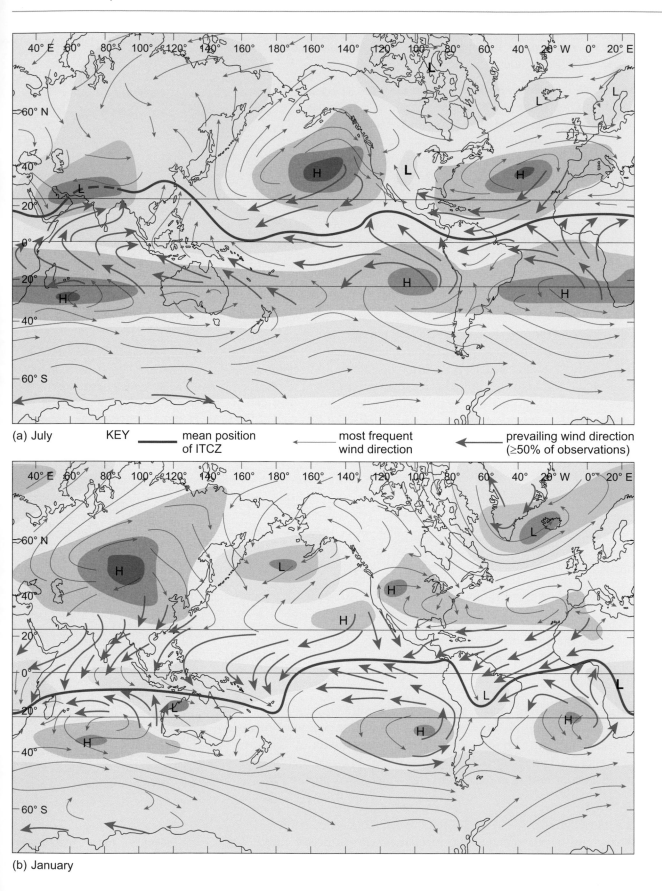

(a) July

KEY ——— mean position of ITCZ ⟵ most frequent wind direction ⟵ prevailing wind direction (≥50% of observations)

(b) January

Figure 4.5 The prevailing winds at the Earth's surface and the position of the Inter-Tropical Convergence Zone (ITCZ), which is where the wind systems of the two hemispheres meet (as in Figure 4.3). Red colours indicate where the air pressure is relatively high and blue where it is relatively low. (a) The prevailing wind in July, and (b) the prevailing wind in January.

deflected by the rotation of the Earth (Figure 4.4) and a mean surface pattern of ocean currents develops (Figure 4.7). Some of the ocean currents in this picture are important enough to have names; for example, the Gulf Stream and the North Atlantic Drift. Compare Figures 4.5a and 4.7 – there are some obvious and clear correlations. The winds in a band from approximately 40°– 50° S form a continuous circulation around the planet – these are the so-called roaring forties and furious fifties that sailors had to contend with before the Panama and Suez Canals were built.

■ Which current do the roaring forties and furious fifties correlate with?

□ In Figure 4.7 you can see these winds correspond to a continuous current around the planet called the Antarctic Circumpolar Current (ACC).

Figure 4.6 A sailing boat is pushed along by the winds.

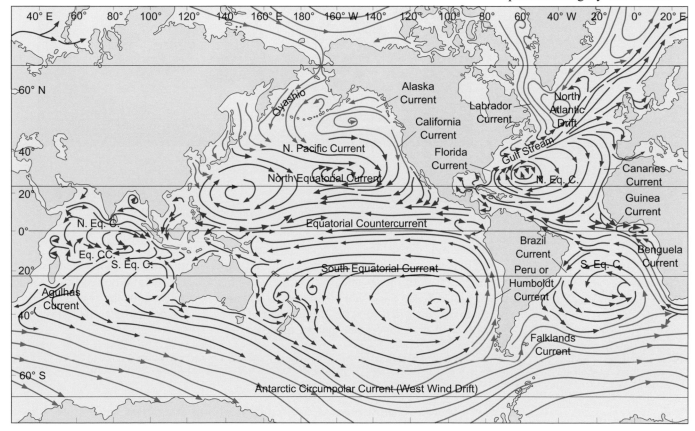

Figure 4.7 A schematic diagram of the surface currents of the Earth for the northern summer. Red arrows represent warm currents, and blue arrows represent cool ones. In some regions there are large seasonal differences.

The ACC is sometimes called the West Wind Drift because the wind that is driving the current comes from the west – meteorologists give directions based on where the wind is coming from, so the roaring forties are a west wind. However, a marine scientist would give directions based on the direction the current is flowing to – so the ACC is an easterly current. To avoid this confusion only the term ACC will be used. The volume of water in the ACC is huge, and roughly 100 000 000 m^3 of water squeezes through the gap between South America and Antarctica every second.

The effects of the circulation patterns shown in Figure 4.7 are clear when compared with maps of sea surface temperature. Figure 4.8 shows the average sea surface temperature (SST) derived using measurements from satellites and ships but displayed using a projection that shows both poles (see Section 1.3). As this projection is most likely unfamiliar, take a few moments to check you understand it. First focus on the South Pole in Figure 4.8.

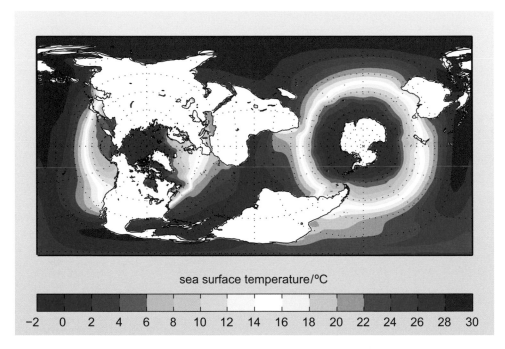

sea surface temperature/°C

−2 0 2 4 6 8 10 12 14 16 18 20 22 24 26 28 30

Figure 4.8 The global mean sea surface temperature derived from ship and satellite measurements on a projection that shows both poles. This is a Cassini projection with the 0° and 180° longitudes shown as horizontal dotted lines across the plot. Lines of latitude are shown as expanding circles from the two poles which are distorted towards the Equator. The white regions close to the coasts are areas with no temperature data in this data set.

■ Comparing Figures 4.7 and 4.8, what is the surface temperature of the ACC?

☐ Figure 4.7 shows the ACC circumnavigating Antarctica and Figure 4.8 shows that this region has a sea surface temperature of generally less than 4 °C but down to −2 °C close to the continent.

In the Southern Hemisphere the isotherms (colours) shown in Figure 4.8 are approximately circular with temperature rising with an increasing distance from the pole. This means that if you started a journey in any of the great oceans from the Equator and headed directly southwards to approximately 50° S (Figure 4.8), the surface temperature would decrease from ~30 °C to ~16 °C. The changing colours are widely spaced so the temperature change is gradual across this latitude range. Further south the change from white (indicating temperatures in the range 14–16 °C) to darker shades of blue (indicating temperatures less than 6 °C) is very rapid and the colour changes are packed closely together. Within the blue-coloured region the temperature only changes a few degrees all the way to the coast of Antarctica.

> Isotherms are lines of equal temperature. Different colours in Figure 4.8 mark regions between isotherms.

Question 4.3

In no more than 100 words, explain whether the sea surface temperature in Figure 4.8 varies with distance from the North Pole in the same way as it does from the South Pole?

The rapid Southern Hemisphere circumpolar temperature fall from a white to blue colour (Figure 4.8) marks the northern boundary of the Antarctic Circumpolar Current and it is called the Polar Front (Figure 1.16). In the historic literature it was called the Convergence and the phrase 'south of the Convergence' meant sailing into icy seas. As a consequence it marked the beginning of the adventure for explorers, whalers and sealers. But what difference does the cold ocean temperature make to the climate?

You have seen that South Georgia is mostly ice-covered as it is south of the Polar Front (Figure 1.16 and Question 3.4). The United Kingdom is approximately the same distance from the Equator but is not surrounded by cold waters; as a result the UK has no glaciers.

Making your own notes

Now close the book and using your notes on this section try to write a paragraph of four or five sentences that encapsulate the main ideas. You could title your paragraph 'Summary of section on the winds and the waves' and keep it until you have worked through the rest of the chapter. Continue to keep notes as you study the chapter, as you will be asked to write further summaries later.

4.3 The frozen seas

The cold Antarctic seas have a tremendous climate impact on the rest of the planet. Closer to the continent, the SST falls but the salt in seawater prevents it freezing until well below 0 °C. At close to freezing temperature, there is an effect which you can see in your kitchen when cooking dinner. Before a heated pan of water boils, water vapour rises as steam into the cooler air above. Exactly the same happens in the oceans: the polar air is cold and the ocean is relatively warm and when the temperature difference is sufficient, the water vapour is visible as sea smoke (Figure 4.9). It can make navigation difficult and must have added to the mysterious reputation of the polar seas in works such as Shelley's *Frankenstein* or Coleridge's *Rime of the Ancient Mariner*.

The exact freezing temperature of seawater depends on the amount of dissolved salt but typically it is around −1.8 °C.

As the temperature falls, small ice crystals called frazil ice form at the ocean surface and develop a layer that looks similar to an oil slick (Figure 4.10a). Just like the expression 'pouring oil on troubled water', the ice crystals make for calm seas.

- When you put ice in a glass of water why does the ice float?
- □ The ice floats because its density is less than that of water.

Figure 4.9 Sea smoke rising from the surface of the relatively warm ocean in a polar sea.

(a)

(b)

(c)

(d)

Figure 4.10 Sea ice growing on the surface of the ocean. (a) The first stage of ice formation is frazil ice forming a 'slick' on the surface; (b) pancake ice which has developed from the frazil; (c) older pack ice with a covering of snow; (d) the dark region in the centre is thin ice which has grown in the gaps between the older, thicker pack ice.

The fact that ice floats on water may not seem particularly significant, but it means that solid water is less dense than liquid water. That sounds simple but it is usually the other way round: the liquid form of a substance is usually less dense than the solid form. For example, if you melt some wax in a pan, the solid stays at the bottom until it has all melted. Usually in a solid the particles (atoms or molecules) that make up the substance are packed together more tightly than in a liquid. More particles in the same volume mean the solid is denser. However, for water it is the other way round: in ice (the solid form) the molecules are packed together more loosely than in water (the liquid form).

■ If there are fewer molecules in the same volume what happens to the density?

□ The density is lower.

The result is that ice floats. In lakes, rivers and the sea the freezing occurs from the top down and not the bottom up and, in a frozen lake, there is liquid water beneath the ice and consequently fish can survive. Can you imagine what would happen to the fish if ice was denser than water?

If solid water is less dense than liquid water, what about the liquid and steam?

■ If you keep a pan of water boiling on a stove what will happen to the water level?

□ As the water vaporises into steam, the water level in the pan will decrease.

The water molecules are more spaced out in steam than they are in the liquid water and the steam is less dense and can rise up from the pan. So in the liquid to gas change, the properties of water are more typical of other materials. However, there are few substances that have a solid phase that is less dense than the liquid, and this property has been critical to the development of life on Earth (see for example Section 2.3.2 on the Cryogenian).

The weight of the floating ice crystals stops the ocean waves breaking and it becomes calmer. This leads to the crystals coalescing and forming small plates that are rounded by constantly being bumped into each other (Figure 4.10b). These plates are pancake ice and they have raised edges caused by the constant bumping. As more seawater freezes, the pancakes grow up to 3 m in diameter and eventually freeze together or are piled up on top of each other by storms to form larger ice floes. Water can freeze onto the bottom and snow falls on the surface increasing their thickness to typically more than 2 m (Figure 4.10c). A large area of this ice is called pack ice or simply 'the pack'. When conditions are calm the frazil ice can develop directly into large sheets of ice and so miss out the pancake stage. The ice floes can be kilometres wide and in the gaps between individual floes, when it is very cold, sheets of ice can grow. The break-up of sea ice is not the reverse of the sequence shown in Figure 4.10. The large ice floes break up into small floes and then melt directly into water.

Question 4.4
Summarise the different stages of sea ice growth in your own words (one or two sentences each), and place them in order of age. You may like to include a diagram to illustrate your answer.

Activity 4.1 Sea ice and sea level

The estimated time for this activity is 1 hour 15 minutes although the experiment can be done whilst you do other things.

Fill a glass with tap water and then place an ice cube in it. Mark the water level on the side of the glass (using for example a felt pen/lipstick or tape). Watching the ice melt could be a little like watching paint dry, so leave it and come back in 20 minutes, then 40 minutes and then 1 hour, by which time all of the ice will most probably have melted. Take a few minutes to think about the answers to the following questions.

(a) What happened to the water level in the glass as the ice melted?

(b) Imagine that part way through the melting you managed to add a teaspoon of snow to the top of your ice cube. What do you think would have happened to the water level in the glass as the ice and snow melted?

(c) If you added another ice cube part way through the melting what would have happened to the water level in the glass as it all melted?

As you would expect from the SST picture in Figure 4.8 and from previous chapters, the Southern Ocean is covered by a lot of sea ice. Satellites such as the one that captured the image shown in Figure 3.17 have mapped the global sea ice on a daily basis since 1978. Figure 4.11 shows the extent and concentration of sea ice in Antarctica in March and September 2010 as these match up with the time when the sea ice extent is close to its minimum and maximum, respectively. In these images, the shades of blue through to white represent the mean percentage ice cover over that entire month for an area of about 20 km^2. A value of 50% ice concentration means that half of the area (10 km^2) is covered with sea ice and the other 10 km^2 is open water. The difference in the ocean area covered in sea ice is striking.

> The satellite which collected the data in Figure 4.11 has a relatively low resolution compared with the one that collected the image in Figure 3.19.

Question 4.5

Given that the area of the land in Antarctica is approximately 14 million km^2, how does the amount of sea ice growth in winter compare with this?

Figure 4.12a shows the area of Antarctic ice with each dot corresponding to the average for that month, and Figure 4.12b shows the ice area over one annual cycle.

■ How do the maximums (peaks) and minimums (troughs) shown in Figure 4.12a compare with the specific values shown in Figure 4.11?

☐ The 2010 maximum (Figure 4.11b) is lower than the peaks in Figure 4.12a, whilst the minimum (Figure 4.11a) is similar to other low values (troughs).

Figure 4.12a shows that from the satellite data the area of Antarctic sea ice has increased very slightly since 1978 and you will revisit this again in Chapter 9.

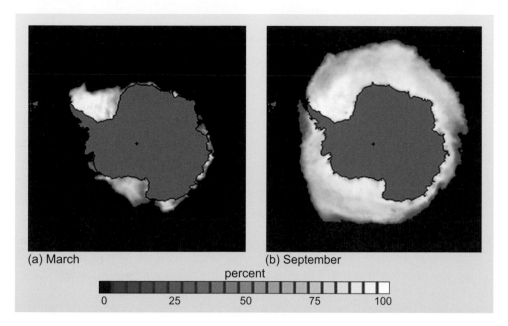

(a) March   (b) September

percent
0   25   50   75   100

Figure 4.11 The sea ice extent and concentration in the Southern Hemisphere in 2010. (a) March (summer) when the sea ice extent is at a minimum (total area 2.6 million km^2), and (b) September (winter) when the sea ice extent is at a maximum (total area 14.2 million km^2).

■ From Chapter 2, how long has Antarctica had a similar climate to the one we observe today?

□ Figure 2.10 shows that both the West Antarctic Ice Sheet and East Antarctic Ice Sheet have been in permanent existence for approximately the last 3 million years.

It seems reasonable to suggest that the cycle shown in Figure 4.12 has been going on for a very long time.

■ Looking at Figure 4.12b, does the cycle of sea ice growth take place over an equal amount of time compared with sea ice melt?

□ No. In 2005, for 8 months (February to September) the ice is increasing in area, whereas for only 4 months (October to January) it decreases in area.

The seasonal cycle of sea ice growth and decay in the Antarctic is asymmetric (Figure 4.12b); it grows relatively slowly but there is a relatively rapid retreat period. By implication, the Antarctic spring and summer are much shorter than the autumn and winter. The impact of the changes in the amount of ocean covered by sea ice, as the following section shows, is profound.

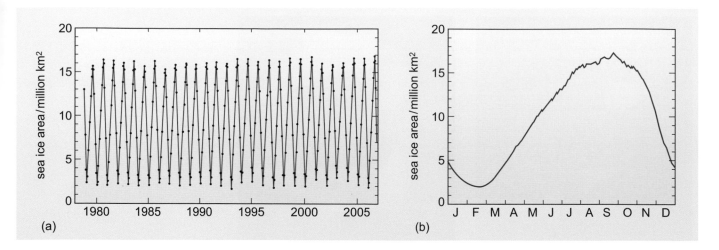

Figure 4.12 (a) The area of Antarctic sea ice from 1978 to 2007 as measured from several different satellites. (b) The area of sea ice in the Southern Hemisphere in 2005.

Sea ice also grows in the Arctic and Figure 4.13 shows the sea ice extent and concentration for September and March 2010. Figure 4.14 presents the Arctic time series and the seasonal cycle of Arctic ice growth and decay. Again, the months are chosen to show when the ice area is at a minimum and maximum.

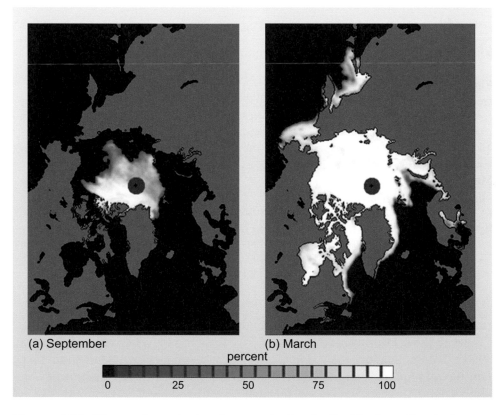

Figure 4.13 The sea ice extent and concentration in the Northern Hemisphere in 2010. (a) September when the sea ice extent is at a minimum (3 million km^2), and (b) March when the sea ice extent is at a maximum (13.1 million km^2). The grey circle over the North Pole is a region where the satellite cannot measure.

Question 4.6

By comparing Figures 4.12 and 4.14, which hemisphere has the greatest seasonal growth and decay of sea ice?

■   Can you identify one major difference in the plots of Antarctic sea ice (Figure 4.12a) compared with the plots of the Arctic sea ice (Figure 4.14a)?

☐   In the Arctic from the late 1990s to the present, Figure 4.14a shows that the area of sea ice is decreasing.

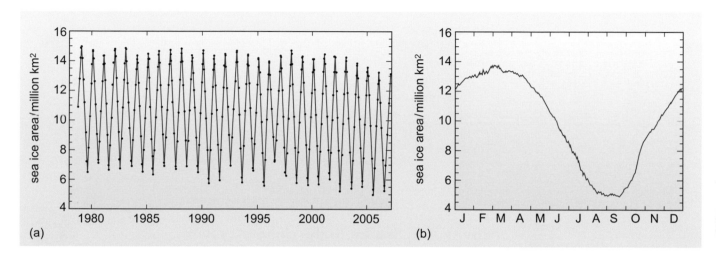

Figure 4.14   (a) The area of Arctic sea ice from 1978 to 2007 as measured from several different satellites. (b) The area of sea ice in the Northern Hemisphere in 2005.

You can see from Figure 4.14a that in March 1979, the maximum ice area was just over 15 million km^2 compared with just over 13 million km^2 in March 2007. For context this is very approximately the area of Greenland and this reduction will be revisited in Chapter 9.

■   Looking at Figure 4.14b, does the cycle of Arctic sea ice growth take place over an equal amount of time compared with sea ice melt?

☐   Yes. There are six months (September to March) when the ice is increasing in area and six months (March to September) when the ice is in retreat.

Whilst the periods of ice growing and melting in the Arctic are of similar duration, Figure 4.14b shows that the rates of the two processes are different. The freezing takes place more rapidly initially and then slows from January to March, whereas the melting occurs at a similar rate throughout the six-month period.

Question 4.7

The plot in Figure 4.13a shows that the minimum area of Arctic sea ice in September 2010 was ~3 million km². How does this compare with the minimums of the entire record shown in Figure 4.14a?

Sea ice generation is a process that happens at the scale of ice crystals only a few millimetres long. But as you have seen in this section, the process is occurring over millions of square kilometres. The next section investigates the effect of the ice and cold temperatures on oceans and the global ocean circulation.

> Sea ice covers vast areas of the polar seas with a layer of ice only a few metres thick. In the Antarctic the area of sea ice changes from ~3 to ~16 million km² every year and the seasonal cycle is asymmetric with a slower growth period than retreat. In the Arctic the area of sea ice changes from ~5 to ~14 million km² every year and the seasonal cycle is symmetric. In contrast with the Antarctic, there is compelling evidence that the area of Arctic sea ice is decreasing.

Activity 4.2 Sea ice in the climate system
The estimated time for this activity is 60 minutes.

You have read a description of the formation of sea ice in the polar seas, but it is hard to convey the beauty and dynamic nature of the system in writing. Now is a good time to visit the S175 website to watch video clips showing critical aspects of sea ice within the climate system.

The detailed notes for this activity are in the 'Activities' section of the S175 website.

Practising writing a summary
Practise the same technique as before to write a summary paragraph about sea ice. Five to ten sentences should be sufficient to summarise Section 4.3. Give your summary a title and keep it with your other notes.

4.4 Small-scale processes, big results: the effect of sea ice on the ocean

The molecules of water have small gaps between them and in seawater these gaps are filled with molecules of salt.

■　What would happen to the density of a given volume of freshwater if salt were added?

☐　Because salt molecules fit between water molecules there would be more molecules in the same volume. As a result the density of salty water is higher than that of freshwater.

As seawater freezes and ice is formed (Figure 4.10), salt is squeezed from between the ice crystals into the ocean beneath in a process called salt rejection. The result is that if you take one pancake ice floe (Figure 4.10b) and melt it in a bucket, the water that results is fresher than the seawater you started with. So what happened to the salt? It has increased the density of the seawater just beneath the ice. This is a small-scale physical process but the effects are global, profound, and clear to see in a plot of the water temperature along the entire length of the Atlantic Ocean (Figure 4.15). The data in Figure 4.15 were collected by a ship stopping and lowering a temperature recorder along the length of the ocean. The depth of the ocean is marked on the vertical axis with 0 (the surface of the ocean) at the top and 6000 m depth in the ocean at the bottom. Latitude is marked on the horizontal axis running from ~55° S on the left to ~63° N on the right. The grey colour along the horizontal axis is the depth of the sea floor. The inset on the lower right-hand side is a map which shows with a red line the track of the ship.

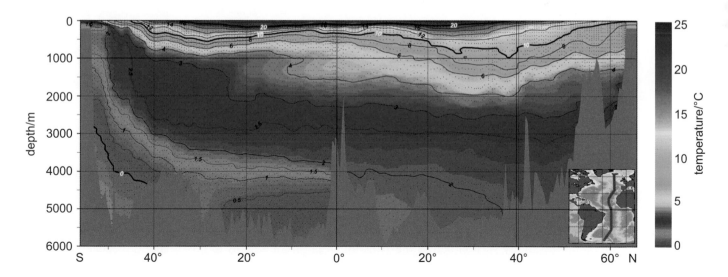

Figure 4.15 A south–north temperature section across the Atlantic Ocean from ~55° S to ~63° N. The Southern Hemisphere is on the left of this plot and the Northern Hemisphere on the right. You only need to focus on the colours on this map and not the lines.

- ■ What is the depth of the sea floor at the Equator (marked '0°' on the horizontal axis)?

- ☐ At the Equator on the horizontal axis you can see that the grey colour extends upwards to ~3000 m. So the depth of water at the Equator is 6000 m − ~3000 m = ~3000 m.

The different shades of colours represent ocean temperatures. The scale is given in the vertical bar on the right-hand side, with purples indicating cold water and red shades indicating warm. This type of plot is called a temperature section of the ocean and at the very top, at a depth of 0 m, there is the sea surface temperature just like in Figure 4.8, albeit using a different colour scale.

- ■ In Figure 4.15, where in the Atlantic Ocean is the water below 0 °C (indicated by pink–purple colours)?

- ☐ The coldest temperatures are on the left of the plot which is close to the Antarctic continent. They then apparently slope away from Antarctica to flood out in a layer across the bottom of the South Atlantic.

Unlike temperature, salinity does not have any units and, for reference, freshwater rivers have salinity very close to 0 on this scale.

The salt rejection from sea ice generation in the Antarctic creates very saline dense water, which sinks and floods away from the continent (Figure 4.15). Figure 4.16 shows the salinity distribution measured along the same section as that shown in Figure 4.15 with this time the colours indicating dissolved salt concentration. Purples indicate the lowest salinity whilst red shades represent the highest.

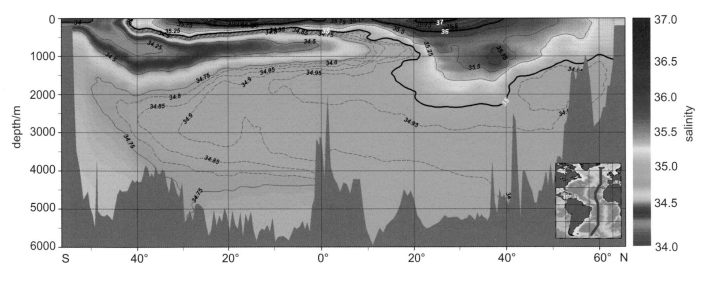

Figure 4.16 A south–north salinity section across the Atlantic Ocean from ~55° S to 63° N along the same section as that shown in Figure 4.15. This time the colours indicate the concentration of dissolved salt in the ocean as measured by the ship.

At first glance, Figure 4.16 shows that the pattern of salinity appears to have a more complicated structure than that shown by the temperature section. Close to the Equator, high atmospheric temperatures evaporate the water to leave the salt behind – so for the surface ocean waters the colours are red.

■ In Figure 4.16, what approximately is the salinity in the location of the pink–purple cold temperatures below ~1.5 °C in Figure 4.15?

□ The salinity corresponding to water with the coldest temperatures is shaded light green, which corresponds to values around 34.7 units.

Comparing Figures 4.15 and 4.16, the coldest water is not the most saline. Salt rejection is a very important process but it is the combination of the cold temperatures and increased salinity that make the water dense enough to sink to the sea floor. The very large volume of water of uniform temperature and salinity flooding away from Antarctica is called Antarctic Bottom Water (AABW) because it is formed in the Antarctic and is dense enough to reach the bottom of the ocean and flow away from the continent. The lowest salinity water, at ~1000 m depth and ~40° S (coloured purple and blue in Figure 4.16), is formed by the climatic conditions in the mid latitudes of the Southern Hemisphere and is not as dense as AABW.

> When a large volume of water has uniform temperature and salinity it is called a water mass, and can be named based on where it obtained the temperature and salinity.

You have investigated a section through the Atlantic, but had you looked at any section radiating from Antarctica along a particular longitude, then the picture would have been broadly similar – the sea ice generation and resulting salt rejection is driving a cold, relatively salty, dense water current northwards along the sea floor at great depth.

If a deep cold salty current is flowing away at depth, then there has to be water flowing towards Antarctica to replace it. Arctic salt rejection increases the density of the waters at the other end of the planet, but because of the shallow sea floor between Greenland, Iceland and the UK (see for example Figure 1.7a), the densest water is restricted and cannot flow south. What can escape into the North Atlantic floods to the sea floor, and so is called North Atlantic Deep Water (NADW). The resulting picture of ocean circulation in the Atlantic when these water masses meet is shown in Figure 4.17. You have seen this pattern in the temperature and salinity, but a similar one is seen if, for example, the oxygen dissolved in the water is shown (Box 4.1).

> To visualise how the layers come about, you could use a jam jar with a layer of honey, a layer of water and a layer of vegetable oil. The different densities mean that one layer sits on top of another.

The dense AABW (coloured blue) spreads northwards along the sea floor and the NADW spreads south.

■ Based on Figure 4.17, which water mass is the densest, AABW or NADW?

□ As the NADW rides up over the AABW it must be less dense. It is both warmer (Figure 4.15) and more saline (Figure 4.16) than AABW.

The NADW is denser than the water mass coloured white and the result is that it is sandwiched between these two Southern Ocean ones. The actual boundaries between the layers are not as distinct as the colours in the picture would suggest, but overall there is an overturning circulation along the length of the Atlantic Ocean.

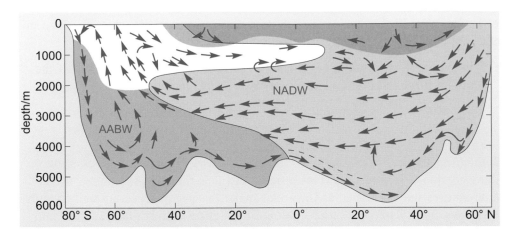

Figure 4.17 A two-dimensional cross-section of the circulation pattern in the Atlantic Ocean. Colours represent different water masses and blue arrows within them represent their movement. AABW is dense enough to fill up the deep basins of the South Atlantic. The NADW is less dense and so it rises up over the AABW and fills up the mid depths of the South Atlantic when the water masses meet.

In the Pacific and Indian Oceans the picture would be similar to Figure 4.17 south of the Equator, but the northern end would be different. The Indian Ocean does not reach the Arctic, and in the Pacific Ocean the gap between Asia and North America is so narrow and shallow that the ocean is virtually closed off to the north. This means that all of the deep waters being formed in the Arctic are entering the global ocean in the North Atlantic. The result is a vast three-dimensional circulation across the entire global ocean called the thermohaline circulation, which was proposed in the 1980s by American climate scientist Wallace Broecker (Figure 4.18).

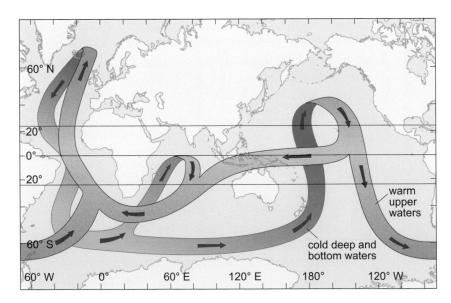

Figure 4.18 A schematic of the thermohaline circulation that moves both heat and salt around the planet. A large component of the forcing in this conceptual circulation is coming from processes happening in the Arctic and the Antarctic.

The picture is a gross simplification of the overall circulation but it makes it clear that the polar processes such as the sea ice growth described in Section 4.3 are driving the global ocean circulation and moving vast quantities of heat and salt around the planet. An example of the result of this is in the answer to Question 4.3. You may have noted that the North Atlantic isotherms of SST are not orientated along lines of latitude like in the south, but they are distorted as shown in Figure 4.19. On the east of the basin north of the coast of Spain, isotherms are deflected by the warm water pushed by the result of processes occurring in the polar regions. The result is that it is warmer in the UK and Norway compared with similar latitudes on the west side of the Atlantic. Take away the sea ice generation at the poles and there is evidence to suggest the ocean temperatures around the UK could be more similar to those around South Georgia in the Southern Hemisphere (Figure 1.13).

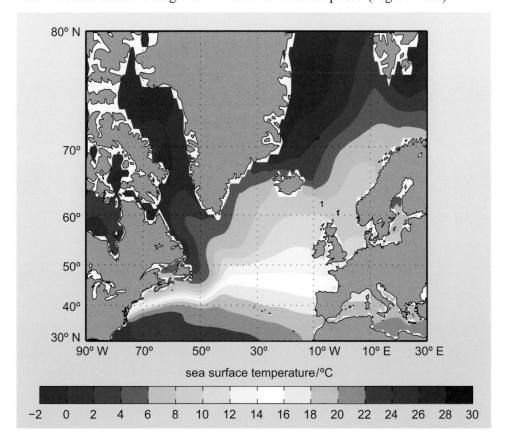

Figure 4.19 An enlargement of the mean sea surface temperature derived from ship and satellite measurements in the North Atlantic and Greenland seas. The colour scale is identical to that of Figure 4.8. The white regions close to the coasts are areas with no temperature data in this data set.

Sea ice growth in the polar oceans increases the density of the surface waters which become dense enough in places to sink to the sea floor. In high latitudes the forcing drives a global circulation of heat and salt that can be thought of as a conveyor belt. The results are clear to someone living on the coast in northern Europe and the warm ocean moderates the air temperatures.

Box 4.1 Dissolved oxygen in seawater

Fish and other animals in the sea require oxygen to live, but where does it come from? The gases that make up the atmosphere can be dissolved in seawater (particularly in breaking waves), but for most gases the amount that can be absorbed is strongly dependent on temperature. Colder waters can absorb much more oxygen than warmer waters. Animals and algae in the ocean use oxygen to live. At the sea surface there is a constant exchange of gases into and out of the seawater so the concentration of biologically important gases dissolved in the water stays more or less constant and is dependent on the sea surface temperature. Away from the surface and isolated, the concentration of gases such as oxygen decrease as it is used up, and the longer it is away from the surface then the lower the concentration.

■   Using Figure 4.17, how would you expect the amount of oxygen dissolved in water to vary at 40° S between the surface and the sea floor?

Animals that live on the sea floor are called benthic animals.

☐   Dissolved oxygen would be high at the surface, but then increase down to 1 km depth because the white-coloured water mass is colder (Figure 4.15) and so can hold more dissolved oxygen. The NADW at 2.5 km will have been at the surface in the high Arctic latitudes, but as it has travelled a long way from its source the dissolved oxygen will be much lower as it will have been partially used up. Finally, from 3 km depth to the sea floor the dissolved oxygen will increase as the water is both cold and was relatively recently at the surface in Antarctica.

The amount of dissolved oxygen is profoundly important for oceanic life and Chapter 7 shows that it is responsible for allowing some species to grow much larger than similar ones in more temperate waters.

Activity 4.3 The polar oceans

The estimated time for this activity is 60 minutes.

In the previous section you saw that the Arctic and Southern Oceans are driving the global ocean circulation. In this activity you will watch animations of the processes and their effect, and listen to an interview with an Arctic-based polar oceanographer talking about their importance.

The detailed notes for this activity are in the 'Activities' section of the S175 website.

A more ambitious summary

Now try writing a more ambitious summary. Try to write a paragraph entitled 'The polar oceans'. You should explain what salt rejection is, how it changes the density of the water, and the result on the global ocean. This is a more difficult task than the previous summaries, because you are trying to cover a longer section of text. Don't be tempted to write a long essay! Try to condense the really key points into between six and ten sentences. Keep this summary along with the others.

4.5 The frozen climate of the frozen planet

In this section you will consider the climate of various representative regions in the Antarctic and Arctic that come about as a result of the energy balance and underlying planetary heat flows. In the Antarctic you will see that there are two clear climatic zones whilst in the Arctic there are four.

4.5.1 The Antarctic

Figure 4.20 shows the mean Antarctic surface temperatures for summer and winter. In summer conditions (Figure 4.20a) the South Pole lies between the −20 °C and −30 °C isotherms. Because it is closer to the −30 °C isotherm, the mean summer temperature is most likely about −28 °C (you can look back at Figure 1.2 to see if this is sensible).

- Find the 0 °C degree atmospheric temperature isotherm in Figure 4.20a and follow it around the continent. In general how close is this to land?

- In some regions such as the Antarctic Peninsula the 0 °C temperature isotherm is very close to the land. In other regions such as the Weddell Sea and Ross Sea it is a long way from land.

In the Weddell Sea the lines of equal temperature are widely spaced and you could move a few hundred kilometres towards the South Pole from the 0 °C isotherm and the mean summer atmospheric temperature would only change by 2–3 °C. In contrast, at a longitude of 90° W, moving a similar distance would lead to a temperature change as much as 20 °C. Excluding the Weddell and Ross Seas, most of the coast of Antarctica has mean summer temperature of around −2 °C. Whilst this is not comfortable for humans, it is not spectacularly cold and not outside the range experienced in the UK in recent winters.

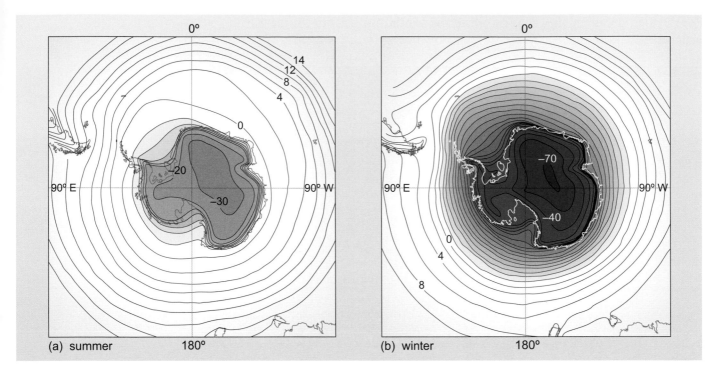

Figure 4.20 The mean atmospheric surface temperatures for the Southern Hemisphere. The circular contours labelled −30, −20, 0, etc., are in °C and are isotherms (lines of equal temperature) just like those in the ocean in Figure 4.8. (a) Summer: the isotherms are in 2 °C steps from 14 °C to −10 °C, and then in steps of −10 °C. (b) Winter: the isotherms are in 2 °C steps from 10 °C to 0 °C, in 1 °C steps from 0 °C to −10 °C, and in 5 °C steps from −10 °C to −40 °C, and then in −10 °C steps to −70 °C.

■ How well does the extent of sea ice in the Antarctic summer shown in Figure 4.11a correlate with the atmospheric temperature shown in Figure 4.20a?

□ The large regions of sea ice only remain in the regions where the 0 °C isotherm is a very long way from the coast.

But what of the Antarctic winter (Figure 4.20b)? The South Pole is at a temperature in the region of −60 °C (see also Figure 1.2). There is also a region of the continent with temperatures below −70 °C. However, whilst there is no doubt that on land the Antarctic winter is very severe, it is hardly representative of the entire continent.

■ In the winter (Figure 4.20b) what is the mean winter temperature at the coast of Antarctica?

□ The mean winter temperature at the coast is in the range −10 to −15 °C.

The change in mean atmospheric winter temperature appears to be related to the distance from the coast out to the 0 °C isotherm which, like in summer, corresponds reasonably well to the maximum extent of the winter sea ice (Figure 4.11b). Between summer and winter, there is an extraordinary seasonal change which is the major difference between the Antarctic continent away from the oceans, and the rest of the planet. This is the so-called coreless winter (Figure 4.21). It arises because of the energy balance and the tilt of the

Earth's axis. As winter approaches, the disappearance of the Sun means that at high latitudes temperatures rapidly fall. The coastal regions are relatively warm as they gain heat from the sea. But inland the heat loss is so great that the temperature drops very rapidly to effectively the lowest temperature it can reach. With no further cooling possible and no heating from the Sun or the ocean, the temperature stays approximately constant in the coreless winter (Box 4.2). The difference in temperature between summer and winter is astonishing at over 40 °C, and as you will see in successive chapters, it has bearing on what wildlife can prosper.

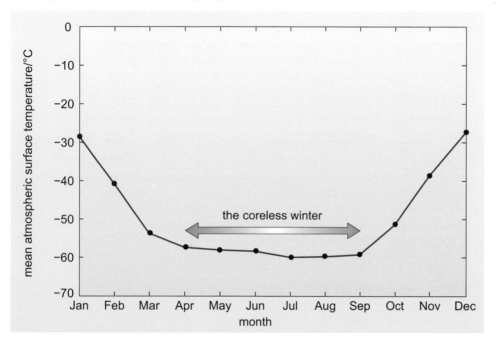

Figure 4.21 The mean monthly atmospheric surface temperature recorded at a research station based at the South Pole showing the coreless winter.

A summary of the Antarctic climate

The Antarctic Circumpolar Current isolates the continent and you can summarise the climate as being dependent on two factors: firstly, very roughly the distance from the highest point on the continent which is the summit of the East Antarctic Ice Sheet; and secondly, proximity to the Southern Ocean. This creates two clear climatic zones in Antarctica. Inland there is the polar desert and it is awe-inspiringly cold in winter; but in contrast, the polar maritime climate in the coastal regions is not particularly extreme.

You will see in subsequent chapters that the wind direction at the coastal regions is very important for the wildlife. Winds from the north are from the ocean and so are relatively warm, but winds from the south are potentially super-cold and even coastal conditions can be for short periods truly awful.

Box 4.2 Did the weather kill Captain Scott and his team?

In 1911 at the peak of the Heroic Age, two nations had teams heading for the South Pole. The Norwegian Roald Amundsen led a team of five using huskies to drag sledges containing their supplies, whilst the Royal Navy officer Captain Scott led a team of five who man-hauled their equipment to the pole. Both teams reached the pole, but famously Captain Scott and his colleagues died on their return. There have been many books criticising Scott's choice to pull his own sledges as being responsible for his team's disaster, but many expeditions since have shown that man-hauling is not a completely irrational way to travel in the polar regions. Could there have been other contributory factors? Amundsen and his team reached the South Pole on 14 December 1911 and Scott and his team arrived 35 days later on 17 January 1912.

There have been automatic weather stations recording the conditions in Antarctica over the last few decades and the polar meteorologist Professor Susan Solomon analysed these records and compared them with the weather experienced by Scott and Amundsen. Figure 4.22 shows her analysis of their data close to the pole.

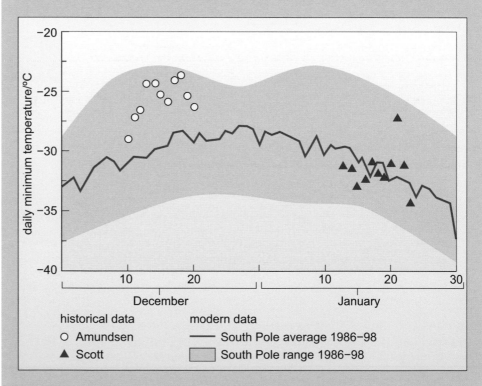

Figure 4.22 The daily minimum temperature recorded by Amundsen (circles) and Scott (triangles) whilst close to the South Pole, plotted against the time they visited. The solid blue line is the average temperature along this time period from 12 years' data collected by an automatic weather station close to the pole and the blue shaded region is the range of temperature for each day over the entire record.

■ From Figure 4.22, how do the conditions Amundsen's team experienced compare with those experienced by Scott's team relative to the data collected by the automatic weather station?

□ Amundsen's team experienced conditions that were warmer than average, whereas Scott's experienced conditions close to or colder than the average winter temperature.

From Figure 4.21 and the dates on the horizontal axis in Figure 4.22, one can see that Amundsen was fortunate in the time he arrived at the pole, whereas Scott experienced the start of the coreless winter. Amundsen was back at his coastal base by 25 January 1912, but Professor Solomon demonstrates in her analysis that Scott's team suffered unseasonably bad weather as well as the coreless winter. After 150 days of continual marching and temperatures below −40 °C, Scott and the last of his party perished on 29 March 1912. As Professor Solomon said of Scott and his men:

A few scant miles from the footprints these men left in the snow in 1912, machines were put in place almost three quarters of a century later to gather new data that would ultimately shed fresh light on their struggle, the strength of their characters and the reasons for their deaths.

Solomon (2001)

4.5.2 The Arctic

In the Arctic the climate can be summarised with four representative regions. More are needed than for the Antarctic because of the circulation of the Arctic Ocean and the winds. The mean atmospheric winter and summer Arctic temperatures are shown in Figure 4.23 and the influence of the ocean currents (e.g. Figures 4.18 and 4.19) is clear. Because of this, the winter isotherm orientation is not along lines of latitude like the Antarctic (Figure 4.20).

Question 4.8

In no more than 100 words compare the winter atmospheric temperatures of the west coast of Norway and the east coast of Greenland, and explain the reason for the difference.

You may have thought that the coldest place in the Arctic would have been the Greenland Ice Sheet but the coldest regions are in fact over northern Russia. But at just below −40 °C they are a full 30 °C warmer than temperatures seen on the East Antarctic Ice Sheet. The summit of the Greenland Ice Sheet is only just below −30 °C in winter and a straight comparison with the Antarctic would suggest that the Arctic was relatively benign. This impression is reinforced in the northern summer (Figure 4.23a) and the 0 °C isotherm is well north of the continental land masses.

The definition of the Arctic from the location of the 10 °C isotherm in summer is shown in Figure 4.23a. Note that this isotherm is not exactly in the same place as those shown in Chapter 1 as a different temperature data set has been used.

The summit of the Greenland Ice Sheet is not within the Arctic according to the 10 °C isotherm definition!

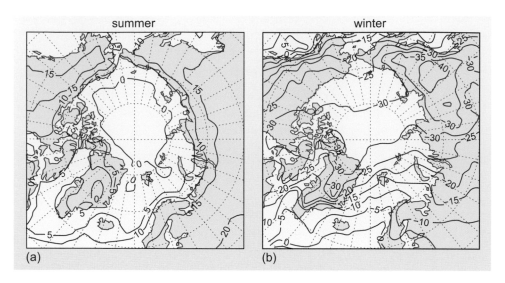

Figure 4.23 The mean atmospheric surface temperature in 5 °C steps across the Arctic in (a) northern summer and (b) northern winter.

■   What is the mean summer temperature of the North Pole in Figure 4.23a?

□   The isotherms are clearly widely spaced across the Arctic Ocean and so the temperature is not changing a great deal. There is no −5 °C contour, so the temperature must be between 0 and −5 °C. Given that the pole is reasonably close to the zero line, then it would seem likely that the surface atmospheric temperature is close to 0 °C.

Just like in the Antarctic, the seasonal temperature changes define the habitats that animals can survive in. The areas of Northern Russia that are below −40 °C in winter are above 15 °C in summer so the seasonal contrast is greater than that in the Antarctic coreless winter. In contrast, on the coast the temperature range is lower; for example, at the coast of Norway the range is approximately 17 °C (−5 °C in winter to ~12 °C in summer).

Figure 4.24 shows two extremes of the Arctic climate – that on the Greenland Ice Sheet and that in the central Arctic Ocean. Both of these sites show similar differences between the summer and winter temperatures but they lack the coreless winter.

Figure 4.24a has two sites with winter temperatures of ~−38 °C. These are much lower than Figure 4.23 shows but the difference is because they are for six specific sites rather than the whole of Greenland and the entire winter. Overall the Greenland Ice Sheet is clearly not as severe as Antarctica. In the central Arctic Ocean (Figure 4.24b) the seasonal change in temperature is large with a smooth seasonal cycle of winter to summer of over 30 °C. Figure 4.13 shows that even in summer the North Pole is usually covered with sea ice, and so heating from the ocean is only going through relatively small gaps in the ice floes like those shown in Figure 4.10c and d.

The remaining two climatic zones of the Arctic are summarised in Figure 4.25. One site is at Resolute Bay in the Canadian Arctic at 74° N, and the second site on the west coast of the Svalbard archipelago and at 78° N.

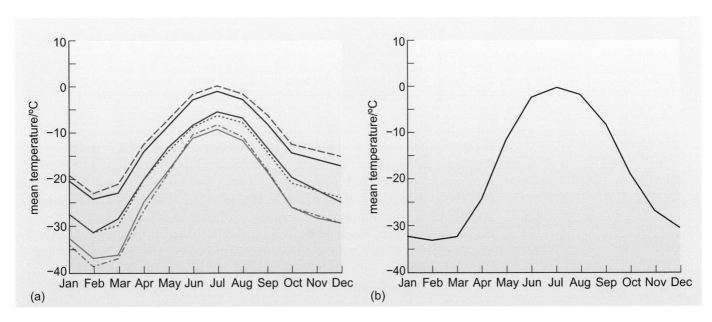

Figure 4.24 The mean monthly temperature at (a) six locations on the Greenland Ice Sheet, and (b) on the sea ice in the central Arctic Ocean.

Resolute Bay is close to the North-West Passage (Figure 3.6) and the temperatures are not dissimilar to those on the Greenland Ice Sheet. With a summer/winter difference of greater than 30 °C even in the absence of the coreless winter, the conditions the Victorian sailors coped with were truly horrendous.

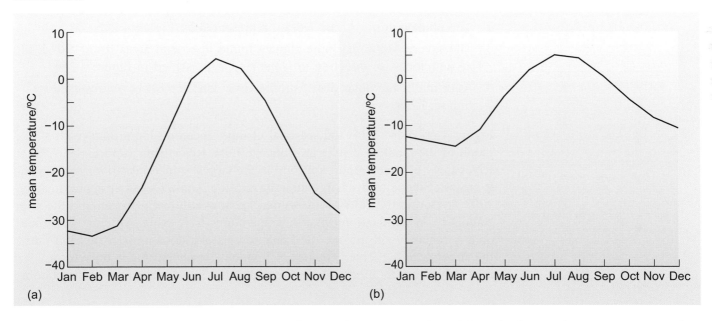

Figure 4.25 The mean monthly temperature at (a) Resolute Bay at 74° N, 94° W in the North-West Passage, and (b) the west coast of Svalbard, the small archipelago to the north of Norway at 78° N, 15° E.

■ At Resolute Bay how much does the temperature change each month from March to July?

☐ From March to April the temperature increases by ~5 °C; from each month onwards from April to July the temperature increases by ~10 °C.

If one compares the conditions shown in Figure 4.25 with those you experience for example in the UK, the seasonal changes are extraordinary, with extreme rates of both warming and cooling. They are similar to those experienced on the EAIS (Figure 4.21) but in the South the temperature never gets above zero. Comparing Resolute Bay with the record from Svalbard (Figure 4.25b), the difference is striking. Svalbard is over 400 km closer to the North Pole than Resolute Bay and a similar distance from the sea. Based on the energy balance, one would expect it to be cooler – but in winter the coldest temperatures do not fall below −15 °C. In summer, Svalbard is only one or two degrees warmer than Resolute Bay. With this greatly reduced atmospheric temperature range, the rates of cooling and warming are closer to the UK winter than the rest of the Arctic.

Question 4.9

Is there sea ice on the coast of Svalbard in the northern winter? Remember to give a reason for your answer.

The four Arctic climatic zones shown in Figures 4.24 and 4.25 can be placed in the following order of climatic severity:

1 The moderate Arctic maritime climate which is found in coastal areas from approximately 0–90° E and represented by Figure 4.25b.

2 The climate in the Arctic Ocean, represented by Figure 4.24b.

3 The severe Arctic maritime climate found in coastal areas from ~90° E in an anticlockwise direction to Greenland, represented in Figure 4.25a.

4 And finally, the polar desert on the Greenland Ice Sheet, represented by Figure 4.24a.

Figure 4.26 shows what the seasonal changes mean on the ground with a graph of the monthly discharge from the Lena River from 1935 to 1999. The River Lena at almost 4500 km long is the largest undammed river in Asia and it crosses Siberia to discharge straight into the Arctic Ocean at approximately 129° E. During the cold Arctic winter the flow is literally frozen and the river stationary. When the atmospheric temperatures have risen sufficiently, the ice dam is released and in June the Lena flows at a rate of more than 1500 times the strength of the River Thames in London. However, this is only for a relatively short duration and by November the Lena is again not a functioning river.

A summary of the Arctic climate

There are four climatic zones determined in part by the influence of the ocean. The northern extremity of the thermohaline circulation moderates the eastern Arctic from approximately 0° to 90° E, making it significantly warmer in winter. In complete contrast, the remaining quadrant of the eastern Arctic and the western Arctic has a winter almost as severe as Antarctica – although it is not the coreless winter of the south. Greenland has a different climate although again it is not comparable with the Antarctic.

In summer, with the exception of the Greenland Ice Sheet, for a short period conditions are benign and you could expect wildlife to prosper.

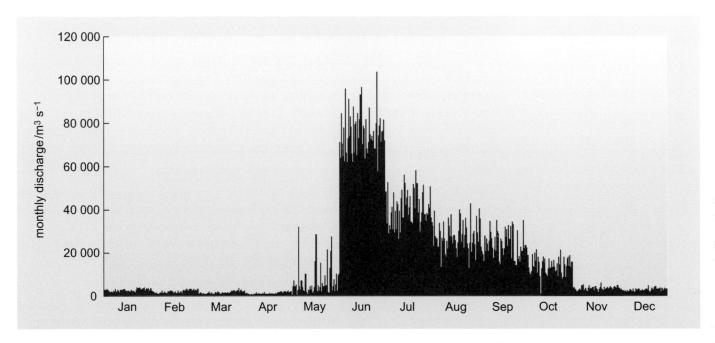

Figure 4.26 The monthly discharge from the Lena River (Russia). Each individual very thin bar in the graph represents one monthly value for each year during the period 1935–1999, so there are 64 bars for each month.

Activity 4.4 The polar climate
The estimated time for this activity is 30 minutes.

The previous sections have described the polar climate. In this activity you will listen and respond to an interview with a leading polar meteorologist discussing the polar climate.

The detailed notes for this activity are in the 'Activities' section of the S175 website.

4.6 Conclusions

In both polar regions the oceans provide a strong moderating effect on the climate. The main difference between the two is that the Antarctic has the coreless winter and the land remains cold all year round. In turn, the sea ice generation in the high latitudes and resulting salt rejection forces the global ocean circulation and is responsible for moving heat and salt around the planet. This is the reason northern Europe has such a moderate climate compared with similar latitudes in Canada or Asia. The fact is that, although the poles are remote, their effects on the climate at lower latitudes are felt on a daily basis.

This chapter began asking how representative popular impressions of the polar climate are. As with most things, there is an element of truth and in Antarctica it does get down to −70 °C, although this is well away from the coast and under special conditions. However, it is not representative of the wider climate. A similar impression emerges for the north and whilst winters are severe, the summers can be actually fairly mild in many locations.

In the following chapter you will investigate how the climate and the physical manifestations of it, such as that shown in the Lena River, impose stress on the wildlife. As a result, there have been biological adaptations.

4.7 Summary of Chapter 4

- The energy to generate wind comes from differential heating of the Earth by the Sun. The surface currents of the ocean correlate reasonably well with the wind patterns and a map reveals that the polar regions have low sea surface temperatures.

- Sea ice develops through frazil ice generation, which then forms pancake ice and finally larger ice floes, although its development can miss the pancake phase.

- Sea ice covers vast areas of the polar seas with a layer of ice only a few metres thick. In the Antarctic the area of sea ice changes from ~3 to ~16 million km^2 every year and the seasonal cycle is asymmetric with a slower growth period than retreat. In the Arctic the area of sea ice changes from ~5 to ~14 million km^2 every year and the seasonal cycle is symmetric. In contrast with the Antarctic, there is compelling evidence that the area of Arctic sea ice is reducing.

- Sea ice growth increases the density of the surface waters which can become dense enough in places to sink to the sea floor. This drives a global circulation of heat and salt that can be thought of as a conveyor belt. The result is clear to someone living on the coast in northern Europe and the warm ocean moderates the air temperatures.

- There are two clear climatic zones in Antarctica: the continental polar desert and the polar maritime climate. Inland in winter it is bitterly cold and there is the distinctive coreless winter. In contrast the coastal regions are not particularly extreme.

- There are four climatic zones in the Arctic determined in part by the influence of the ocean. The northern extremity of the thermohaline circulation moderates the eastern Arctic from approximately 0° to 90° E, making it significantly warmer in winter. In complete contrast, the remaining quadrant of the eastern Arctic and the western Arctic has a winter almost as severe as Antarctica – although it lacks the coreless winter. Greenland has a different climate although again it is not comparable with the Antarctic.

5 Life in the polar regions

5.1 Introduction

So far in this module you have considered the physical conditions that exist within the polar regions, their relationship to the rest of the planet and how and why humans populated them. In this chapter you will consider life within the polar regions and the physiological adaptations developed through evolution and natural selection that have enabled life to prosper.

Activity 1.1 considered your initial views and impressions of the high latitudes. Take a moment now to look back at your answer to this activity and see if you mentioned wildlife. Did you think of whales and polar bears? Perhaps you thought of penguins? One feature common to all of these species is that not only do they cope with the harsh polar conditions, but they also prosper – and have done so for perhaps millions of years.

■ From what you have learned so far, where do most of the animals in the polar regions appear to live?

☐ In both hemispheres they appear to live on the edge of the polar regions.

The charismatic polar bear hunts seals and creates dens on the edges of the Arctic Ocean and penguins live on the coasts in the Antarctic. Whilst it is true that coastlines can still have very poor weather (Chapter 4), they are much more amenable to habitation and conditions are not as severe as those inland. This means that the coastal environments put less physical stress on the animals. Stress in this context refers to the impact of the conditions presented by the environment on the animal. A simple example of this is sitting on a very hot sunny beach in a swimming costume with no shade – the Sun is providing a stress and soon the skin becomes sunburnt. Human bodies are adapted to cope with some exposure to bright sunlight.

■ Can you think of a simple adaptation that a person with light-coloured skin may exhibit in response to bright sunlight?

☐ The person's skin can darken and go brown.

This is an example of an adaptation. The brown colour is a pigment called melanin which protects skin from the radiation in the Sun's rays. It takes time for melanin to develop and so people usually build up their exposure to sunlight, with some developing the pigment so slowly that they are not comfortable in the Sun at all. As a consequence some people are not well adapted to this particular physical stress. A simple example of a stress that humans are not well adapted to is lack of drinking water. With no water, in just a few days a person would die.

■ Besides low temperatures, can you think of two physical conditions that put stress on polar organisms?

☐ Organisms have to cope with huge variations in day length – from continuous darkness during the winter periods, to continuous light in summer (see Section 1.5.1). There is also the lack of liquid water on land, at least at some times of the year, as demonstrated by the flow of the River Lena (Figure 4.26). You may also have thought about the effect of the wind, which reduces the apparent temperature still further, and dries the surface of animals and plants exposed to it (Box 5.1).

One simple adaptation to avoid the worst of the weather is migration; however, this chapter focuses on animals that remain in the polar regions and concentrates on the adaptations that enable some species to cope with what would be a major stress for humans – the cold temperatures. To understand the adaptations to life in very low temperatures one needs to consider them in two separate groups. First, there are those species, including humans, that can regulate their body temperature (within certain limits) keeping it at a constant level. These are known as the endotherms and comprise mammals (animals with fur or hair that feed their young on milk) and birds. The second group controls their body temperature through external means and so are called ectotherms. Almost all animal species (excluding birds and mammals) that live in the polar regions are ectotherms, including fish and plants. Clearly, the adaptations needed to survive the cold will vary in these two groups.

To answer this question you may need to review some of the activities on the S175 website and the climatic zones described in Chapter 4.

Question 5.1

What are the typical temperature conditions experienced by an animal or plant on (a) Svalbard and (b) the Antarctic Peninsula? Try and answer this question in a short paragraph of no more than 150 words in total.

Box 5.1 Wind chill

In cold air humans and other animals lose heat by conduction and convection (described in Chapter 4). However, air is a relatively poor conductor and in still air, the thin, warm layer close to the skin means heat is lost slowly. Windy conditions remove this thin layer of warm air next to the skin, and so heat loss increases in a process called wind chill. The apparent temperature – that is, the temperature it feels like – depends on how rapidly the insulating layer of warm air is lost, which in turn depends on the wind speed. The higher the wind speed the colder it feels.

■   Imagine standing outdoors on a cold day. Which part of your body would wind chill affect the most?

□   Wind chill only affects areas of skin that are exposed to the wind. On a cold day you would probably be wearing warm clothing, a hat and gloves. Most likely the only region of your body where wind chill would increase heat loss substantially would be your face.

Wind chill is only an issue for unprotected skin but in cold conditions it can be very significant. The amount of wind chill on exposed skin is summarised in Figure 5.1 in a plot called a nomogram. The picture consists of three lines and to use it you need a ruler. Line A is the actual measured air temperature, line B is the measured wind speed and finally line C is the equivalent temperature caused by the wind chill. To use the nomogram you lay the ruler on Figure 5.1 using the values represented on lines A and B, and then read off where the ruler crosses line C for the answer. For example, in Figure 5.1 the dashed line shows how to use the nomogram when the air temperature is −25 °C and the wind speed is 8 m s^{-1}. The ruler meets line A at −25 °C, and line B at 8 m s^{-1}. The equivalent temperature caused by the wind chill is then given by the point where the ruler crosses the line labelled C − in this case it is ∼−36 °C.

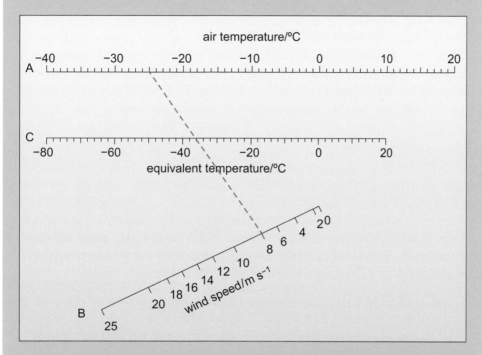

Figure 5.1 A nomogram for determining wind chill in terms of equivalent temperature given the ambient air temperature and the wind speed. A description of how to use this plot is within the text.

■ What is the equivalent wind chill temperature when the air temperature is 20 °C and the wind speed 0 m s^{-1}?

☐ Overlaying a ruler on Figure 5.1 shows that unsurprisingly when there is no wind, then there is no wind chill and the equivalent temperature is the actual temperature, i.e. 20 °C.

Establishing what works for you

Before starting to study the rest of the material in this chapter, now would be a good point at which to think about the various techniques you have practised while studying previous chapters (scanning ahead, making notes, highlighting, and writing a summary of the main points of particular sections). Decide which techniques have worked best for you, and try to make these a regular part of your study routine for this and subsequent chapters.

5.2 Endothermic animals

Most mammals maintain a core body temperature in the range 37–38 °C and in birds it is often slightly higher. To live in polar conditions endothermic animals must have special ways to maintain their bodies at a very much higher temperature than their surroundings. When a human gets cold, one of our reflex mechanisms is to shiver. Groups of muscles begin to shake in very small movements using up energy in the body and creating heat as a by-product. Other endothermic animals also shiver as a quick way of generating heat but it can use up vital energy reserves in wild animals.

One adaptation for avoiding the worst of the cold winter weather is the ability to hibernate. This is when the energy-producing processes in an animal's body slow down. Its body temperature and breathing rate are lower than normal and the animal falls into a deep sleep. Such a state can last several days or weeks and it can save a lot of energy. However, it is only possible in a frost-free environment. Breeding female polar bears have limited winter sleep (called dormancy) which they are thought to have inherited from their ancestor brown bears when the species diverged. However, their body temperature only falls for a few days at a time, so this is not true hibernation.

■ Two well-known polar species are emperor penguins from Antarctica and polar bears from the Arctic. They do not hibernate nor do they shiver. What features do you think have evolved in these species that enable them to cope with extremely cold temperatures?

☐ You probably first thought about insulation; they have feathers and thick fur, respectively. You may have also considered their behaviour – emperor penguins often huddle together in groups, with those on the outside gradually working their way to the middle where they are kept warm by their fellow animals. You may recall that female polar bears build themselves a den in the snow where they remain during the winter and give birth to their cubs. You may also have noticed that both of these species are relatively large animals. All these points are significant in the discussion that follows.

5.2.1 Insulation by fur, feathers and fat

Polar bears are of course not the only terrestrial mammals in the Arctic. Previously you came across the arctic fox and Figure 5.2 shows a cross-section through its skin, highlighting some of the structures that are involved in keeping the animal warm in cold conditions. The fur of Arctic mammals, such as the arctic fox, usually consists of many closely spaced relatively short hairs, with fewer longer hairs forming an outer layer (Figure 5.2a). The insulation is provided not by the hairs themselves, but by a layer of still air trapped by them close to the skin. As noted in Box 5.1, air is a relatively poor heat conductor so it acts as a good insulator. The air close to the skin gets warmed, but because it is trapped in the fur, the heat is only very slowly transferred towards the outside of the fur. The same principle is used in the clothes that you wear to keep warm – they trap a layer of air which is heated and then insulates against the cold.

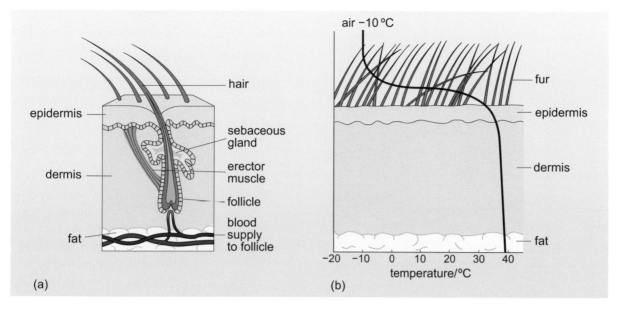

(a)   (b)

Figure 5.2 (a) Cross-section through a small area of skin of an arctic fox. (b) The temperature at different sites within and outside the fur of an arctic fox.

Figure 5.2b shows a graph of temperature overlaid on the cross-section of the skin of the arctic fox, with the coldest temperature outside the fur being typical of that in a Svalbard winter. The insulating effect of the fur is clear.

■ What is the difference in Figure 5.2b between the temperature near the surface of the skin (the epidermis), and at the top of the fur?

If you need help with negative numbers, then study Section 2 in the Maths Skills ebook.

☐ The temperature at the skin surface is approximately 32 °C whilst at the top of the fur, it is −10 °C. This means the temperature difference is 32 °C − (−10 °C) = 42 °C.

The fur of the fox and polar bear clearly provide very good insulation and you will not be surprised to know that longer fur is better at trapping heat (Figure 5.3). In this figure the vertical axis shows the relative insulative value of the fur – the higher up this axis then the more the heat is retained. The horizontal axis shows the hair length. The graph has two data sets presented on it: the first consists of blue dots which show values for some Arctic-dwelling mammals, and the red dots are for some tropical-dwelling mammals.

■ Using Figure 5.3, how much longer is the fur of an arctic fox compared with that of a tropical rabbit?

☐ The arctic fox has hair approximately 51 mm long, whereas the tropical rabbit has fur ~8 mm long. Therefore the arctic fox has fur that is ~43 mm longer than that of the tropical rabbit.

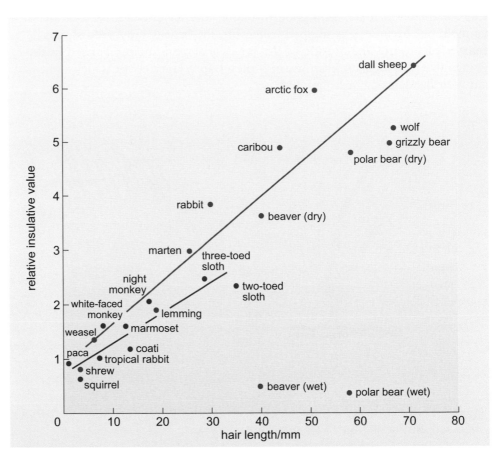

Figure 5.3 The relationship between the length of fur in Arctic mammals (blue dots) (some tropical animals are shown in red dots for comparison) and the relative amount of insulation the fur provides.

The blue and red lines drawn on Figure 5.3 are called best-fit lines. They represent the best relationship between the fur length and insulative value.

Figure 5.3 also suggests that the hairs of Arctic-dwelling mammals are apparently better at insulating than those of tropical mammals. For example, the Arctic-dwelling weasel has slightly shorter hair than the tropical-dwelling rabbit (~8 mm) but has a relative insulative value that is higher. The blue best-fit line is above the red best-fit line, so this seems to apply in general for all of the Arctic animals shown here.

It is not just the length of the hair that controls the amount of insulation. Each hair on a mammal can be made to stand up by contraction of the tiny erector muscle attached near its base within the skin (Figure 5.2a). The result is that the fur appears fluffier and more air can be trapped, providing increased insulation in particularly cold conditions. The erector muscles in Figure 5.2a are present in human skin as well and their contraction is responsible for 'goose bumps' when you are cold, but there is not enough body hair for this to have any useful effect. Clearly the furs are important and they are kept in good condition, and are somewhat waterproofed by the oily secretions from the sebaceous glands (Figure 5.2a). Human hair is coloured by pigments deposited in them, but Arctic mammals, like the arctic fox and polar bear, have transparent hair with hollow cores. These hollow cores provide additional insulation and visible light is scattered and reflected due to an absence of colour, making the coat appear white. As a result, the animals are camouflaged against the snow, which is advantageous both for hunting prey and for avoiding being hunted themselves. In summer the arctic fox acquires a brown pigment which camouflages it against rocks.

Birds have evolved a similar adaptation and they have a dual layer of feathers similar to the long and short mammalian fur shown in Figure 5.2a. They have tough outer feathers with soft downy feathers closer to the skin. One well-known Arctic species is the eider duck and its downy feathers are known for being particularly good at providing insulation and so are collected and used in bedding ('eiderdowns'), sleeping bags and outdoor clothing. Antarctic species such as penguins have the same adaptation: their outer feathers are stiff and broad and relatively short but very closely spaced, with some species having more than 15 feathers per square centimetre (cm^2) of skin (Figure 5.4). The relatively high feather density means the feathers overlap uniformly to cover the entire skin and trap air beneath them. Tiny tufts of down on the shafts of these larger feathers add to the insulation provided and, just like hairs, each feather has a tiny muscle enabling it to be lifted away from the body, thereby trapping even more air.

■ Using Figure 5.3, what happens to the insulating ability of fur when it gets wet? Can you suggest why this might be?

☐ Figure 5.3 shows that wet fur (in polar bears and beavers) is very much less effective as an insulator than dry fur. The insulative value of beaver fur drops from ~3.7 when dry to ~0.5 when wet; and for polar bear fur, from ~4.9 dry to ~0.4 wet. The insulative value falls because in water, the layer of air that provides the insulation is compressed and can be squeezed out by the water pressure. This reduces the insulating effect.

Figure 5.4 An Adélie penguin which has a relatively high feather density compared with other bird species.

A consequence of the reduced insulation of wet fur or feathers would result in the animal cooling down relatively quickly compared with when dry. In polar conditions this obviously could cause problems, and this is why many polar animals, including the Adélie penguin, have additional insulation in the form of a thick layer of fat beneath the dermis of the skin. This is known as subcutaneous fat (Figure 5.2). Fat is a relatively good insulator and heat travels less well in it compared with other body tissue, retaining the heat within the body.

The combination of ~58 mm long fur and a subcutaneous fat layer of up to 11 cm thick provides near-perfect insulation for polar bears on land. Given that the internal temperature of the bear is ~37 °C, you can see from Figure 5.5 how effective it is. The colours in this figure indicate the surface temperature of the bear and the black background is snow.

■ From Figure 4.8 what is the sea surface temperature where polar bears live?

☐ The sea surface temperature is in the range approximately −2 °C to +2 °C.

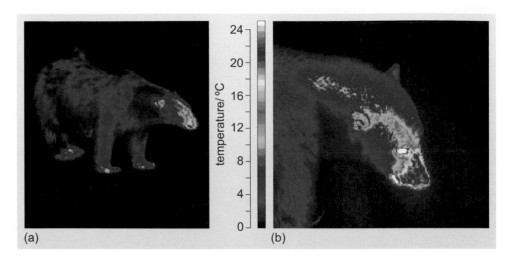

Figure 5.5 The heat emitted from a wild polar bear, photographed using a technique called infrared thermography. The colours and scale indicate the surface temperatures inferred from the amount of heat radiated by the bear. The background snow radiates so little heat compared to the bear that it appears black in these pictures. (a) The whole polar bear; (b) an enlargement of the face and shoulders.

The symbol > in mathematics is shorthand for greater than, so >10 °C means greater than 10 °C.

Figure 5.6 The underside of a hind paw of an arctic fox in winter coat, showing paw pads covered with short dense fur.

Although the temperature difference between the animal and the ocean may be much less than that between the animal and polar atmospheric conditions, heat travels much more easily through water, so its cooling effect is more significant. However, the excellent insulation from subcutaneous fat is sufficiently effective to offset the heat loss and bears have been tracked swimming for many hours across more than 75 km of open water hunting for prey such as seals. Figure 3.19b showed one remarkable example of this.

There is, however, a disadvantage for animals that are so well insulated – high temperatures can cause them stress. For example, a polar bear can overheat when the external temperature is >10 °C and, even at low temperatures, adult polar bears overheat very quickly when they run. For this reason, they tend to move relatively slowly with regular rests (for the same reason, humans are banned from chasing them using vehicles). Finally, fur or feathers often extend over parts of the body that are usually naked in temperate-zone species, in order to reduce wind chill. For example, the feathers of polar species such as ptarmigan (a relatively large bird in the grouse family) and snowy owls extend along the legs and over the feet. Adélie penguins have feathers that cover most of their red bill (Figure 5.4) and the paw pads of arctic foxes and arctic hares are covered in short, tough fur (Figure 5.6).

Question 5.2

Use Figure 5.5 to estimate the average surface temperature of the polar bear. Where on the body is the bear losing the most heat?

Whilst polar bears spend only part of their lives in water, other mammals such as seals and walruses (which belong to a group of mammals called pinnipeds, Figure 5.7) spend almost all of their lives in water, coming onto land only to breed.

(a)

(b)

Figure 5.7 Two species of pinniped: (a) the southern fur seal; and (b) the arctic walrus. Both species are perfectly adapted to the polar marine conditions.

Fur seals, as their name implies, do have fur – which is easily seen in Figure 5.7a. But the fur is especially adapted with outer hairs (called guard hairs) that repel water, coupled to an insulating layer of under-fur which keeps the skin dry by trapping small bubbles of air within it. This dense fur was prized by the early hunters and, as noted in Chapter 3, it was one of the key factors in the drive to reach the poles. Adults of other seal species such as sea lions and walruses have much less fur and so the pinnipeds primarily rely on a thick layer of fat to provide insulation. However, the fat is much firmer, tougher and more fibrous than that of the land-dwelling animals, and it is known as blubber. The blubber also provides buoyancy to the animal and helps to produce a streamlined shape. When they are born on land, most pinniped pups have a different type of fur that protects them from the weather whilst they are fed on rich milk by their mothers. The milk enables them to put on weight mostly in the form of blubber that ultimately insulates them at sea, but before they enter the sea for the first time this fur is moulted.

■ What would be the likely consequences if a pinniped seal pup entered the water before its first moult?

□ The fur, while providing good insulation on land, would become waterlogged in the sea and once the trapped air was lost, it would lose much of its insulating properties as demonstrated in Figure 5.3. Additionally, the pup would not have developed a sufficiently thick layer of blubber and so would have little insulation. As a result its body temperature would fall and it may not survive.

Penguins have a similar issue. Figure 5.8 shows a king penguin chick with downy feathers that protect it as it grows sufficient subcutaneous fat and the high density of specialised feathers that it needs to survive in the ocean. The more time a polar animal spends in water, the greater the relative importance of the blubber. Mammals that spend all their time in water such as dolphins, porpoises and whales – collectively called cetaceans – have a particularly

Figure 5.8 A king penguin chick covered in downy feathers which insulate it from the weather. When it moults it will resemble the adult penguins in the background.

Activity 3.1 discussed the value and uses of pinniped and cetacean blubber by humans.

thick and dense blubber layer, but little if any hair. Whilst the insulating properties of fur, feathers and fat discussed above are important, they are not the only adaptations of polar wildlife, and in the following section you will investigate how mechanisms that control blood flow around the body conserve heat.

Activity 5.1 Adaptations to the polar environment
The estimated time for this activity is 45 minutes.

Often people think only of polar bears and penguins when asked to name different species of polar wildlife. At this stage in the module, you are developing a more complex understanding, and in this activity you will see the range of animals that have adapted to what would be for humans, very harsh conditions.

The detailed notes for this activity are in the 'Activities' section of the S175 website.

5.2.2 Keeping warm by varying blood flow

With the internal temperature of an animal being in the range 37–38 °C, how this heat is moved around the body by blood flow is important. For example, is there an additional heat conservation mechanism that leads to low heat being emitted by the polar bear in Figure 5.5?

You have probably noticed that, even if your hands are cold at the start of a walk, once you have been walking briskly for some time, your hands warm up. This is the effect of the blood circulating around the body and bringing some of the heat generated in your leg muscles, to the hands. However, this creates a problem in very cold conditions, as vital heat can be lost from areas exposed to the cold air. As well as fur, feathers and fat, many polar animals have a very efficient way of preventing significant heat reaching their skin in the first place. Arteries are blood vessels that carry warm blood from the core of the body towards the skin, but they lie very close to veins, blood vessels that carry the cold blood away from the skin and back towards the heart. So the warm blood flowing in the arteries loses much of its heat on the way to the skin, by warming up the returning cold blood in the veins which is moving in the opposite direction. This heat exchange system is called a countercurrent and it keeps most of the heat within the body. As a result, the extremities can often be quite cold – but the animal suffers no ill-effects. Figure 5.9 shows how effective this process is in a husky dog.

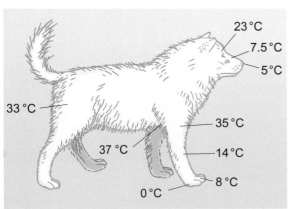

Figure 5.9 The temperature recorded at different parts of the body in a husky dog in an environmental temperature of −30 °C.

Question 5.3
Use Figure 5.9 to briefly answer the following three questions.

(a) What is the coldest part of the dog's body?

(b) How much colder is it than the core temperature (the highest temperature recorded)?

(c) How much warmer is it than the temperature of the surrounding air?

Countercurrent heat exchange systems are relatively common in polar wildlife. For example, whilst the main insulation for cetaceans and pinnipeds is a thick layer of insulating blubber, the flippers and tail have to be thin and blubber free to function effectively. As a result the efficient countercurrent heat exchange system prevents heat loss (Figure 5.10). Antarctic scientists often get asked questions such as: why don't penguins have cold feet? The answer is simply because of the countercurrent exchange systems within their exposed feet and thin flippers (seen in Figures 5.4 and 5.8). A further penguin adaptation is that the muscles that move the feet and flippers are located within the warmer regions of the body and tendons pass from the muscles to operate the feet, toes and flippers remotely. The result is that the limbs can function properly even when they are very cold. The countercurrent system is a physiological adaptation. Penguins also have behavioural adaptations and some species rock backwards on their feet and lift their toes up so that only the minimum area of the foot is in contact with the ice. Stiff tail feathers prevent them from falling backwards, and, of course, with no blood flow in the tail, no heat is lost through it (you can see one of these tails in Figure 5.8). If it is very cold and windy, penguins can squat down slightly, so that the tops of the feet are shielded from the cold air by feathers and body fat and the effect of wind chill is reduced. Such fine adjustments of the blood flow to the feet mean that their temperature is always kept above freezing. In complete contrast, if a human stood barefoot on ice there would soon be physical damage to the feet.

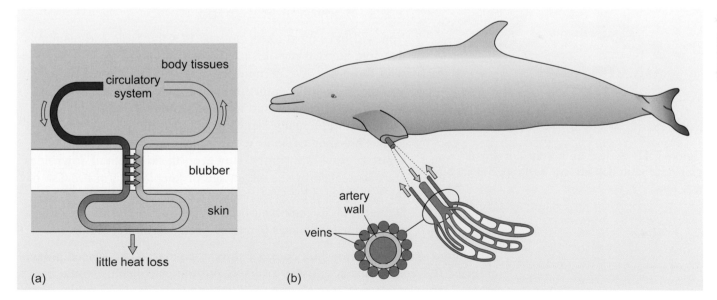

Figure 5.10 A countercurrent heat exchange system. (a) Schematic representation. (b) Blood supply to the flipper of a cetacean, with a schematic cross-section of an artery and the surrounding veins to the left. Arterial blood is shown in red, venous blood in blue. Pink arrows denote heat flow; yellow arrows show direction of blood flow.

Like polar bears with their fur and fat, these very efficient heat retention systems can cause problems when animals are too hot if, for example, they are very active and so generating a lot of heat, or when the physical environment changes due to increasing air or water temperatures. However, the countercurrent exchange system has its own control mechanism: the arteries can expand.

■ Look back to Figure 5.10b. What effect could the expansion of the central artery in the enlarged region have on the flow of blood through the flipper?

□ The expanding artery compresses the veins surrounding it. This would slow down the overall blood flow.

This effect can completely close the veins, so the blood would have to use another (non-countercurrent) route back to the heart. Overall, no heat would be lost from the arterial blood (to the veins) on its way to the surface, and the cool blood would not be warmed up as it returns. In hotter temperatures on land, seals often extend one of their flippers into the air to increase the amount of air flowing around it, and so lose more heat (Figure 5.11). Within water, blood vessels in the blubber of marine mammals can open up, so that the blubber gets warmer and relatively more heat is lost from the skin than normal.

Figure 5.11 A seal on a very hot day at temperate latitudes raising its flipper to increase heat loss.

There is one more feature common to many of the polar animals that reduces heat loss. If you consider the shape of the penguins (Figures 5.4 and 5.8), the seals (Figures 5.7 and 5.11), the polar bear (Figure 5.5) and the cetacean (Figure 5.10), they all have a similar stocky body shape.

5.2.3 Body size and shape

You will have most likely noticed that the birds and mammals that live in polar regions are often relatively large compared with those that live in more temperate climates. At first sight, you might find this surprising since there is not a lot of food available and perhaps sustaining a large body could be a problem. Additionally, being large generally results in a much longer breeding cycle as the offspring can take a number of years to grow to maturity. However, these potential downsides are outweighed by the advantage of keeping warm because of the relationship between the surface area and volume of an animal. This is important because heat is lost from the surface of an animal, whereas it retains heat within its volume.

If you are not familiar with calculating areas and volumes, you should read Section 6 of the Maths Skills ebook before you go any further.

To demonstrate the relationship, consider three imaginary cube-shaped polar animals. (Of course this is not very realistic, but the calculations would be more complicated if real animals were chosen and this simple example demonstrates the concept.) The first is the small animal A which has sides of its cube 1 cm long (Figure 5.12a). The second is animal B which is larger with the sides of its cube being 2 cm long (Figure 5.12b). Finally, the largest animal is C which has sides of length 3 cm (Figure 5.12c).

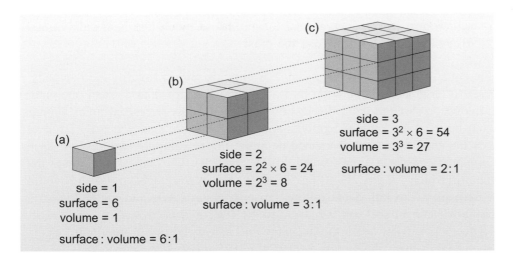

Figure 5.12 The linear dimensions, surface areas and volumes of three different-sized cubes representing animals, compared to how the surface area to volume ratio decreases as they increase in size.

For each animal, one needs to work out its surface area compared to its volume. If you know how to do this, then you might like to do the calculations yourself. If not, then follow these arithmetic steps carefully:

- for animal A:
  - the area of one face of the cube is 1 cm × 1 cm = 1 cm^2
  - there are 6 faces to the cube, so the total surface area is 1 cm^2 × 6 = 6 cm^2
  - the volume of the cube is 1 cm × 1 cm × 1 cm = 1 cm^3
  - so the ratio of the surface area to the volume is 6 : 1.

- for animal B:
  - the area of the 6 faces of the cube is 2 cm × 2 cm × 6 = 24 cm^2
  - the volume of the cube is 2 cm × 2 cm × 2 cm = 8 cm^3
  - so the ratio of the surface area to the volume is 24 : 8, which, dividing both sides by 8, gives a ratio of 3 : 1.

- for animal C:
  - the area of the 6 faces of the cube is 3 cm × 3 cm × 6 = 54 cm^2
  - the volume of the cube is 3 cm × 3 cm × 3 cm = 27 cm^3
  - so the ratio of the surface area to the volume is 54 : 27, which, dividing both sides by 27, gives a ratio of 2 : 1.

■ Bearing in mind that heat is generated within the volume of the animal (mainly by its muscles) but lost through the surface of the animal, what can you conclude from these results about the amount of heat that would be lost by these three animals, assuming they had no fur and were under the same environmental conditions?

□ Looking at the ratios, for animal A, the surface area is six times the volume (ratio 6 : 1); for animal B, the surface area is three times the volume (ratio 3 : 1); and for animal C, the surface area is twice the volume (ratio is 2 : 1). So, with relatively much less surface through which heat can be lost, animal C would lose much less heat than animal B, and animal A would lose the most.

This conclusion can be generalised. For animals with a roughly similar body shape, a large animal can keep its warmth more easily than a small one, and so evolution through natural selection has led to most terrestrial polar animals being large. With some exceptions, Antarctic birds are also generally large and even the smallest so-called crested penguin, the rockhopper, weighs 2–4 kg (comparable with an oven-ready roasting chicken). The largest penguin is the emperor which weighs 20–40 kg. A 40 kg bird is very substantial and would be perhaps 1.3 m tall. Seals follow the same general rule and the male southern elephant seal can weigh up to 4000 kg and be over 4 m long (Figure 5.13). Polar bears too are large and can weigh more than 600 kg, which makes them the largest terrestrial carnivores (meat-eaters). But compared with other bears, polar bears have short, stocky limbs, short tails and short ears.

Figure 5.13 Southern elephant seals on an Antarctic beach. That they look like fat slugs is not through chance – the body shape gives a large volume compared with surface area, so minimising heat loss.

■ What is the advantage of these physical features in the polar bear?

□ Longer limbs, tails and ears would increase the surface area to volume ratio and so increase the area over which heat could be lost. Short limbs, tails and ears help to conserve heat.

Due to the dependence of heat loss on surface area, very small animals that live in areas with very cold winters face a real problem. They have an advantage in that being lighter, they need less energy to move but their surface area is large in relation to their volume (and so their mass). This means they rapidly lose heat in cold conditions and the amount of extra fur or feathers they would need to insulate themselves would simply make them unable to move. However, the dwarf hamsters of Siberia and Mongolia, which are only ~5 cm long, remain active in winter. They can manage this as they have a network of tunnels beneath the deep snow through which they can run in search of seeds and vegetation to feed on. This adaptation means that they are sheltered from the wind and extremes of cold – but over the course of a winter they do get markedly lighter and leaner, losing up to 50% of their body weight. The emperor penguin has also evolved a behavioural adaptation to go with its physiological adaptations (Box 5.2).

Box 5.2 An extreme endotherm – the emperor penguin

In Box 3.3 you discovered the story of the quest for eggs of the emperor penguin by three British scientists/explorers.

■   Why did they want to collect eggs in the middle of the Antarctic winter?

☐   They wanted eggs containing the embryo at a stage of development that could suggest a link between reptiles and birds.

Birds are endotherms and reptiles are ectotherms, so this was a radical idea. It is often said that emperor penguins live and breed in the most extreme conditions encountered by any endothermic animal on Earth. They live on the Antarctic coast which, as you saw in Section 4.5.1, varies between ~0 °C in summer and ~−15 °C in winter. The problem for this penguin, as Activity 1.2 showed, is that when the wind blows from the centre of the continent towards the coast, it brings cold air from the coreless winter.

■   From Figure 4.20, what temperatures would the penguins have to endure under these conditions?

☐   Winds blowing from the centre of the continent could bring air that was colder than −50 °C towards them.

These are staggeringly poor conditions, and yet the penguins have evolved a strategy that allows them to keep eggs warm throughout. So how do they do this? Emperor penguins are large but even if all the stored fat was used to generate heat, an individual would not be able to maintain its body temperature, let alone incubate an egg. Their survival secret is huddling together.

■   Using what you have learned in Section 5.2.3, what would be the benefit of several thousand penguins huddling into one big group?

☐   Effectively it turns them into one large animal. The group has a much lower surface area compared to volume than each individual penguin. As a result the heat loss is greatly reduced.

In the huddle (Figure 5.14) the only penguins that feel the full force of the low temperature and the wind, are those on the outside of the group. The ones in the middle are surrounded by other warm penguins. There is of course a continual movement of penguins from the outside of the group into the middle, so that no individual remains exposed to the worst of the weather on the outside of the huddle for long. Whilst the penguins exploit the adaptation in extreme conditions, elephant seals and other species, as Figure 5.13 demonstrates, use similar heat-conserving techniques.

The life cycle of the emperor penguin is described in Activity 5.2.

Figure 5.14 Emperor penguins huddling to conserve heat in the depths of the Antarctic winter.

Question 5.4

Write a brief summary of no more than 100 words listing the three major adaptations of polar endotherms that enable them to live in the extreme conditions.

Activity 5.2 The hardest life: the breeding cycle of the emperor penguin

The estimated time for this activity is 60 minutes.

The emperor penguin has been highlighted as a polar animal which has a life cycle filled with formidable environmental challenges. In this activity you will watch wildlife documentary clips to see how well this species is adapted to the Antarctic winter.

The detailed notes for this activity are in the 'Activities' section of the S175 website.

5.3 Marine ectotherms

Ectotherms cannot control their body heat through internal processes and this means that the successful adaptations of the endotherms are not applicable to them.

■　What is the main problem that ectotherms face when the temperature of their surroundings falls below freezing? You may find it useful to look back to Section 5.1 to remind yourself of the meaning of 'ectotherm'.

☐ The main problem for ectotherms is the risk of their body tissues freezing when temperatures fall below zero. If this happens it may result in their death.

In Activity 5.3 you will consider the adaptations that enable some ectotherms to survive winter at the high latitudes. Here the focus is on the fish that live at very low temperatures. Most of these fish are marine (i.e. saltwater-dwelling) and you have already encountered one species in Box 3.2.

■ What are the lowest temperatures that marine fish will have to cope with in polar conditions?

☐ Although freshwater freezes at 0 °C, seawater does not freeze until the temperature falls to approximately −1.8 °C, and Figure 4.8 suggests large areas of the polar oceans are below 0 °C.

Because fish are ectotherms and cannot control their body temperature in the way that endotherms can, their body temperatures follow the temperature of the environment. But it is important that no ice forms in the cells that make up their bodies because ice water crystals could damage them. Just as for snow (described in Section 4.2), ice crystals need to form around a nucleus and these nuclei can be dust grains, other particles, or other ice crystals. The blood of marine fish freezes at between −0.9 °C and −1.0 °C, but they can live in seawater close to its freezing point at −1.8 °C because there are no ice-forming nuclei in their blood. Under these conditions the fish are said to be supercooled as they are living below their freezing point. However, if ice is introduced near to the fish, ice crystals can enter through the mouth and gills and these provide the nuclei for more crystals to rapidly form. The result is that the fish will freeze solid and die very quickly (Figure 5.15).

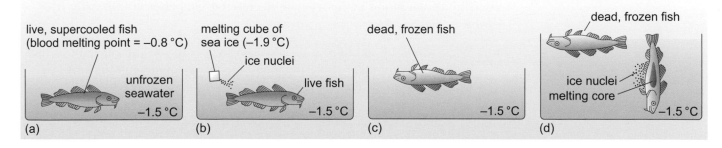

Figure 5.15 The effects of 'seeding' ice crystals into water containing a supercooled arctic cod. (a) The fish can remain indefinitely at −1.5 °C, because its blood is supercooled but contains no ice nuclei, but if (b) a piece of frozen seawater at −1.9 °C is put near it, the supercooling is destroyed, and the fish freezes and dies (c) in a few minutes, even though the seawater itself remains liquid at −1.5 °C. Similar processes (d) occur if the fish comes into contact with another already frozen fish that contains ice crystals.

One way of preventing a liquid from freezing is to add antifreeze, just as might be done for water in a car radiator or screen wash. In Box 3.2 you saw that some species of fish in cold waters produce chemical substances in their blood (glycerol, some types of sugars and glycoproteins) that act as a natural antifreeze. The antifreeze proteins are absorbed onto the surface of the initial forming ice crystals and prevent them growing any larger, so they do not damage the fish. You have already met the cod icefish in Figure 3.10, and there are many similar species (Figure 5.16).

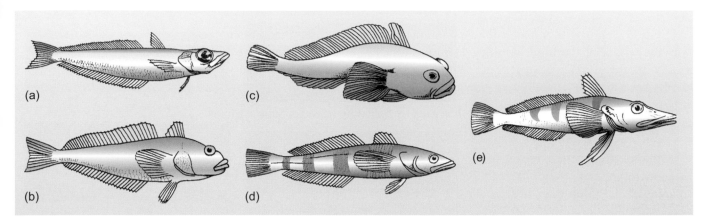

Figure 5.16 Some icefish native to the Southern Ocean. (a) The Antarctic silver fish which is 12–17 cm long. (b) The yellow belly rock cod which is 25–40 cm long. (c) The emerald rock cod approximately 20 cm long. (d) The toothfish, which at up to 1.25 m long is the largest fish in Antarctic coastal waters. (e) The mackerel icefish which is up to 1 m long and similar to that in Figure 3.10.

The lack of red blood cells, or more accurately, the absence of the red pigment haemoglobin which gives the colour to the blood of other vertebrates (animals with backbones), is a characteristic of a group of 16 species of Antarctic fish, and six of these lack the ability to produce another important oxygen-carrying protein called myoglobin. For different species the loss has occurred in different ways through evolution, but the result is the same. These are significant physiological adaptations and to see their advantages and disadvantages, the physical properties of blood must be addressed. The viscosity of the blood increases with decreasing temperature – literally it is harder to make it flow.

■   What would be the impact of increasing viscosity on the capacity of the heart of an animal to drive the blood around a countercurrent heat exchange system like in Figure 5.10?

☐   The heart would have to work harder to pump the blood.

Capillaries are the smallest blood vessels.

The absence of red blood cells reduces the viscosity of the blood so that it flows more easily at low temperatures. In icefish the heart is able to pump 3 to 4 times more blood compared with a fish of similar size that has red blood cells, and the result is that large volumes of this low viscosity blood flow through wide capillaries. The final ingredient that enables the fish to prosper is that, as you saw in Box 4.1, the polar waters are rich in dissolved oxygen. This is a significant advantage – but without myoglobin, oxygen cannot be stored so the fish quickly run out of oxygen (i.e. become anoxic) after a brief burst of swimming. As a result, like polar bears, icefish move relatively slowly with regular rests. In temperate waters the lack of movement could be a problem in seeking food, but in Chapter 7 you will see that the polar waters are rich biological systems. So, unsurprisingly perhaps, the combined effects of high oxygen concentrations and low viscosity blood make the icefish species perfectly adapted to their polar environment. However, in warmer, less oxygen-rich waters their lack of red blood cells means they would become anoxic and suffocate, and so they are confined to the high latitudes.

5.4 Adaptations of plants

Like animals, plants face unique problems in cold, snowy and windy conditions, where there is little or no sunlight for some months each year. But they too have successfully adapted, particularly in the Arctic, which has over 100 species of flowering plants. The Antarctic has only two species that are currently limited to Antarctic Peninsula (Figure 5.17).

(a)

(b)

Figure 5.17 (a) The white dryas, a common Arctic flower. (b) Antarctic hair grass, one of the two flowering Antarctic plants.

Question 5.5

Considering the previous chapters, why are there so few species of flowering plants in Antarctica? (Answer in no more than 100 words.)

You met the white dryas in Section 2.4.

■   Spend a few moments looking at the two plants in Figure 5.17 and make a note of the features that are different from plants typical of warmer climates.

□   You may have noted that the plant is growing very close to the ground and the leaves appear to be very small.

Plants that grow close to the ground, and particularly if they are in gaps between stones and rocks, are protected from the worst of the weather. Strong winds would bend and possibly break the stems of taller plants, but just as importantly, they would cause the plant to dry out. To enable valuable nutrients to move from the soil to the rest of the plant, there has to be a continuous upward movement of water through the plant which is taken up through the roots, and then escapes by evaporation through pores in the leaves called stomata (Figure 5.18). These stomata need to be open for at least some of the day, because, as well as being important for water flow, they are also the routes by which plants can exchange gases with the atmosphere (you will see the importance of this below). However, when the stomata are open in very windy conditions, the speed of evaporation is increased and the plant can dry out very rapidly. Additionally, if the soil is very cold, or worse still, if the water in it is partly frozen, then it will be difficult for the plants to take up liquid water through their roots, so preventing loss of water through the leaves is even more problematic.

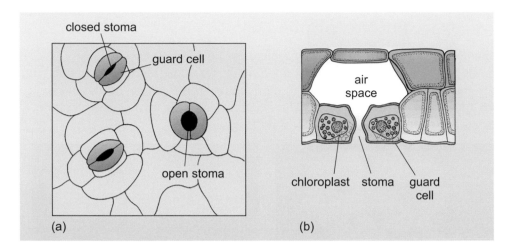

Figure 5.18 (a) The underside of a leaf surface showing three stoma, each of which is surrounded by two guard cells. (b) One of these stomata has been cut and is viewed from the side. Guard cells can change in size and so alter the size of the stomata and the amount of gas exchanged with the environment.

There are some adaptations that enable plants to limit water loss. If they grow close to the ground in a cushion (rosette) as shown in Figure 5.17a, then they can create a tiny microclimate where the moisture stays between the leaves and there is less risk of drying out. It has been found that the cushion insulates the base from the cold air above, by trapping energy from the Sun; the temperature at the base of the plant can be more than 10 °C higher than in the surrounding air. Also the leaves are often small and chunky, and so like the animals (Section 5.2.3), there is a reduced surface area – although in this case it reduces water loss through evaporation. Being fleshy also means that the leaves can retain more water for when it is in short supply. Chemical reactions are faster at higher temperatures and the microclimate enables plants to rapidly produce more flowers and as a result seeds. Some plants, such as the glacial buttercup (Figure 5.19a), can swivel their flowers on their stems to track the Sun around the sky and so absorb the maximum possible amount of solar energy. Close up you can see that the flowers are shaped like a parabolic reflector which focuses the warmth of the Sun's rays at the centre of the flower where the seeds will develop, in the same way that a solar cooker uses the energy from the Sun to heat food (Figure 5.19b).

The Sun is not just important to plants for warmth, it is critical for photosynthesis. This is a complex process, involving the plant absorbing the energy from sunlight, using the green pigment in their leaves called chlorophyll. This energy is then in turn used to combine atmospheric carbon dioxide (CO_2) with water (H_2O) to produce a range of carbohydrate compounds (e.g. starches and sugars) which power all the other chemical

(a)   (b)

Figure 5.19 The Arctic glacial buttercup tracks the Sun around the sky to maximise the solar energy it receives. (a) The glacial buttercup on a stamp from the Faroe Islands. (b) A parabolic reflector in the Nepalese Himalayas which also focuses sunlight but this time to cook food.

reactions that go on in the plant cells. Expressed in words, the process of photosynthesis can be written as follows:

$$\text{carbon dioxide} + \text{water} + \text{light energy} \rightarrow \text{carbohydrate} + \text{oxygen} \quad (5.1a)$$

The number next to the equation is like a figure number and it means that it can be easily referred to in subsequent sections.

Animals cannot harness the energy from the Sun for photosynthesis and so they have to rely on plants, either directly if they are herbivores or indirectly if they are carnivores. For plants and animals to make use of organic material such as carbohydrate, it has to be broken down (metabolised) into the different substances that an organism requires in order to live. The energy needed for all of these living processes is released from carbohydrate (and other organic molecules) by a process known as respiration which can be expressed in a 'word equation' as follows:

$$\text{carbohydrate} + \text{oxygen} \rightarrow \text{energy} + \text{carbon dioxide} + \text{water} \quad (5.1b)$$

■   Do you notice anything interesting about Equations 5.1a and 5.1b?

□   The equation for respiration (5.1b) is the *reverse* of the equation for photosynthesis (5.1a). Note also that while photosynthesis captures or *fixes* energy, respiration releases it.

You most likely also noticed that both equations involved two gases, carbon dioxide and oxygen, which in plants are obtained from and returned to the air via the stomata in the leaves (Figure 5.18). It is for this reason that plants need to keep these pores open for as long as possible, particularly during daylight hours when photosynthesis is rapid, despite the risk of water loss. Without sunlight, there is no photosynthesis and polar plants have a problem when there are either very short days with only a few hours of light or, as in the middle of winter at high latitudes, when there is no daylight at all (see Section 1.5).

■   What options are available to plants for surviving the winter darkness?

☐   There are two main options that you may have considered. They could produce seeds at the end of the summer, which then lie dormant on the ground, probably protected by a covering of snow from the worst of the weather (like the dwarf hamster in Section 5.2.3) and then germinate the following spring. Another option is for the plant itself to become dormant, where the above-ground portion may die off leaving only the roots to survive. These then develop new shoots when the weather improves.

Plants and animals are just two of the groups of living organisms in the animal kingdom. Algae are also found in the polar regions (Box 5.3).

Box 5.3 A mysterious observation – red snow

In May 1818, the North-West Passage expedition, led by Captain Sir John Ross, left England to map the coastline of North America. On 4 December 1818, the following article appeared in *The Times* in London:

Captain Sir John Ross has brought from Baffin's Bay a quantity of red snow, or rather snow-water, which has been submitted to chymical analysis in this country, in order to the discovery of the nature of its colouring matter. Our credulity is put to an extreme test upon this occasion, but we cannot learn that there is any reason to doubt the fact as stated. Sir John Ross did not see any red snow fall; but he saw large tracts overspread with it. The colour of the fields of snow was not uniform; but, on the contrary, there were patches or streaks more or less red, and of various depths of tint. The liquor, or dissolved snow, is of so dark a red as to resemble red port wine. It is stated, that the liquor deposits a sediment; and that the question is not answered, whether that sediment is of an animal or vegetable nature. It is suggested that the colour is derived from the soil on which the snow falls: in this case, no red snow can have been seen on the ice.

The Times (1818)

At the time, it was suggested that the red colour was due to iron from meteorites which had fallen on the snow, and it was not until the end of the 19th century that the correct interpretation was made. The red colour was the result of the growth of a very primitive sort of plant called the snow alga (Figure 5.20). Close relatives of this species live in soil and in ponds in the UK, where they contribute to the greenish colour often seen in pond water. Each individual alga is microscopic in size, consisting of just a single cell, and they can only be seen when large numbers are present together. But instead of appearing green due to the presence of chlorophyll, as would be expected for plant cells, the cells of the snow alga are red. The green pigment chlorophyll can be damaged by the very high intensity of light from the Sun at high latitudes, if it is in cells where there is very little protection. In the cells of leaves of flowering plants, the chlorophyll has some protection by the tough outside 'skin' of the leaf, but this is not possible in a single-celled organism. An extra pigment, a bright red carotenoid (related to the red pigments in carrots) has arisen through natural selection in them, which protects the cell, including the chlorophyll, from damage by absorbing some of the radiation. Because the pigments in the alga absorb sunlight, the algal cells warm up slightly and melt the snow around them. Thus they are often found in small depressions in the snow, which are called 'sun cups'. During the winter, when the algae are covered with snow, they form spores. When the temperatures rise in spring, and slight melting begins, these spores germinate and release tiny green cells each with a tiny twisting thread (a flagellum) on their surface, which they use to propel themselves towards the surface of the snow. Some may fuse in pairs in a simple form of sexual reproduction. The cells then develop the red pigment and the annual cycle is repeated.

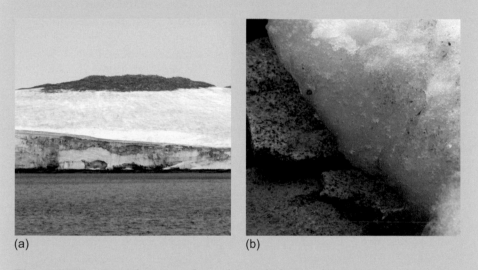

(a)   (b)

Figure 5.20 Antarctic snow algae. (a) Red algae colour the snow bank whilst green algae are on the vertical wall. (b) A close-up picture of the red algae showing the strong pigmentation.

Activity 5.3 The adaptations of tiny animals

The estimated time for this activity is 45 minutes.

This chapter has concentrated on relatively large animals and plants. What about the smaller animals such as insects which are vital to the life cycle of the plants? In this activity you will listen and respond to an interview with a polar terrestrial biologist and learn how animals such as bees survive through the polar winter. The detailed notes for this activity are in the 'Activities' section of the S175 website.

5.5 Conclusions

This chapter has not been a comprehensive survey of life in the polar regions – rather it has highlighted some key physiological and behavioural adaptations that particular species use to their advantage. What is clear is that the polar regions are not devoid of life and as you found in Activity 5.3, there are even species of bees that survive the polar winter.

The following chapter is about terrestrial habitats and ecosystems of the polar environment and you will learn how the animals are interdependent.

5.6 Summary of Chapter 5

- Polar wildlife consists of endotherms which can control their internal body temperature and ectotherms which cannot. Both types have developed through natural selection both structural and physiological adaptations, as well as behavioural adaptations that cope with what would to us be environmental stress.

- Endothermic animals maintain their core body temperature by insulation through fur and feathers and by controlling their blood flow, and natural selection has meant larger body shapes are preferred as they are more effective at retaining heat.

- Some marine ectotherms have an antifreeze system which combined with the environmental conditions enables them to prosper in the sub-zero waters of the Arctic and Antarctic.

- Plants have adaptations that enable them to create their own microclimate and prevent water loss, and some can even track the Sun around the sky to maximise their energy intake.

6 Habitats and ecosystems

6.1 Introduction

In Chapter 4, climatic regions within the two polar regions were identified and Chapter 5 discussed some of the adaptations of plants and animals to climatic variations.

■ How many climatic regions are there in the Arctic and how many in the Antarctic?

□ There are four climatic zones in the Arctic and two in the Antarctic (Section 4.5).

In this and the subsequent chapter you will investigate the habitats and ecosystems that have arisen in the polar regions through the combination of the climate and evolution. 'Habitat' and 'ecosystem' are words that you may have come across before, but in this chapter you will investigate the scientific meaning of these terms and their significance in more detail.

6.2 Defining an ecosystem

So far you have encountered many different environments, of which the classic 'polar' environment is one. The biological meaning of 'polar' is actually rather vague and so the term will not be used in this chapter. Instead it is helpful to introduce some new terms, which will aid understanding of the complexity of the connections of life on the frozen planet. The term 'environment' refers to the surroundings of a particular organism. Generally, when this word is used it refers to our environment; that is, the environment as experienced or perceived by humans. Investigating non-human environments means that a more precise meaning has to be given, and a set of terms will be used that identify more clearly the different attributes of these environments. Four of these key terms are introduced below.

Habitat The term habitat is used to indicate the area where an organism lives. The habitats of the polar bear are sea ice and Arctic coasts. Within those habitats, there will be many other animals living alongside the bear.

Community A combination of plants, animals and other organisms interacting together is described as a community or, more accurately, a biological community.

Niche Ecological niche is a term used to describe the place and role of a species within a community and describes more than the precise place where it lives. It also includes what the species does there; that is, its behaviour, its mode of feeding and its role in the community. Different species may occupy the same ecological niche in different communities. For example, the polar bear occupies the ecological niche of large mobile species feeding on animals on the sea ice. In Britain a similar niche is filled by many different animals including a fox or a grey seal.

Ecosystem If all the non-living elements of a community (e.g. dead wood, non-living parts of the soil, the air in that area, and so on), and the interactions between them are included within the community, the term ecosystem is used. Thus ecosystem is the highest level of description of all the components within a given area. The study of ecosystems includes consideration of the way in which elements such as carbon move between different parts of the whole. An ecosystem might link together several different habitats. A bird that feeds on a plant in the Arctic and drops it or defecates in a grassland area during a migration is providing a biological link between the two habitats.

6.2.1 Biological interactions

Animals and other organisms interact in many ways, but one common way between individuals of different species includes feeding interactions. This is where the different species form part of a so-called food chain or web. Food chains and food webs indicate the feeding relationships between different species and can be shown as a simple linear series of feeding relationships. For example:

Arctic plant (primary producer) → bird (herbivore) → arctic fox (carnivore)

The first step in this chain is labelled 'primary producer' and it is called this because plants are fundamentally different from animals and fungi, in that they are capable of building their tissues using light energy from the Sun and simple inorganic substances from the environment, including water, carbon dioxide and mineral salts.

■ What is the process called whereby plants obtain energy from the Sun and simple inorganic substances? Refer back to Section 5.4 if you need to.

☐ The process is called photosynthesis.

Animals cannot use photosynthesis to obtain their energy and materials for building their bodies; they have to get these by consuming other living things, either plants or other animals. For this reason plants are called autotrophs (from the Greek *auto* meaning 'self' and *troph* meaning 'feed'). In contrast, animals are termed heterotrophs (*hetero*, from the Greek for 'different'). Ultimately all animals depend on plants or other autotrophs for the energy and materials with which to build and maintain their bodies.

Herbivores, or primary consumers, are animals that eat plants and in turn use the plant materials they absorb to sustain their own growth. Secondary consumers, or carnivores, in turn, eat these animals, which in turn are eaten by tertiary consumers. Omnivores eat both plants and animals. These kind of feeding relationships are summarised in Figure 6.1 as a food chain, which is a hierarchy of plants and animals where each is food for the next member of the sequence. Each level or link in the food chain is called a trophic level, with the primary producers on the first level.

■ How many trophic levels are there in Figure 6.1?

□ There are three trophic levels: the Arctic plant, the goose and the fox.

Simple food chains such as the one shown in Figure 6.1 are rare. Herbivores generally feed on a range of different plants (primary producers) which occupy the same niche. In turn, the herbivores are preyed on by a wide range of carnivores, which again are occupying the same niche. For example, an arctic goose which subsists on plants could be eaten by another type of bird, a fox, a polar bear, and so on. The carnivores in turn prey on a wide range of herbivores, either dead or alive.

Consumers at each trophic level only convert on average about 10% of the chemical energy in their food to their own organic tissue – the rest of the food provides energy for warmth and activities such as hunting. For this reason, food chains rarely extend for more than five or six levels as there is so little of the energy from the primary producer left.

6.2.2 Food webs and energy

Complex feeding relationships between organisms are described as food webs, and a food web is essentially a map of many simple, connected food chains (e.g. Figure 6.1). An example of an Arctic food web is shown in Figure 6.2 – although this is by no means a complete picture of all the interactions that occur within this system.

■ In Figure 6.2, why are there arrows pointing towards and away from the arctic fox?

□ The arrows pointing towards the arctic fox indicate that it is consuming those organisms. The fox catches and eats arctic hare and snowy owl, and also eats dead arctic hare. The arrow from the fox to the arctic wolf means the fox is consumed by the wolf. In both cases the arrows indicate the direction of the energy flow.

Because there are arrows going in two directions, Figure 6.2 shows more complex interactions than Figure 6.1.

■ Look carefully at Figure 6.2: how does it differ in another significant way from the simple food chain in Figure 6.1?

□ Below the primary producers there is an additional level called detritus.

The detritus level in a food web contains the dead remains of plants and animals which form the food for many different animals, fungi and bacteria. These detritivores (detritus feeders) break down plant and animal tissue into simple substances such as CO_2 and soluble nutrients, which can then be used by primary producers. The result is that organic molecules move from plant to primary consumer to secondary and perhaps also a tertiary consumer through a food web as each component of the web is consumed in turn. The basis of

Figure 6.1 A simple example of an Arctic food chain.

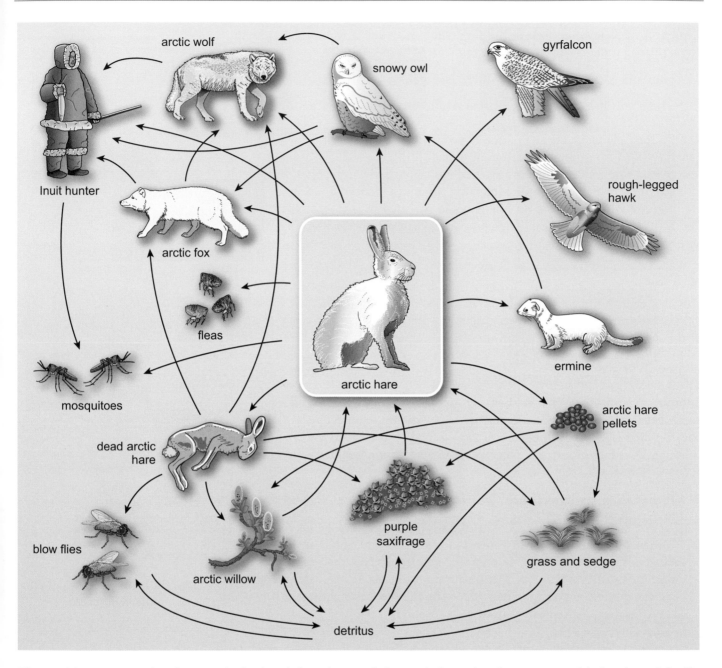

Figure 6.2 An example of an Arctic food web based around the arctic hare showing more trophic levels and feeding relationships than in the simple food chain in Figure 6.1.

life on Earth is carbon and because the common chemical constituent of organic molecules is carbon, food webs provide a way for carbon to cycle around an ecosystem.

When plants manufacture carbohydrates (glucose) during photosynthesis they are producing the compound from which whole food webs can be sustained.

■ Where does the energy for photosynthesis come from? Look back to Equation 5.1a if you need a reminder.

□ The energy used in photosynthesis is in the form of light from the Sun.

Within each molecule of glucose produced, energy from sunlight is fixed as chemical energy in the chemical bonds of the molecule. So not only does carbon move through food chains but so does energy.

When the glucose molecules are broken down, energy is liberated through the process of respiration (Section 5.4). One of the waste products of respiration is CO_2, which is returned back to the atmosphere. Similarly, when a primary consumer eats a plant, some of the compounds that are absorbed into the animal will be broken down during respiration, to power the functions of the animal – movement, chemical reactions, and so on – and CO_2 is again released. And this is the reason why the transfer of energy between trophic levels is relatively inefficient.

Some of the interactions in a relatively simple ecosystem like that in Figure 6.2 may not be obvious. For example, when the snowy owl defecates, the waste may be consumed by the arctic fox, or the three species of plants may compete for sheltered areas with high light levels, and so on. In a similar way, the outcomes of interactions between species are not always obvious. When a polar bear eats a seal, there is clearly only one winner. However, when a fly takes nectar from an Arctic flower like that shown in Figure 5.17a, it is not only helping itself to a sugar-rich meal, but also benefiting the plant by spreading its pollen to other members of the same species, thereby allowing seeds to be formed. Similarly, a plant may benefit by having its seeds eaten by birds because the seed will be dispersed to a new location by passing through the bird's digestive system.

Question 6.1

Without looking back, write down your own very brief definitions for the four key terms: habitat, biological community, ecosystem and niche.

Question 6.2

Which components in Figure 6.2 are occupying the same ecological niche of primary producers?

More on note-taking

To help you make notes on this discussion of ecological concepts, three techniques are presented in Figure 6.3. These are: a simple list, a simple line diagram and a more complex diagram. Using the example of a food chain that is part of a food web you can see that, depending on the content, one technique may be more appropriate than another. So a simple list would be sufficient to describe the animals that live in a particular ecosystem, a relatively simple food chain would show the one-way interactions, but a flow chart of a food web is a much better tool for visualising the complexities of an ecosystem of which a particular food chain is a part.

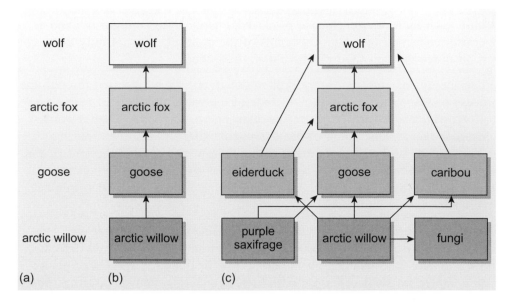

Figure 6.3 Different ways to describe trophic interactions: (a) a list of organisms; (b) a simple food chain; (c) a food web.

Activity 6.1 Note-taking techniques

The estimated time for this activity is 10 minutes.

In the three examples shown in Figure 6.3, the information is presented in different ways. In no more than 100 words, describe the different stories that are being told in each of the three examples.

6.2.3 The boundaries of an ecosystem

In the definition of 'ecosystem' given above, there was the example of a bird creating a connection between two habitats or ecosystems by eating seeds in one, whilst defecating in another. This reveals a problem with the concept of ecosystems — where does one ecosystem end and another one begin? There is no easy answer to this question, and it could be argued that the question itself is flawed because any given ecosystem is how you define it. For example, a lake within a meadow could be considered as comprising two separate ecosystems, or just one with two habitats. Another example is the ecosystem containing the red snow in Figure 5.20. The foreground of that picture shows the ocean and when the sunlight melts the snow with the algae ecosystem in it, the melt-water will flow into the sea and another ecosystem. Whether the algae can survive in the salt water is another question.

Overall, placing a boundary on an ecosystem, habitat or community is a difficult and essentially subjective exercise. It is therefore a good idea to be clear about the definition and boundaries that have been used when considering ecological information in any detail. So, can the Arctic or the Antarctic be considered as a single ecosystem? Not really, because different species live in different parts of it. There are soil-living organisms and so the soil can be regarded as one habitat; there are sea icc-dwelling organisms so the sea ice is a second habitat; there are ocean-dwelling organisms, and so on. On top of this, there are animals that easily move from one habitat into another; for example, a polar bear moves easily both on land and in the ocean (Figure 3.19b).

6.2.4 Large-scale ecosystem classification

At the beginning of Section 6.2 there was a detailed discussion of the key concepts needed for making sense of the relationships that make up the biological components of the frozen planet. As in all subjects, categorisation aids communication; in this case, allowing consistent identification of types of environment is important because ecosystems operate (function) in different ways or at different rates.

Major ecosystems with similar chemical and physical characteristics such as light, temperature, water and soil (called abiotic factors) and similar living organisms (called biotic factors) are known as biomes. But the terms 'ecosystem' and 'biome' can be considered interchangeable at large scales. Biomes are vast regions with climatically and geographically similar conditions, and can support similar communities of plants, animals and other organisms. But as with the example of the polar bear, you must always be aware that individual species are not restricted to particular ecosystems.

The next section will discuss the three major ecosystems that cover virtually the entire frozen planet. They are the ice sheet and polar desert, the tundra and the taiga.

Taiga is pronounced 'tiger'.

6.3 The biomes of the frozen planet

Large-scale mapping of the biotic and abiotic factors has allowed the construction of global biome maps (Figure 6.4). You may recognise some of the names of biomes such as arid desert or tropical rainforest, but the ice sheet and polar desert, the tundra and the taiga are limited to the higher latitudes and are probably less familiar. Broadly speaking, biological diversity within terrestrial biomes increases with the net primary productivity (through photosynthesis), the availability of moisture, and temperature. So in Figure 6.4, the most biologically diverse places would be expected to be the tropical rainforests, and the least diverse the ice sheets and polar deserts.

Net primary productivity is total primary productivity (i.e. the rate of biomass production) minus what the plant requires.

- Antarctica is missing from Figure 6.4; what biome would it fall into?

□ It would be similar to Greenland and contain ice sheet and polar desert biomes.

- What key ecosystem is missing from Figure 6.4?

□ The marine ecosystem is missing.

Figure 6.4 is a map of the terrestrial biomes and so it does not show any marine information. There is of course a similar complexity of biomes in the

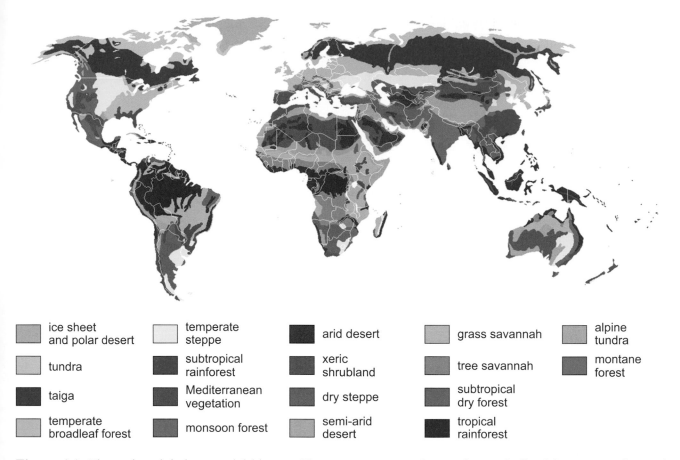

ice sheet and polar desert	temperate steppe	arid desert	grass savannah	alpine tundra
tundra	subtropical rainforest	xeric shrubland	tree savannah	montane forest
taiga	Mediterranean vegetation	dry steppe	subtropical dry forest	
temperate broadleaf forest	monsoon forest	semi-arid desert	tropical rainforest	

Figure 6.4 The major global terrestrial biomes. You are not expected to understand all of these terms, but to just concentrate on the ones relevant to the polar regions.

ocean, and Chapter 7 discusses the polar oceans and marine food chains. The following sections discuss the terrestrial biomes of the polar regions in order of increasing levels of net primary productivity.

6.3.1 The ice sheet and polar desert

The polar desert is a unique environment limited to the ice sheets and mostly comprises the continent of Antarctica and inner Greenland. In total it makes up almost 17 million km², which for context is approximately the area of Russia.

■ From Chapter 4, what are the extreme (i.e. the highest and lowest) temperatures on the Greenland Ice Sheet and the Antarctic ice sheets?

□ From Figure 4.24a, the lowest temperatures experienced on the Greenland Ice Sheet are below −35 °C and the highest just below 0 °C. From Figures 4.20 and 4.21, the lowest temperatures in the Antarctic ice sheets are below −60 °C and the highest ∼−30 °C.

In the case of Antarctica it is not just the temperatures that are significant, but the sustained and extreme cold of the coreless winter. Clearly the temperatures in this biome are severe and overall it appears extremely bleak (Figure 6.5). As a result, it is virtually impossible to draw a food web like Figure 6.2 as there is not a wide diversity of life. However, the severe temperatures are not the only factor that limits the biological activity.

Question 6.3

With the exception of temperatures, can you think of other factors you have learnt about that could affect biological productivity in this biome?

In the environment of Figure 6.5 there is a short supply of nutrients within the ice which any primary producers could use. As a result, the polar desert has no equivalent of lush meadows where, for example, large herbivores such as deer could graze. In fact, even the true polar survivors such as the emperor penguin could not sustain life here; a scarcity of resources means the only organisms that can live in the polar desert must be very small, and very well adapted.

The organisms that do occupy these harsh environments are called psychrophiles, and are capable of survival, growth or reproduction at temperatures of −15 °C or lower for extended periods. Most psychrophiles are bacteria that have become adapted to survive through evolution and natural selection. Like the ice fish, they have a protein which acts as an 'antifreeze' to keep their internal space liquid and to protect their genetic material at these very low temperatures. In Chapter 2 you saw that ice cores have been extracted from the ice sheets, and researchers have found that 400 000-year-old bacteria can be revived once thawed.

Figure 6.5 A typical view of the ice sheet and polar desert biome in Antarctica. The patterns visible are caused by the winds moving the snow.

Psychrophiles are of great interest to astrobiologists, who study the possibility of extraterrestrial life.

A more extreme psychrophile has been found in one location of the East Antarctic Ice Sheet. There is a feature that looks like a waterfall – but it is red in colour and has been named Blood Falls (Figure 6.6). Water from Blood Falls is salty and microbes that cause the colouration are similar to marine species, which suggests they have evolved from marine microbes. In an environment without light, the microbes cannot photosynthesise; instead they produce carbohydrates utilising sulfur and iron compounds as energy sources in a process called chemosynthesis. It is these reactions that are responsible for the colouration in Figure 6.6.

Figure 6.6 Blood Falls in East Antarctica. The colour is caused by microbes that use energy not from sunlight, but from inorganic chemicals (in this case iron and sulfur) in a process called chemosynthesis.

- ■ The microbes (actually bacteria) that form Blood Falls are thought to have become isolated when the East Antarctic Ice Sheet became permanent. From Figure 2.10, when did this happen?

- ▢ The EAIS became permanent ~10 million years ago. So the microbes could have been isolated for this extremely long time.

The processes that have led to this so-called chemosynthetic system have been relatively isolated for a long time, and such organisms are rare on Earth. They do however prove that photosynthesis is not the only route to sustain life and

Microbes are very small organisms. They are very diverse and include fungi and bacteria.

that sunlight is not a prerequisite. As a result, some scientists believe that similar chemosynthesis may support life in extreme environments on other planets; for example, below the surface of Mars and Europa (a moon of the giant planet Jupiter).

Within the polar desert there can be small habitats that provide a relatively temporary refuge for microbes. As you saw in Chapter 2, glaciers can reshape the landscape by eroding mountains and transporting rocks.

■   If a rock trapped within the ice reaches the surface, what will happen as solar energy falls on it?

☐   The rock will have a lower albedo than the surrounding ice, so it will absorb more solar radiation and as a result it will heat up. As a consequence, the ice in contact with the rock can melt.

Cryoconite holes can also be formed by low albedo volcanic ash and dust falling on the ice sheets.

The result of the melting is a hole filled with water just below the rock, called a cryoconite hole. In the summer months, such a pool of water can provide a temporary habitat for minute aquatic animals, green algae and bacteria. But when the sunlight – and so relative warmth – disappears, so do the holes and, if able, the organisms will enter a dormant state.

Finally, in Box 5.3 and Figure 5.20 you have already met one other organism able to survive in the polar desert – snow algae.

■   What adaptations do snow algae have that enable them to survive?

☐   Snow algae have a bright red carotenoid pigment which protects them from a high intensity of solar radiation, and the spores germinate into cells that have a flagellum to propel themselves towards the surface of the snow to reach the light.

Activity 6.2 The habitats of Antarctica

The estimated time for this activity is 60 minutes.

The Antarctic ice sheets are clearly a bleak environment. But evolution of adaptations through natural selection means that even apparent wastelands like those in Figure 6.5 can sustain life. In this activity you will investigate different Antarctic habitats and learn how valuable the ice-free areas can be for different wildlife.

The detailed notes for this activity are in the 'Activities' section of the S175 website.

Clearly the large Antarctic and Greenland polar ice sheets are bleak to humans (Figure 6.5) and biologically unproductive. It should therefore come as no surprise that humans have never survived there by living off the environment. In fact, long-term habitation has only been achieved in scientific research stations that are supplied with food.

At the edges of the ice sheets is the polar desert. This is a relatively dry stony environment where strong winds can sculpture the rocks into shapes called ventifacts, and the only significant life larger than microbes are the lichens which can grow on sheltered sunny rock faces (Figure 6.7). For the famed polar wildlife and inhabited environments, one has to head to the next biome: the tundra.

(a)

(b)

Figure 6.7 (a) A ventifact sculptured in the Antarctic wind (approximately 75 cm across). (b) The most advanced form of life in the polar desert are lichens which live on sheltered sunny rock faces.

6.3.2 The tundra

Tundra is a major Arctic biome of the frozen planet and it is characterised by areas free of glacial ice and a summer mean maximum temperature below 10 °C.

■ With temperatures below 10 °C in summer, would you expect to find trees in the tundra?

□ Figure 1.14 shows the 10 °C July isotherm and the treeline. Because the isotherm is virtually always north of the treeline you would not expect to find trees.

This biome is not as large as the polar desert in area, but it makes up virtually all of the land between the ice sheets and the treeline (Figure 6.4). North of the treeline it again looks bleak (Figure 6.8). However, there are plants visible on the ground living in the thin soil.

■ Are there any components of the frozen planet (the so-called cryosphere) visible in the photograph in Figure 6.8?

□ With the exception of the mountains in the far distance, there is no snow visible in Figure 6.8.

Snow and glaciers are very obvious parts of the cryosphere. But the cryosphere also extends below the surface of the land. In the UK, weather forecasters will often warn of 'ground frost' on sufficiently cold nights, when soils will freeze to some depth,

Figure 6.8 A landscape view across the Alaskan tundra with a mountain range in the background.

potentially causing problems for gardeners, for sporting events that rely on turf pitches and, in extreme cases, for utility pipelines. Such conditions are usually short-lived in the UK, but in colder parts of the world such as the tundra, subsurface freezing can often be permanent, freezing the land to surprising depths. This is called permafrost. Figure 4.25a showed the climate of a location called Resolute Bay at 74° N 94° W in the North-West Passage, where the depth of the permafrost has been measured to be ~400 m. Unsurprisingly, such conditions affect the physical processes within the environment as well as the plants and animals that might live there. With the ground frozen, when the winter snows melt, the water cannot drain away from the ground; so the summer tundra is often boggy and soft, as the very near surface (called the active layer) melts whilst deeper soils remain frozen. This is yet another environmental factor, along with light, temperature and winds, that makes it impossible for trees to grow. Overall, to humans the tundra is a very inhospitable place, with great extremes in both temperature and light and relatively strong winds. In fact, it is not hard to be filled with admiration for the explorers of the North-West Passage (Section 3.3.1) who had to contend with the hardships it presented in winter.

However, although humans have found the environment challenging, this does not mean that it is not biologically rich. The tundra is a habitat for large plant and animal communities, which have evolved some of the adaptations already seen in Chapter 5.

■ What are the main adaptations that enable the Arctic glacial buttercup (Figure 5.19a) to cope with the short growing season?

□ The Arctic glacial buttercup has a flower that concentrates the solar energy within its centre and can track the Sun around the sky.

Compared with more temperate climates, the tundra has a low diversity of primary producers (plants), but there are still over 1700 species of mostly shrubs, mosses, lichens, grasses and an additional 400 varieties of flowers which prosper. With short growing seasons, the tundra in summer can be very beautiful with spectacular displays of flowering plants and berries (Figure 6.9).

Question 6.4

Assuming a particular plant in Svalbard could only grow when atmospheric temperatures are above 0 °C, what is the length of its growing season? (*Hint*: see Figure 4.25.)

The food chain is dependent on the limited vegetation and there are just 48 species of land mammals. The primary consumers are smaller mammals such as the arctic hare and lemming, and also larger mammals including musk ox, caribou, bison and reindeer. The secondary consumers, the carnivores, are the arctic wolf, arctic fox, wolverine, ermine and snowy owl as well as – in certain regions – the polar bear. Figure 6.2 shows a typical tundra food web.

The continuous light of the Arctic summer drives a very short but intensive breeding season and millions of migratory birds arrive at wetlands and coastal shores of the tundra. Their food is not only the plants and berries but insects

Figure 6.9 In the short summer the tundra can have a surprisingly wide range of plants and flowers. This photo from Greenland shows mainly flowering grey-leaf willow. There is a polar bear skull in the foreground.

as well, for the wet surface habitats (Figure 6.8) are a breeding ground for black flies, deer flies and mosquitoes – all of which survive the winter using strategies described in Activity 5.3. The abundant feeding opportunities have led to epic animal migrations with, for example, a small bird called the arctic tern flying from the Arctic to the Antarctic every year to feed.

■ What could be the advantage for the tern of flying the huge distance from the Arctic to the Antarctic?

☐ The tern can spend summer in both hemispheres and so never suffer the hardship and relative scarcity of food in winter.

Large animals also migrate, with approximately 3 million caribou migrating more than 3000 km southwards across the tundra to find grazing away from the worst of the winter. No carnivorous mammals have regular migrations, but some wolf packs may track caribou if food becomes scarce in their home territory.

The animal and plant communities that are supported in the tundra have significant adaptations to cope with the extreme conditions. As a result, the ecosystem is sensitive to climatic stress.

■ What would be an example of a climatic stress on the tundra?

☐ Increasing temperatures could melt the permafrost and adversely affect the organisms that are adapted to the current freezing conditions.

During the short summer, the plants absorb CO_2, sunlight and water in the process of photosynthesis. Usually, when plants die and decompose they release the CO_2 back into the environment. However, in the tundra with the short summers and freezing winter temperatures, plants do not decompose – in fact, their remains from thousands of years ago can still be found in the permafrost. This means that the tundra is effectively removing CO_2 from the atmosphere and the soil is carbon-rich. Amazingly, it has been estimated that approximately one-third of all the carbon trapped in soil globally is trapped within the Arctic tundra.

The Antarctic provides a very different environment and in contrast to the vast swathe of Arctic tundra, the habitat is very limited and mostly restricted to the islands of the Antarctic and sub-Antarctic.

Overall, the tundra, with relatively few well-adapted species, is vulnerable to human impacts despite its large area. Figure 3.19 showed the track of a polar bear from satellite data. Attaching such equipment to bears gives an opportunity for them to be weighed, measured and tagged, and samples such as hair and fat can be taken for chemical analysis. The amount of body fat on a bear indicates whether it has been eating well or is starving. But a chemical analysis of the body fat of polar bears produced a surprise: they have measurable amounts of a family of chemicals called polybrominated diphenyl ethers (PBDEs) in their fat. The same discovery was made in arctic ringed seals (Figure 6.10). PBDEs are a group of synthetic chemicals developed during the 20th century as fire retardants. Fabrics and furniture are impregnated with them for the purpose of slowing the rate at which they burn, and with great success. However, once created, PBDEs are very difficult to destroy and will not break down into simple harmless components over time. For this reason, they are considered a persistent organic pollutant (POP) (Box 6.1).

Box 6.1 Pollution and bioaccumulation

The term 'pollutant' is a very wide-ranging term. When the introduction or action of something into our environment causes harm it is considered a pollutant. This could be a harmful chemical such as smoke from a chimney, or it could be a more subtle and transient effect, such as floodlights at an evening football match preventing stargazing (so called 'light-pollution') . There are many examples of how society has responded to pollution, such as the removal of lead in petrol which adversely affected human health, or the modification of floodlights so they only shine downwards. In both of these examples, when the pollution source was removed the levels of pollutant in the environment were reduced and consequently so were the effects – albeit with a time delay. By definition, persistent organic pollutants (POPs) such as PBDEs do not break down, so continued introduction of even minute levels of them into an environment leads to accumulation and perhaps magnification of potential harm. For example, Figure 6.10 shows that ringed seals have a PBDE level that is likely to increase with time. But the concentration of PBDE that accumulates in their tissues may be so small that it does not cause problems. However, a predator such as a polar bear may eat many seals, so it would receive the combined dose that each of these seals had within it. If this were absorbed by the bear, then the resulting accumulated level could be significantly more harmful. The concentration of pollutants at higher trophic levels in the food chain is called bioaccumulation, and the result is that higher predators can be poisoned while animals at lower levels in the food chain are apparently unaffected.

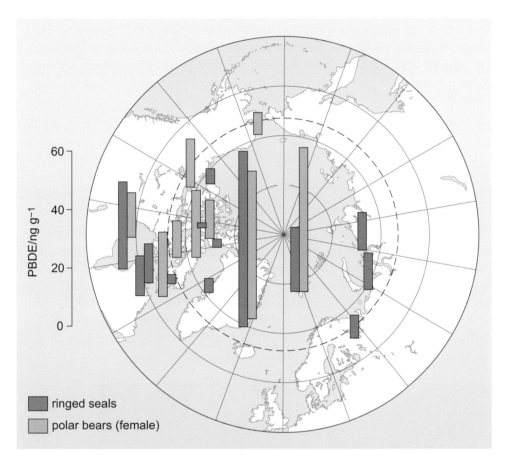

Figure 6.10 The concentration of PBDEs in the fat of polar bears and ringed seals (one of their main prey species) at different sites across the Arctic. The base of each bar indicates where the sample was taken. The dashed line shows the Arctic Circle. Concentrations are expressed in units of ng g^{-1}, and 1 ng = 10^{-9} g.

In the early 1980s, scientists began to detect POPs in the tissues of fish and shellfish close to populated areas. Concentrations were then detected in human breast milk, and the levels were shown to be increasing with time – perhaps through direct exposure to PBDEs or through bioaccumulation (see Box 6.1). The scale in Figure 6.10 is given in nanograms per gram. So, in every gram of the sample of bear and seal fat in East Greenland there are about 50 nanograms of PBDE. This is 0.000 000 05 grams in every gram of sample. It may seem an extremely small amount, but PBDEs are potentially very toxic and have been shown to hinder development of nerves in mammals. The migration of PBDEs into humans and shellfish was explained by proximity to where they were used. That they appear in the fats of Arctic animals that

The European Union has banned several PBDEs in the 21st century.

dwell on and around the tundra demonstrates the global connections by the winds, and the global ocean circulation described in Chapter 4.

Activity 6.3 The habitats of the Arctic

The estimated time for this activity is 60 minutes.

The tundra is a landscape with large differences between the seasons. It is covered by snow and ice in winter and then completely ice-free in summer. In this activity you will learn how different animals such as polar bear and musk ox have adapted to cope with these changes and succeed in landscapes that would be at the limits of human endurance.

The detailed notes for this activity are in the 'Activities' section of the S175 website.

6.3.3 The taiga

To the south of the tundra is the last ecosystem of the frozen planet. This is the taiga or boreal forest. The word 'taiga' is derived from the Russian for forest and it is the largest global biome (Figure 6.4), containing just over a quarter of the world's forests (Figure 6.11). Stretching over Eurasia and North America, it is usually found at latitudes between 50° and 70° N and the more northern parts consist mainly of conifer trees. The taiga only exists in the Northern Hemisphere since there is no land mass in the Southern Hemisphere that is large enough to create a 'taiga-type' biome.

Figure 6.11 The Russian taiga at 67° N in the region of the coldest winter Arctic temperatures shown in Figure 4.23b. However, in summer the temperatures here will be above 15 °C in July.

■   Why is the taiga not strictly a polar habitat?

□   The boundary of the Arctic is often defined as the isotherm where the mean July temperature is 10 °C and this generally coincides with the northernmost treeline (Section 1.6.1, Figure 1.14). The taiga is a forest environment, characterised by coniferous trees, so it is, of course, south of the treeline.

This accepted, the taiga can be considered part of the frozen planet in as much as it has the coldest recorded sea-level temperatures in the world, and a very strong seasonal cycle between summer and winter with only a very swift transition through spring and autumn. In essence, the taiga is the link between the tundra to the north and temperate forests to the south; consequently it is home to a wide range of species of plants and animals.

Despite relatively warm summers, the taiga is a harsh environment and the vegetation is relatively homogenous, dominated by hardy coniferous evergreens. These typically have long, thin, waxy needles which limit their water loss and give protection from freezing temperatures or from drying out. As evergreens, they retain their needles throughout the year and a dark-green colour allows them to absorb heat from the Sun and photosynthesise as soon as there is enough light. Towards the treeline in the northernmost part of the taiga, the forest cover is sparse, trees are stunted in growth and there is a lichen ground cover. Further south, it becomes a closed-canopy forest with densely packed trees and a mossy ground cover. This means that within the forest, the ambient temperature is usually higher than outside and the branches reduce wind chill in a similar way to penguins and seals huddling. In this way, the trees – and animals – gain protection from both the cold and the wind.

■   Why could the conical shape with downward pointing branches be an advantageous adaptation in the taiga?

□   Winter snow would slide off the downward-slanted branches and so not build up. As a result, they would be less likely to break under the weight of the snow.

In the clearings between trees, shrubs and wildflowers are common, and berries too – including bilberry, cranberry, cloudberry and lingonberry – form an important part of the ecosystem. Lakes and standing water are common, and several of the world's largest rivers including the Ob, Yenisei and Lena in Russia, and the Mackenzie and Yukon in North America flow through the taiga into the Arctic Ocean (Figure 6.12) – although, as you saw in Figure 4.26, the flow is strongly linked to the season.

Figure 6.12 The Yukon River flowing through the North American taiga.

The animals of the taiga have adapted to the strong seasonality and in comparison with the tundra, there are a large number of animal species. The boreal forest of Canada, for example, has 85 species of mammals, 130 species of fish, and more than 32 000 insect species which play a crucial role as pollinators and decomposers, as well as providing food for nesting birds. There are many large herbivorous mammals including moose and caribou and other deer species. Smaller herbivores include the snowshoe rabbit, red squirrel and vole which provide food for predators such as the lynx, wolverine, bobcat, mink and wolf, as well as food for omnivores such as bear and racoon. To survive the winters, larger mammals such as bears gain weight in the summer to take them through the winter. Other adaptations are described in Section 5.2. The biggest change in animal population is in springtime. For example, only about 30 species of birds spend the winter in the taiga and they are generally seed eaters such as the grouse and crossbill, large raptors such as the golden eagle and scavengers like ravens. In springtime vast numbers of migrating birds increase the number of species up to ~300 as they are attracted by the insect populations. With so many species, drawing a food web detailing the links is complicated and an example from the Canadian taiga is shown in Figure 6.13.

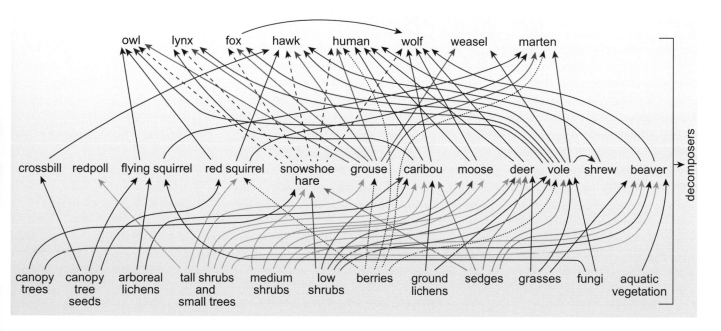

Figure 6.13 An example of a food web based on data collected at a Canadian research station in the taiga.

■ From Figure 6.13, suggest which herbivore is at the centre of this particular food web.

☐ The vole appears to be at the centre of this food web as it has the most arrows going towards and away from it.

Question 6.5

There are some species of reptiles and amphibians in the taiga. In no more than 50 words, explain why these animals would find it hard to cope in the conditions.

Question 6.6

Make a list of the different species in the ecological niche of the highest trophic level in Figure 6.13.

The taiga is susceptible to wildfire, partly due to the profusion of coniferous trees which produce a flammable resin. But this is a natural part of the forest life cycle and the way it periodically regenerates. Burning away the upper tree canopy allows sunlight to reach the ground and stimulate new growth on the forest floor. There are significant challenges for the habitat in the near future though. It is threatened both by the changing climate and also directly by human activities. Forestry is an important industry for the Russian Federation, and in North America forest fires, wood pulp manufacture, logging, spraying and clearing for agriculture are all major factors in habitat loss. This of course threatens many animal species, such as the woodland caribou, the American black bear, the grizzly bear and wolverine.

Question 6.7

Compare Figure 1.15 and Figure 6.4 to identify in which biome the Arctic peoples mostly live.

Activity 6.4 Reindeer evolution and adaptation

The estimated time for this activity is 60 minutes.

Like the polar bear, the reindeer is an iconic animal of the north. In this activity you will investigate how the reindeer of the high Arctic land of Svalbard has evolved relatively rapidly to cope with the changing climate of the planet, and its local environment compared with that of reindeer in mainland Europe.

The detailed notes for this activity are in the 'Activities' section of the S175 website.

6.4 Conclusions

When mapped, the major ecosystems and biomes can be used to categorise the different regions of the frozen planet where organisms can exist. At one end of the diversity scale is the ice sheet and polar desert, where life is barely visible. The tundra is arguably the true polar habitat as it is where the Arctic peoples and animals such as the polar bear live. The taiga is for large parts of the year frozen, but as Figure 6.4 shows, it extends to relatively low latitudes and into populated areas of the planet. At the start of the chapter you identified that there were four climatic regions of the Arctic, but these do not map easily onto biomes. However, in Figure 6.4 you can see that away from the influence of the warm ocean currents described in Chapter 4, the tundra and the taiga do extend further south on the eastern edge of Asia compared with northern Europe. In this way, the two chapters present a consistent story. In the Antarctic, Chapter 4 identified two climatic zones – the inner continent which is the ice sheet and polar desert, and the coastal regions and these do map onto biomes. You have seen that the ice sheet and polar desert is not a productive biological system. But Antarctica does not get its justified reputation for biological productivity from the ice sheets – it gets this reputation from the coastal climatic zone. Ecosystems here are supported by the polar seas, and this is the subject of Chapter 7.

6.5 Summary of Chapter 6

- Ecosystems can be defined by habitat, community and ecological niche. Individuals in particular niches make up a trophic level. The lowest trophic level are the primary producers, and they are consumed by herbivores, which are then in turn consumed by carnivores and/or omnivores.

- As energy moves between different trophic levels, only a small fraction is changed into organic tissue. The rest is used by the organism to live. Overall, it is not a very efficient transfer process.

- The boundaries between ecosystems are often not clear, but at the largest scale, biomes/ecosystems can be mapped out on the basis of similar biotic and abiotic factors.

- The three major biomes of the polar regions ordered in terms of increasing productivity are the ice sheet and polar desert, the tundra and the taiga.

- The distribution of biomes is at the larger scale consistent with the discussion of climate in Chapter 4.

7 Polar oceans and food chains

7.1 Introduction

In the previous chapter you considered the various distinct ecological habitats on land. A major habitat that remains to be discussed is created by the polar oceans. The oceans and their sea ice are a large component of the polar environment and in this chapter you will learn more about the types of small organism that exist there and the interactions that occur between them.

You saw in Chapter 4 that the two polar oceans are intimately linked through connections in the global ocean circulation and in this chapter you will consider the environment these frozen oceans provide for life. On first impression, the vast fields of sea ice look completely lifeless and barren (Figure 4.10c) – indeed the image of a hungry polar bear pacing across the bleak sea ice is common. However, you will see that the frozen seas contain an ecosystem that is the source of much of the sustenance for life both on land and in the air. In addition, the wind swept sea ice is not quite the wasteland that it first appears to be. The ice is made up of individual crystals, and in the gaps between them there can be quite extraordinary levels of biological activity. Overall, the polar seas are not just a part of the biological system of the high latitudes – they are arguably the key component.

7.2 Seawater and marine biology

Chapter 4 showed the ranges and distribution of both temperature (Figure 4.15) and salinity (Figure 4.16) along a north–south section in the Atlantic Ocean. The cold polar surface waters descend at high latitudes to the ocean depths and drive the overturning circulation (Figure 4.18). You also saw that oxygen is dissolved in the seawater (Box 4.1).

■   How does oxygen become dissolved in seawater?

□   It is absorbed at the sea surface in breaking waves.

Box 4.1 also noted that the amount of oxygen that can be dissolved in seawater is strongly dependent on temperature. The relationship between the two is shown in Figure 7.1a, which shows a plot of a best-fit line of dissolved oxygen and temperature data to create a so-called saturation curve. To use this plot, draw a line vertically upwards from the horizontal (temperature) axis to the point where it meets the saturation curve and the corresponding value on the vertical axis is the maximum amount of oxygen that can be dissolved in the water for any given temperature. For example, a line from 20 °C meets the saturation curve at a point corresponding to an oxygen concentration of approximately 225 μmol kg^{-1}; this means that water of this temperature can have any amount of oxygen below this value dissolved in it – but it cannot have higher values because it is not possible to dissolve any more oxygen. Figure 7.1b shows a vertical profile of dissolved oxygen in seawater versus depth (recorded by a ship lowering a sensor into the ocean) which is discussed below.

The oxygen concentration units are μmol kg^{-1}. A mol is a way of measuring amounts of substances. So it shows the amount of oxygen dissolved in 1 kg of water.

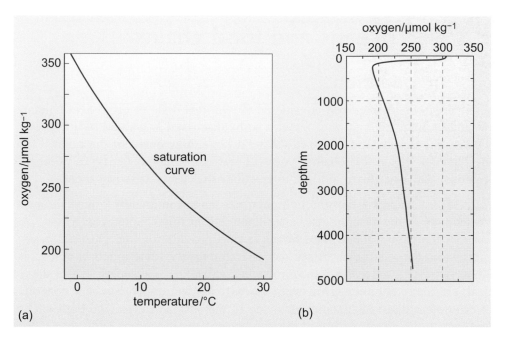

Figure 7.1 (a) A saturation curve showing how much oxygen can be dissolved in seawater at any given temperature. (b) A vertical measurement (profile) of oxygen dissolved in the South Atlantic Ocean.

Question 7.1

Use Figure 7.1a, and other information where required, to answer the following questions.

(a) What would be the maximum amount of dissolved oxygen in surface seawater at the Equator in the North Atlantic? (Hint: use Figure 4.8.)

(b) Why does the oxygen saturation curve show data for temperatures below 0 °C?

Oxygen is not the only gas in the atmosphere and as a consequence seawater contains dissolved quantities of other gases as well, including nitrogen (N_2), oxygen (O_2), argon (Ar) and carbon dioxide (CO_2). However, their relative proportions in the ocean differ from those in the atmosphere because they are soluble to different extents in seawater. There is an additional complication because, with the exception of argon, which is unreactive, these gases are affected by their participation in biological and chemical reactions.

In the ocean, just as on land, there is relatively little chemosynthesis.

As you saw in Chapters 5 and 6, the basis of virtually all life on land is photosynthesis; this is the process whereby plants build their own organic material by harnessing energy from the Sun. In Chapter 6 this was referred to as primary production because it occurs at the first trophic level. The same process is at the base of virtually all marine life, with the primary producers being single-celled marine algae. Collectively these floating organisms are known as phytoplankton (*phyton* = plant) or planktonic algae (Figure 7.2).

■ Which gas would be released into the water as phytoplankton photosynthesise?

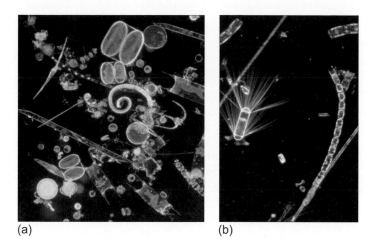

(a)   (b)

Figure 7.2 In high-latitude seas the most conspicuous phytoplankton are often species of diatoms, which have external skeletons made of silica; some diatom species have spines, some have a pill-box shape or are elongated. (a) A collection of phytoplankton. The picture is ~1.25 mm across. (b) Various species of chain-forming diatom, collected in the Southern Ocean.

☐ Equation 5.1a shows that the products of photosynthesis are carbohydrate and oxygen, so planktonic organisms will release oxygen into the seawater.

As a result of photosynthesis and the effect temperature has on the solubility of oxygen, the surface waters are generally supersaturated with oxygen; that is, they contain more dissolved oxygen than would normally be dissolved in seawater at that temperature (and so sit slightly above the curve in Figure 7.1a). However, as oxygen is used by all organisms in respiration including by bacteria in the decomposition of dead material, its concentration generally declines in the top 500–1000 m of the ocean. In the process of respiration, oxygen is taken up from the seawater and the waste carbon dioxide is returned back to it. Like in plants, the green pigment chlorophyll is important for algal photosynthesis and is responsible for the green colouring visible in the phytoplankton in Figure 7.2. Overall, the effect of these processes is demonstrated by Figure 7.1b, a profile showing dissolved oxygen versus depth in the South Atlantic Ocean.

■ Why is the dissolved oxygen in Figure 7.1b higher at depths of greater than 4000 m compared with at 500 m?

☐ At great depths the measurement is recording the dissolved oxygen in water that was once at the surface close to Antarctica and has descended to the deep ocean (Figure 4.17). This water is colder and was at the surface more recently so there has not been as long for biological processes to occur.

Ultimately all organisms die and in the oceans, just as on land, the dead organic material is broken down by bacteria. Where oxygen is present, these bacteria break down dead tissue in a process resembling respiration (Equation 5.1b). The components are then released back into the seawater.

Dead plankton which fall to the sea floor and are buried make up the sediments used to determine climate records like those shown in Chapter 2.

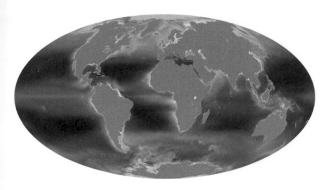

chlorophyll concentration/mg m⁻³

0.01 0.03 0.1 0.3 1 3 10 30 60

Figure 7.3 The average chlorophyll concentration in the Earth's oceans from mid-September 1997 through to the end of August 2007. Areas where phytoplankton thrive are lighter blue and yellow, whilst less productive regions are darker blues. Note that the scale is not linear; that is, the change between different shades of blue is only a tiny fraction of the change in chlorophyll concentration between different shades of yellow.

This includes the carbon, hydrogen and oxygen present in carbohydrates, as well as other constituents essential for life. Below you will see that sometimes these other constituents can be in short supply. Overall, the amount of organic material synthesised from inorganic substances per unit volume or unit area of water is called net primary production.

Individually the phytoplankton are relatively small but collectively, these single-celled and multicellular organisms can be detected from space using a satellite-borne sensor which records the amount of light that the chlorophyll is absorbing during photosynthesis (Figure 7.3).

Question 7.2

Using Figure 7.3, how in general does the mean chlorophyll concentration in the two polar regions compare with that of the warmer tropical oceans at low latitudes over the decade 1997–2007?

Question 7.3

Using Figure 7.3, can you think of any feature of the Earth system that would seriously limit the productivity at higher latitudes? (Hint: look at the components that make up Equation 5.1.)

Activity 7.1 Wildlife in the marine polar food web
The estimated time for this activity is 60 minutes.

In this activity you will view video clips showing the key components and interactions between different elements of the marine-based food web. You will use the information to estimate the number of trophic levels and construct a simple food web. The detailed notes for this activity are in the 'Activities' section of the S175 website.

7.3 The ingredients for primary production: light, mixing and nutrients

The variation in light is a key control on biological production in the polar oceans because the amount varies both seasonally and with latitude. Yet even so, Figure 7.3 shows that the oceans of the frozen planet are very productive compared with the rest of the global oceans. The term 'production' has been used loosely so far and it is possible to be much more precise: as stated previously net primary production is the productivity minus what the animal or plant requires, whereas productivity is the rate of primary production. You will now look at the vital components that together account for the high productivity of the polar oceans.

7.3.1 Light

Visible light is electromagnetic radiation and what is perceived as white light is actually made up of a spectrum of different colours including violet, indigo, blue, green, yellow, orange and red. These are the colours seen in a rainbow. When sunlight enters the ocean, its total intensity decreases very rapidly with increasing depth, and the shape of a graph showing intensity of light plotted against depth is called an exponential decay (Box 7.1).

Box 7.1 Exponential decay and increase

You may have heard the phrases 'exponential decay' and 'exponential increase' before. They are commonly used in science and describe a quantitative change in a particular mathematical way. For instance, in Section 7.3.1 the example of the reduction of intensity of light in water is discussed, and Figure 7.4 shows an example of how the intensity of light changes with depth. In this case, 100 units of light enter the surface of the ocean, but within 5 m of the surface half of the amount that arrived is absorbed by the water and so only 50 units remain. By 10 m depth another half of these 50 units has been absorbed and so 25 units remain. By 15 m depth there are only 12.5 units left, and so on. Every 5 m of depth reduces the intensity of light by one half. By 35 m depth, the intensity of light is below 1 unit compared with the 100 units arriving at the surface. This type of change, where a property reduces by one-half in a fixed interval of distance or time, over and over again, is called an exponential decay.

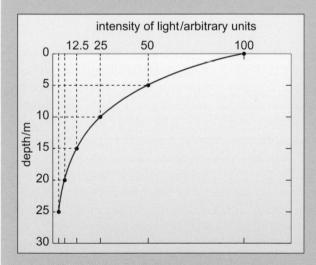

Figure 7.4 An example of exponential decay with 100 units of light entering the surface of the ocean and decreasing by one half in every 5 m of water depth.

Perhaps unsurprisingly, an exponential increase is when something doubles in equal distance or time intervals; for example, if a phytoplankton alga split into two every 5 seconds. This rate would then continue until at 1 minute there would be 4096 algae under this growth condition. To multiply from 1 algal cell to 4096 so quickly is impressive and any increase that follows the rule whereby the number doubles in equal fixed time periods is called exponential growth. A plot of the number of algae against time under exponential growth is shown in Figure 7.5.

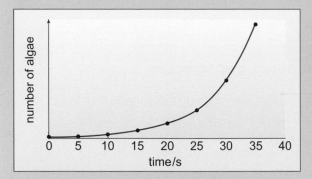

Figure 7.5 An example of exponential growth in number of algae over a period of 40 seconds.

The plot shown in Figure 7.3 does not have a linear colour scale – it changes very little from 0 to 1 mg m^{-3} of chlorophyll, but then it changes relatively rapidly in an exponential way up to 60 mg m^{-3}. This scale is used because, as Figure 7.3 shows, over much of the global ocean, chlorophyll concentration is mostly below 1 mg m^{-3}. By using a colour scale that changes a lot at high values, but very little at low values, the patterns of the chlorophyll over the global ocean can be highlighted.

There is an additional complication because, whilst each colour of the spectrum will reduce in intensity following an exponential decay, the rate of decay is different for each colour. Figures 7.6a and b show typical curves for the absorption of radiation with variation in ocean depth. Figure 7.6a shows the 10 m closest to the ocean surface and Figure 7.6b shows the intensity down to 300 m depth. As plotted, both assume that all the sunlight that reaches the sea surface passes straight into the water. This is not true in practice because some is reflected from the surface, some is absorbed, and some is scattered by sea foam on the surface. The proportion of incoming sunlight reflected from the sea surface also changes over the course of the day and with the seasons because the Sun will be at different locations in the sky. Once in the ocean, the light energy is absorbed both by constituents of living organisms such as chlorophyll in the phytoplankton, and by non-living materials such as sediment. It is also scattered by multiple reflections from these suspended particles.

■ According to the black line in Figure 7.6a, at roughly what depth in the ocean has the total light intensity been reduced to 50% of the incident radiation at the surface? (Ignore the fact that the black profile includes a small contribution from the infrared.)

☐   The incident radiation has reduced to ~50% by about 0.6 m, or 60 cm.
So, in the topmost 60 cm or so of the ocean, the intensity of sunlight
coming down from above is reduced by half!

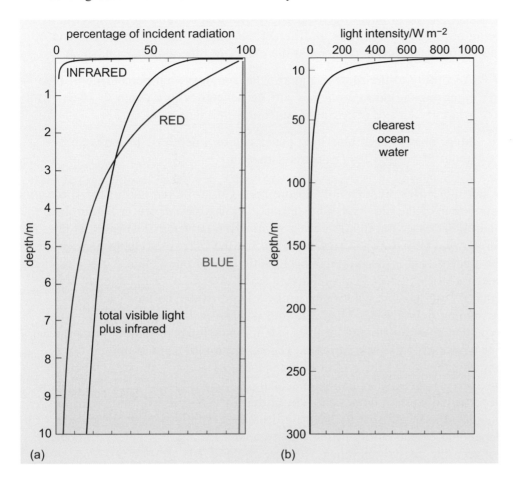

Figure 7.6 (a) The variation with depth in the oceans uppermost 10 m of total
light intensity (black line) and the intensities of red, blue and infrared
(i.e. thermal) radiation (Figure 5.5), relative to their surface intensity assuming
clear waters. (b) The decline of total light intensity with depth in the uppermost
300 m of the ocean, assuming bright sunlight and the clearest open ocean water.

The visibility of animals in the ocean is a matter of contrast – an object may
show up against its background because it is a different colour, because it has
a different brightness, or indeed both. An object viewed under water is seen
by the light rays that travel directly from the object to the eye of the observer.
However, like the light coming down through the sea surface, this will be
absorbed and scattered as described above and some of this light from the
object will be scattered towards the observer, producing a 'veil of light'
behind which the object becomes progressively more indistinct until it
disappears against the background. This is the reason that penguins and other
marine animals tend to be darker on their backs than underneath
(e.g. Figure 5.4). If a penguin is swimming, looking down on it from above,
the dark back will be indistinct against the low light beneath; from underneath
looking upwards the white fronts will be hard to make out against the bright

light from the surface. With the exception of very shallow water, this brightness contrast has a much greater effect on visibility than colour contrast and is an evolutionary adaptation.

There is one additional effect caused by different colours of the spectrum being absorbed by seawater to different extents (Figure 7.6a). At one end of the visible spectrum is red, and at the other are blue/violet (Figure 7.7).

- According to the plots in Figure 7.6a, roughly what percentage of blue light passing through the sea surface penetrates to a depth of 10 m? And what percentage of red light penetrates this far?

□ More than 95% of blue light penetrates to a depth of 10 m, but only about 5% of red light penetrates this far.

Water molecules preferentially absorb the light at the red end of the spectrum rather than at the blue end. This means that, as you can see in Figure 7.6a, the blue light passes through the water relatively unaffected. The result is that the further one gets from the surface of the sea the bluer everything appears, and the light is said to become monochromatic (i.e. of one colour). It is also because of this effect that a relatively small volume of water such as a full kitchen sink appears colourless, whilst a larger water volume such as a swimming pool appears blue. The four profiles in Figure 7.6a show exponential decay (though at this scale the plot for blue light appears linear), but with a different rate for each. The absorption of light is critical for photosynthesis and the region in the uppermost part of the ocean where the intensity of the solar radiation is actually sufficient for net photosynthesis to occur is called the photic zone. Given that light is critically important for photosynthesis and that its intensity decreases rapidly with depth (Figure 7.6), depending on the clarity of the water one can summarise typical differences between the coastal and open ocean as in Table 7.1.

Figure 7.7 The spectrum of white light can be seen by passing the light through a prism.

Table 7.1 Typical approximate depths of light penetration in the ocean.

	Coastal ocean	Open ocean
Limits of phytoplankton growth (below this intensity there is not enough energy for photosynthesis) (~ 10 W m^{-2})	20 m	150 m
Threshold of light perception for many fish (below this intensity there is not enough light for many fish to see) ($\sim 10^{-7}$ W m^{-2})	180 m	700 m
Threshold of light perception for some deep-sea fish (some deep-sea fish can see down to this intensity of light) ($\sim 10^{-11}$ W m^{-2})	N/A	~ 1000 m

- How would the depth of the phytoplankton growth limit in the open ocean change if the water was not very clear?

□ The limit would become shallower because the light would not penetrate as far into the water in the relatively murky coastal ocean.

7.3.2 Mixing: the stratification of the ocean

So far, you have concentrated on the visible light entering the ocean. There is another crucial factor for primary production which is how the density in the ocean changes in relation to depth. This is called the stratification and one needs to consider the forcing at the ocean's surface that is caused by the solar radiation and the winds (see Section 4.2). Figure 7.6a shows that the infrared radiation, which actually heats up the water, decreases extremely rapidly with depth in comparison with the light intensity.

■ From Figure 7.6a, at approximately what depth has the intensity of infrared (thermal) radiation entering the ocean been reduced to 5% of its value at the surface?

□ Thermal radiation has been reduced to 5% of its value at the surface by a depth of about 0.2 m, or 20 cm.

Thermal radiation from the Sun penetratcs only a small distance into the ocean and certainly to nowhere near the depths that light can penetrate. The way in which heat is carried deeper into the ocean is intimately linked to the global wind-system (such as that represented in Figure 4.5) through the process of turbulent mixing. This is where strong winds mix and stir the surface of the seas to ultimately determine the vertical distribution of temperature (Figure 7.8). Figure 7.8 summarises the effect of this turbulent mixing on the mid-latitude oceans in winter and summer. For both Figures 7.8a and 7.8b, the left-hand plot shows the effect of the wind and wave action on the depth of the turbulent mixing in the ocean; the right-hand plot shows a schematic of the variation of temperature with depth (i.e. the temperature profile) that results from this mixing. The uppermost section of the temperature profile where there is almost no change is called the mixed layer; this region also has uniform salinity. Beneath the mixed layer is a region where the temperature decreases relatively sharply with depth, between the surface waters and the cold dense water below; this transition zone is called the thermocline. Below the thermocline (as can be seen in the North Atlantic in Figure 4.15) the temperatures are relatively uniform compared with the change in the surface layers. The situation in the polar seas is slightly more complicated because of sea ice generation and the fact that the surface layers can be colder than the water beneath, but the general principle remains: at the surface of the oceans there is a wind-mixed layer which has uniform temperature and salinity.

7.3.3 Nutrients

Whilst phytoplankton requires carbohydrate and light to photosynthesise, they also require for their existence other non-gaseous components that are dissolved in the seawater. Collectively these ingredients are known as nutrients and the most important are nitrate (NO_3^-), phosphate (PO_4^{3-}) and silica (SiO_2). Of the three, nitrate and phosphate are used to make proteins whilst silicate is used in the external skeletons of certain groups of phytoplankton, notably diatoms (Figure 7.2). These biologically usable forms of nitrogen (N) and phosphorus (P) also occur in the soft tissues of marine

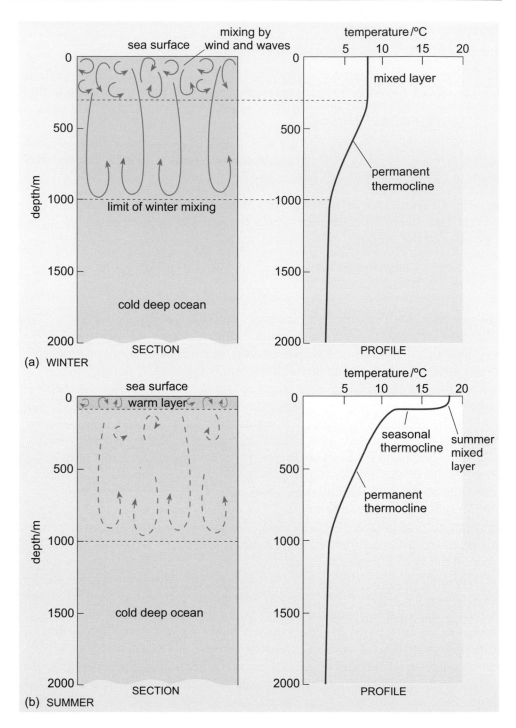

Figure 7.8 Schematic diagrams showing how the vertical distribution of temperature in the oceans in mid-latitudes results from the alternation of winter mixing and summer warming. (a) Cross-section (left) showing winter mixing, and (right) a typical winter temperature profile. (b) Cross-section (left) showing how summer warming produces a thin, warm surface mixed layer, and (right) a typical summer temperature profile, with a seasonal thermocline. The effects of winter mixing (dashed arrows) remain and contribute to the temperature gradient in the permanent thermocline, which is between the well-mixed layer (or seasonal thermocline) and the cold, deep water beneath.

organisms in the same proportions that they are in seawater. Light levels permitting, it is the nutrient concentrations that determine how much phytoplankton production (such as shown by the chlorophyll measurements in Figure 7.3) can take place. There are other seawater constituents used by the plankton; for example, calcium is also used to build shells and skeletons and sodium is one of a number of elements present in soft tissues. However, calcium and sodium are available in great abundance in seawater and so their precise concentrations have no effect on the growth of living organisms. In complete contrast, nitrate, phosphate and silicate are in limited quantities in the oceans and they may be completely used up by phytoplankton as it grows. Figure 7.9 shows the annual mean sea-surface distribution of the three key nutrients for oceanic production. Immediately one can see that the absolute values are small – in all cases they are in mmol m^{-3} (Box 7.2). In addition, the relative ranges are different: for nitrate it is 0–~30 mmol m^{-3}; for silicate the range is 0–~70 mmol m^{-3}; and for phosphate it is much smaller, with the range being 0–~2 mmol m^{-3}. Because all three nutrients are used in different ways in biological production, the relative proportions are not so important. However, they must all be present for phytoplankton production.

Box 7.2 Millimols and micromols

You have already met the unit mole (abbreviated to mol) in Figures 7.1 and 7.9 and it was referred to as a way of measuring the amounts of substances. The strict definition sounds a little more complicated:

One mole of any element (or compound) has a mass in grams equal to the atomic (or molecular) mass of the element (or compound).

But what does this mean? Section 2.3.1 noted that the nucleus of an atom consists of protons and neutrons, and each of these atomic building blocks has an atomic mass of one. In the case of a hydrogen gas molecule, which is given the symbol H$_2$ to indicate two hydrogen atoms (Box 1.3), there is one proton in the nucleus of each hydrogen atom and no neutrons. This means a hydrogen molecule has a molecular mass of 2 and so one mole of hydrogen weighs 2 g.

■ How much will 1 mole of water weigh assuming the oxygen is oxygen-16?

□ A water molecule is H$_2$O, with 2 hydrogen atoms to 1 oxygen atom. In oxygen-16 there are 8 neutrons and 8 protons so the atomic mass of oxygen-16 is 16. In total, the atomic mass of the water molecule is 2 + 16 = 18. So one mole of water weighs 18 grams.

The prefix 'm' in mmol m^{-3} refers to 'milli' which is 10^{-3}. For the case of nitrate (chemical symbol NO$_3^-$), one mole weighs 62 grams, so for a value at the top of the range of 30 mmol m^{-3} (Figure 7.9a) the concentration is calculated as follows:

1 mol = 62 grams

1 mmol = 62 grams × 10^{-3} = 0.062 grams

If you need to revise small numbers and powers of 10 you may wish to consult the Maths Skills ebook.

> So 30 mmol = 30 × 0.062 grams = 1.86 grams of nitrate in every m^3 of the surface waters.
>
> Figure 7.10 shows nutrient profiles using the unit μmol kg^{-1} which are equivalent to the units in Figure 7.9 but the m^{-3} has been converted to kg. There are ~1000 kg of water in a 1 m^{-3} volume, and so the units are 1000 times smaller – micromoles (μmol), which is 10^{-6} moles instead of 10^{-3} moles.
>
> From the scales in Figures 7.9 and 7.10, you can deduce that in absolute terms the nutrient concentrations are small – but they are vital ingredients for life.

■ How do the nutrient values shown in Figure 7.9 in the Arctic and the Antarctic compare with the rest of the global ocean?

☐ The Antarctic has very high values of all three nutrients, which are close to the top end of the scales. In the Arctic the values are lower for nitrate and silicate, whilst for the phosphate there is a correlation between lower values and the warmer water shown in Figure 4.19.

Question 7.4

Figure 7.9 shows the annual mean nutrient concentrations of the global ocean. In no more than 100 words, describe how well these values correlate with the average chlorophyll concentrations shown in Figure 7.3.

As phytoplankton grows, the nutrients shown in Figure 7.9 are used up and in particularly productive regions they can be completely depleted and stop growth. It is important to note that only one nutrient would have to reach zero concentration to limit growth. Figure 7.10 shows the vertical distribution of the three nutrients from a location in the Antarctic Circumpolar Current.

■ Will the profiles of nutrients in Figure 7.10 limit the biological production in the photic zone?

☐ They will not limit production because they do not reach zero concentration at the surface.

Whilst growth is not limited, it is clear in Figure 7.10 that in the upper 200 metres or so the values fall – in the case of phosphate, from ~2.4 μmol kg^{-1} at 500 m depth to below 2 μmol kg^{-1} at the surface. This nutrient decrease is linked to the schematic of the mixed layer shown in Figure 7.8. In the upper layer there is both carbon dioxide and light – the phytoplankton production has used up some of the nutrients (for the phosphate ~0.5 μmol kg^{-1} from ~2.4 μmol kg^{-1} at ~200 m depth to ~1.9 μmol kg^{-1} at the surface); but this only occurs to the depths where the light can penetrate (Table 7.1 and Figure 7.6). The same result can be seen for nitrate and silicate.

■ What will be the result of the increasing depth of the mixed layer in winter on the nutrient concentrations in the photic zone?

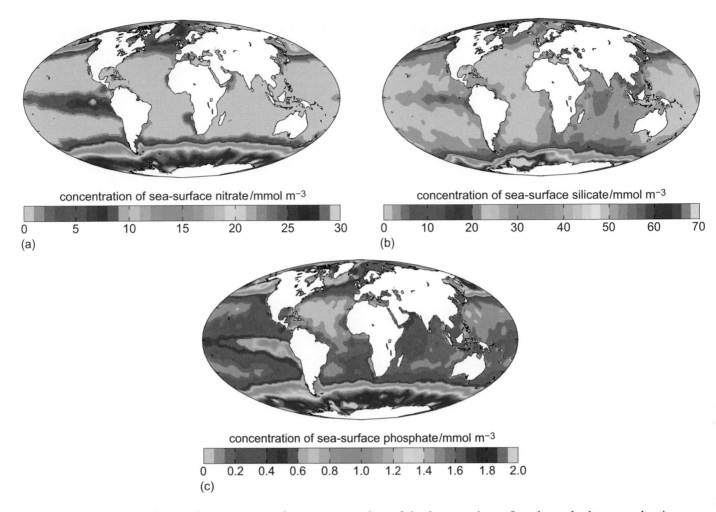

concentration of sea-surface nitrate/mmol m⁻³

0   5   10   15   20   25   30
(a)

concentration of sea-surface silicate/mmol m⁻³

0   10   20   30   40   50   60   70
(b)

concentration of sea-surface phosphate/mmol m⁻³

0   0.2   0.4   0.6   0.8   1.0   1.2   1.4   1.6   1.8   2.0
(c)

Figure 7.9 The global annual mean sea-surface concentration of the key nutrients for phytoplankton production: (a) nitrate, (b) silicate, and (c) phosphate. In all three cases, both the Arctic and the Antarctic show significantly elevated values compared with the global mean.

☐ In winter, stronger winds will deepen the mixed layer (Figure 7.8) and so water with higher nutrient values is mixed upwards into the photic zone. The result is that the concentrations in the photic zone will increase.

In winter however, as you saw in the answer to Question 7.3, the light which is necessary for production is absent or at low levels. Hence the overall biological production is low and the surface layers increase in nutrients as the deeper nutrient-rich waters mix towards the surface. When the light levels increase in spring and summer, all of the components for photosynthesis are in place and phytoplankton production increases. This results in a decrease in nutrient levels at the surface, leaving profiles similar to those in Figure 7.10. Comparing Figures 7.9 and 7.10, you can see that the concentrations of the nutrients do not reach zero at the surface and so, as a result, they cannot be limiting the biological production. It seems reasonable to ask the simple question – what does limit the production in the Southern Ocean when there are high concentrations of nutrients? One proposal is that iron is the missing ingredient (Box 7.3).

The nutrients in dead plankton are also returned to the water as they fall to the sea floor and decompose.

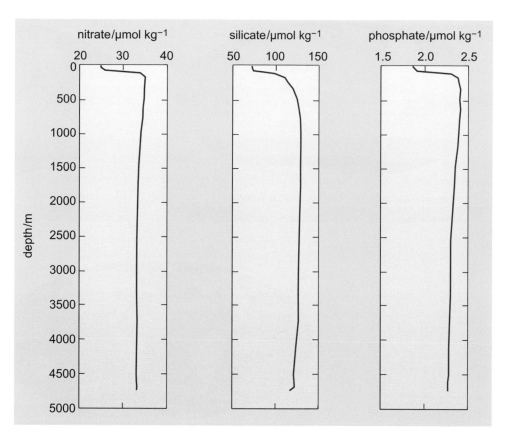

Figure 7.10 Vertical profiles of three nutrients shown in Figure 7.9. The data were recorded in the Antarctic Circumpolar Current and are typical of those at higher latitudes.

Box 7.3 The iron limitation hypothesis

Figure 7.3 shows that the chlorophyll is relatively high in the Southern Ocean compared with most of the global ocean. However, given the data in Figure 7.9 perhaps it could be higher. Regions like this are called high-nutrient low-chlorophyll (HNLC) environments. What else is missing to prevent the phytoplankton growing even more?

There is now strong evidence to suggest that trace elements such as iron play a crucial role in algal growth. This may seem strange as iron is the most abundant element on the planet as a whole, but it is only present in minute concentrations in seawater. Missing iron appears to be the answer because experiments in laboratories and the ocean have shown that the addition of dissolved iron to the environment of Southern Ocean phytoplankton allows them to grow faster and to use up more of the available supply of other nutrients.

■ What gas would be used up by photosynthesis (Equation 5.1a)?

☐ Carbon dioxide dissolved in the water would be used up.

If the CO_2 in the seawater was used up, more CO_2 from the atmosphere would be absorbed into the ocean to re-create the balance of gases noted in Section 7.2. Given the anthropogenic climate change induced by human emissions of CO_2, the process raises an intriguing possibility. Would it be possible to 'seed' the Southern Ocean with iron and engineer a massive phytoplankton bloom with the aim of removing atmospheric CO_2 to the ocean? This idea was originated by the scientist John Martin who named it the 'iron fertilisation hypothesis'. He said:

You give me half a tanker of iron, and I'll give you the next ice age.

(Martin, J., cited in Kunzig, 1999)

■ Based on the evidence presented in Chapter 2, is there any way that promoting the removal of CO_2 from the atmosphere could create a new ice age?

☐ Figure 2.13 shows that there is a correlation between atmospheric CO_2 and global temperature; however, this would have to be combined with variations in the orbit of the Earth around the Sun to recreate an ice age.

It is a dramatic quote and expresses a much disputed and extreme view, so you should be wary of taking it at face value. For example, if it was feasible and if phytoplankton production in the Southern Ocean did increase to levels where it reduced the amount of carbon in the atmosphere, where would the carbon in the phytoplankton finally end up? Nutrients within the plankton are mostly returned to the water as they die and decompose. Wouldn't the same happen to CO_2? Overall, there would only be removal of the carbon if the dead plankton were buried in the sea floor and over deep time turned into sedimentary rocks. In addition, if one fundamentally altered the first trophic level of the marine ecosystem, how would this affect higher trophic levels? You will see in Chapter 8 that in the Southern Ocean there is a legal and political framework to regulate such actions.

7.4 The sea ice and biological production

The opening to this chapter referred to the image of a polar bear wandering across the barren wastes of the sea ice. In the light of the previous section, would you expect the sea ice to be as sterile? It does seem unlikely, doesn't it? Section 4.3 discussed the formation of sea ice in the polar seas whereby small frazil ice crystals coalesce to form eventually large areas of pack ice. There always remain gaps between the original ice crystals and as the ice grows there is a complex network of joined-up channels within the ice. It is easy to think of sea ice as being like the ice cubes in your freezer, solid and impervious, but in fact a better way to think of it would be as a seawater-soaked matrix rather like a sponge sitting in water. If you pick up a piece of sea ice, then sea water will drip from it, and in some cases it will pour out. The ice is internally flooded with high-nutrient liquid (Figure 7.9).

Figure 7.11 Algae growing within the sea ice matrix are seen in the dense brown layer within broken ice. The light white-coloured layer on top is snow that has fallen on the ice and so it is neither seawater-soaked nor does it have the algae within it.

The median is the middle value of a range of values.

■ What could restrict biological production in sea ice?

□ The most critical restriction would be the availability of light.

Phytoplankton have evolved many adaptations throughout the world and there are species that are able to live in the low light and relatively low temperatures within the sea ice. With a yellowish-brown pigment to help them photosynthesise in these conditions, it is very common to break the ice and find a dense layer of brown-coloured phytoplankton algae within (Figure 7.11).

Given that one can clearly see phytoplankton algae in Figure 7.11, it seems reasonable to ask the simple question: how does this concentration of chlorophyll compare with the data shown for the whole of the Earth in Figure 7.3? In the oceanic areas of the Arctic and Antarctic the chlorophyll is typically in the range 3–60 mg m^{-2} compared with, for example, the central Pacific Ocean which has chlorophyll concentration in the range 0–1 mg m^{-2}. A compilation of data from 30 studies in the Arctic Ocean gives a median chlorophyll concentration within sea ice of 25 mg m^{-2}, with a range of 3–>800 mg m^{-2} in Hudson Bay. A similar compilation from 108 studies in the Antarctic gives a median chlorophyll concentration within sea ice of 170 mg m^{-2}, with a range of 4–>6000 mg m^{-2} in McMurdo Sound. To put these extraordinary values into context, the concentration of chlorophyll in a typical vigorously growing field of grass would be approximately 2000 mg m^{-2}. Truly the sea ice, whilst looking barren, is actually acres of white cold storage, and the bear may as well in some places be walking through a field of grass.

7.5 The oceanic food chain

The biological production discussed so far is at the very base of the food chain – the primary producers. What happens next at the higher trophic levels? Figure 7.12 shows a typical simplified food chain for a continental shelf. The phytoplankton is equivalent to grass, and there are two subsequent paths: a benthic path on the sea bed, and a pelagic path in the ocean. Zooplankton, clams and mussels are the herbivores which are subsequently grazed by carnivorous fish.

Just like on land, in the real world predator–prey relationships are usually complicated, with many carnivores feeding on a variety of prey, and themselves being prey for a variety of larger predators. The complexity in the Arctic Ocean food web is shown in Figure 7.13.

■ On the basis of the feeding interactions shown in Figure 7.13, what would you say is the key organism in the Arctic?

□ The food web shows that although some of the animals (including the largest) are feeding on various planktonic organisms, the rest depend directly or indirectly on the arctic cod, which therefore plays a pivotal role in the functioning of the Arctic marine ecosystem.

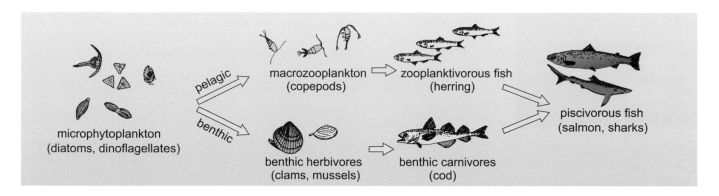

Figure 7.12 A simplified food chain for a shallow-water region. Note: the organisms representing each trophic level are selected examples of the many marine species that could be present at that level. Note also the prefixes indicating different size ranges: microphytoplankton are 20–200 μm across; macrozooplankton may be millimetres to centimetres across/long. Zooplanktivorous fish are fish that eat zooplankton and piscivorous fish are fish that eat other fish.

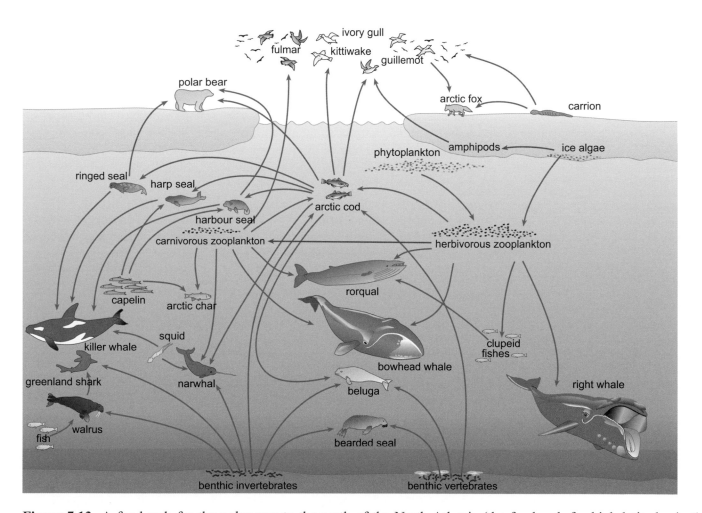

Figure 7.13 A food web for the polar seas to the north of the North Atlantic (the food web for high latitudes in the North Pacific differs from this in important ways). Note that this food web is simplified and not all links and species are shown. Amphipods are small crustaceans. (Not to scale.)

Figure 7.14 Antarctic krill (*Euphausia superba*) — the 'invisible' herbivore of the Southern Ocean which is the keystone species of the region. Average body length 5 cm.

In the Antarctic, the system is somewhat simpler because of the existence of a key species, which is comparable in some ways to the arctic cod: the antarctic krill (Figure 7.14). Krill are one of the most important consumers of phytoplankton in many parts of the ocean around Antarctica. There are several species but the most common is *Euphausia superba*, which grows up to 5–6 cm long when adult and lives for several years. Typically marine herbivores range in size from fractions of a millimetre up to a few millimetres; so the krill is a relative giant and they can successfully graze on other small zooplankton as well as phytoplankton. As a biological 'rule of thumb', small animals are fast-growing and short-lived, whilst big animals tend to have slower growth but live longer — for a comparison think of the activity, growth and movement of a mouse compared with that of an elephant. As a result, one could expect the small herbivores in the oceans to feed and grow rapidly and respond very quickly to an increase in phytoplankton. This means that phytoplankton and grazing zooplankton populations go through very similar cycles and as the amount of phytoplankton increases, the grazers such as krill multiply because of the food 'surplus'. Unsurprisingly, krill are abundant in the parts of the Southern Ocean with a dense food supply of phytoplankton.

You saw in Chapter 1 that the Antarctic Polar Front marked the northern boundary of the Antarctic Circumpolar Current, and south of this is a useful definition for the Antarctic (Figure 1.16). As a consequence, krill are found south of this front. Figure 7.15a shows a map of the mean November–April chlorophyll around Antarctica along with the mean winter and mean summer ice edge. Figure 7.15b shows the location of all of the catches of krill around Antarctica from 1926 to 2003. It is no coincidence that the krill are only found to the south of the Antarctic Polar Front — to the north of this the water is too warm. Together the two maps demonstrate that there is clearly a correlation between the distribution of krill and its main food supply. With a relatively simple Antarctic marine food web it is possible to suggest, based on Figure 7.15, where the predators such as whales and seals will be in high concentration.

Question 7.5

Figure 7.15a shows many areas within the summer sea ice which have a blue colour indicating no data. Why is there no data in this area?

Activity 7.2 Krill in the Southern Ocean food web

The estimated time for this activity is 75 minutes.

Krill are at the centre of the food web in the Southern Ocean. In this activity you will listen to audio and watch video clips about krill, their life cycle and the methods some animals have evolved to exploit them. You will derive the numbers of trophic levels in the Southern Ocean and calculate productivity for each.

The detailed notes for this activity are in the 'Activities' section of the S175 website.

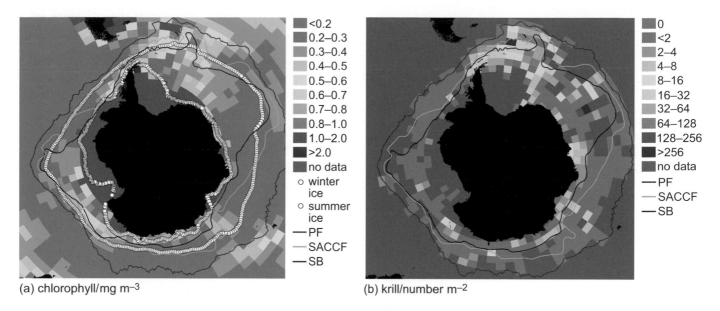

(a) chlorophyll/mg m^{-3}
(b) krill/number m^{-2}

Figure 7.15 (a) The mean November–April chlorophyll from satellite data between 1997 and 2003. On this plot are the mean extent of the summer sea ice and the mean extent of winter sea ice. (b) The mean density of krill derived from 6675 stations over the time period 1926–2003. PF = Polar Front; SACCF and SB are other oceanic fronts.

7.5.1 Oceanic vertical migration

The discussion about light has concentrated on its vertical distribution within the oceans surface. You noted that light is important for photosynthesis and Table 7.1 gave approximate depths for light penetration in the ocean; but the amount of light received at the surface of the ocean changes throughout the course of the day. Could this have any impact on the biological system? The simple answer is yes.

Every evening at dusk, over large parts of the polar oceans, there is a mass migration of marine animals up towards the surface; every morning, around dawn, the animals begin to return to the depths. This amazing phenomenon has been known about for nearly 200 years, but its ecological significance has still not entirely been satisfactorily explained. It is sometimes known as 'diurnal migration', but as diurnal means 'pertaining to the day' (i.e. is the opposite of 'nocturnal'), this behaviour is more properly known as diel migration, meaning migration 'once a day' or 'every 24 hours'.

At night, animals such as krill rise towards the surface. Diel migrations are tuned to the light–dark cycle, and the depth zones occupied by different species are influenced by day length, as well as factors like cloud cover, or even bright moonlight and eclipses. The vertical distance travelled over 24 hours varies, with larger species and better swimmers generally travelling further. However, even small zooplankton can travel several hundred metres twice a day with larger crustaceans such as krill travelling 100–200 m per hour, making a twice-daily journey of perhaps 800 m.

What possible advantages could there be for zooplankton to migrate in this way? Consider for a few minutes, and try to come up with some suggestions.

Many hypotheses have been advanced to explain vertical migrations. Here are three:

1   Food is more abundant as the primary producers are in the sunlit surface layers, but this is also where animals are most vulnerable to predators which hunt by sight. One solution to this might be to hide at depth by day, in darkness or near-darkness, and only rise to the surface to feed at night. The fact that many migrants are transparent, or very small, suggests that the animals that prey on them do hunt by sight.

2   Another possibility is that zooplankton conserve energy by spending non-feeding time in colder, deeper water.

3   Finally, because water at different depths moves at different speeds, and sometimes in different directions, migrating animals can feed in different bodies of water without having to travel horizontally. For example, they could be in plankton-poor waters one night, but when they come to the surface the next evening could well find themselves in a different, more nutrient-rich body of surface water, with more phytoplankton. This could also prevent them overgrazing a particular patch of productive water.

The most likely explanation is the first one, but it is possible that all of these hypotheses are correct, with different factors being more or less important depending on the circumstances. It seems that the migration of zooplankton is the incentive for the vertical migration of other larger animals, including fish and squid.

7.6   Oases in the winter pack ice – polynyas

You have seen that both the ocean and the sea ice can be biologically productive in the polar regions, although the amount of sunlight can limit productivity. However, in the polar seas as spring arrives, the sunlight usually returns long before the light will have enough energy to contribute to the melting and retreat of the sea ice. If there were regions of open water within the pack ice, then there could be enough light for them be productive. Such areas of open water could be useful for air-breathing predators such as seals and whales.

■   From what you have learnt so far, take a moment to come up with two ways in which sea ice can be removed from an area within the pack ice to leave an area of open water.

□   One way could be to melt the ice. Another is that sea ice floats, so a persistent strong wind from one direction could sweep the ice away leaving open water.

Both of these mechanisms happen in the polar seas and the area of open water that remains is called a polynya (pronounced 'poleenya' and from the Russian *polyi* meaning 'open' or 'hollow'). Warm water rising to the surface can contain enough heat to melt the sea ice. As long as there is a continual source of rising warm water then the area will be free of sea ice.

- What would happen to the upper ocean nutrient levels in this type of polynya?

☐ From Figure 7.10, rising warm water would contain elevated nutrient levels, so overall the nutrient levels in a polynya would be higher than the surrounding waters.

The second mechanism, with the strong winds, occurs usually at the coast where strong winds from the continent push the ice out to sea. Air temperatures are still cold and as the water is cold as well, new sea ice is formed – but this too is pushed away from the coast, keeping the water ice-free. A summary of the two methods of formation is shown in Figure 7.16.

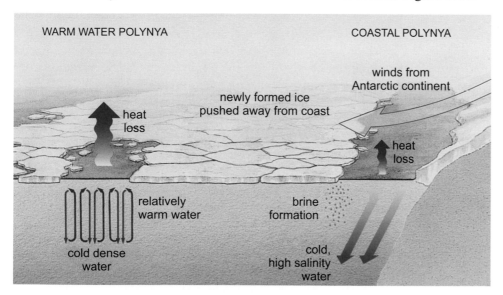

Figure 7.16 Formation mechanisms for two different types of polynya. In the mechanism on the left, a continual supply of warm water is melting the sea ice. In the polynya on the right, a strong coastal wind is blowing the ice away and keeping the water clear.

- What would be the impact of the increased sea ice generation within the coastal polynya?

☐ The sea ice generation will cause salt rejection (Section 4.4) which increases the salinity and therefore the density of the surface waters.

Increasing the density of waters at the edge of the continent in this way is thought to be one of the forces driving the global ocean circulation (Figure 4.18). As the ice is pushed away it also drags deeper water to the surface – but even if these waters are warmer, they are quickly cooled by the strong wind. What then remains is again, a surface layer with enriched nutrients. Coastal polynyas tend to occur in more or less the same place each year because the winds flow down valleys or glaciers out to sea. Figure 7.17 shows a map of Western Antarctica with the land shaded grey and colours indicating the percentage of ice-free days within the period 1 June to 31 October. From Figure 4.12b this is clearly the winter when sea ice is

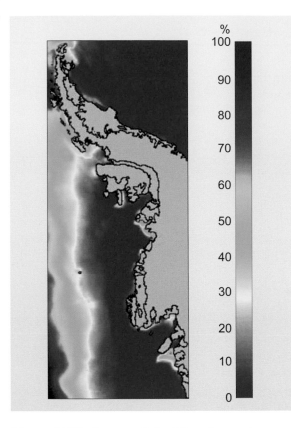

Figure 7.17 A map of the West Antarctic coast showing how much of the coastline is free of sea ice within winter. The colour scale shows the percentage of days between 1 June and 31 October for the years 1997–2001 that a particular location was ice-free.

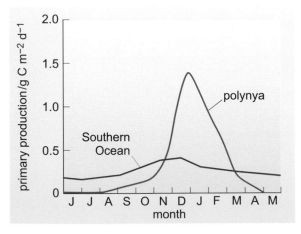

Figure 7.18 A comparison of the primary production of Antarctic polynyas with the entire Southern Ocean waters south of 50° S.

growing or close to its maximum extent – so adjacent to the coastline any region that is not coloured dark red is ice-free for a proportion of the winter.

- Given that there are 153 days between 1 June and 31 October, for how many days between these dates will an area be ice-free if it shows a value of 40% on Figure 7.17?

- For 40%, there would be 153 × 0.40 = 61.2 days. So for over 61 days the area would be ice-free.

Figure 7.17 shows some regions where for more than 60 days in the winter the coasts will be ice-free. In other regions, when the prevailing winds are in a favourable direction, then there are similar polynyas around the rest of Antarctica, and in the Arctic including the coasts of Greenland and Canada. Such regions of open water are persistent polynyas. Figure 7.15a showed the satellite-derived chlorophyll concentration around Antarctica at a large scale. By focusing on the polynya regions revealed by pictures such as Figure 7.17, Figure 7.18 shows the primary production within the polynyas compared with the wider Southern Ocean. In this plot the horizontal axis is month, and the vertical axis is primary production in a unit that indicates grams of carbon produced by each square metre of ocean per day.

- If a region produces 1 gram of carbon per each square metre of ocean each day (written 1 g C m^{-2} d^{-1}), how much carbon will it produce over 1 year?

- There are 365 days in a non leap year so the region will produce 365 × 1 = 365 g C m^{-2} d^{-1}.

Figure 7.18 shows that at certain times of the year the primary production within the polynyas is much greater than the background production of the Southern Ocean.

- How much more productive are the polynyas compared with the background productivity in January?

- In January, the Southern Ocean primary productivity is ~0.3 g C m^{-2} d^{-1}; within the polynyas the primary productivity is almost ~1.5 g C m^{-2} d^{-1}, so the polynyas are more than 1 g C m^{-2} d^{-1} more productive.

Although in Figure 7.17 the areas of the polynyas are relatively small compared with the wider Southern Ocean, clearly they stand out as being potentially important at the base of the food web. If so much primary production is being generated, surely it must have some affect on the higher trophic levels? Figure 7.19 shows a graph of mean Adélie penguin colony size on the vertical axis and annual primary production on the horizontal axis for colonies close to reoccurring polynyas.

- ■ The annual production on the horizontal axis in Figure 7.19 goes from 0 to ~100 mg C m^{-2} which is much lower than 365 times the 1.5 g C m^{-2} d^{-1} in January noted above. Why is this so?

- □ The value for January only exists for a short period of time – not the whole year. When you add up the annual production for the entire year overall, it is lower.

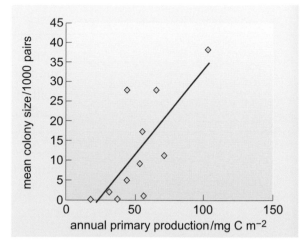

Figure 7.19 Mean Adélie penguin colony size versus annual polynya primary production in Eastern Antarctica.

Figure 7.19 has data points showing the results for individual Adélie penguin colonies with a mathematically derived best-fit line. There is a clear positive relationship whereby the higher the annual production within the polynyas, then the larger the penguin colony. Penguins do not feed on the primary producer, so it is safe to assume that their main food source – the krill – are thriving in the high productivity of the polynya waters. In turn, there will be other higher predators enjoying the benefits. Figures 7.17–7.19 referred to polynyas in Antarctica but similar relationships exist in the higher trophic levels of the Arctic polynyas as well. Indeed, there is strong archaeological evidence to suggest that Inuit peoples inhabited regions close to polynyas to exploit the increased biological production for thousands of years. As Figure 7.17 shows, a polynya may not be geographically large in extent, but oasis is an apt description.

7.7 Conclusions

The contrast between the images of the polar regions as isolated, bleak and empty, and as biological hot spots is stark. Much of the wildlife is dependent on the ocean and so marine processes are vital. Productivity is variable depending on season, but when in full swing the polar oceans are rich compared with the rest of the planet and they provide an explanation for the proliferation of the regions' large animals. Within the seasonal pack ice, the image of a sterile sea ice system is perhaps as far from reality as it is possible to be. Break open sea ice and the algae can colour the water chocolate brown (Figure 7.20). Finally, close to the continent polynyas provide an environment that is extremely productive and is exploited by animals including humans at higher trophic levels. In the following chapter you will see how this high biological productivity has led to profound implications for the management and protection of the polar regions.

Figure 7.20 Brown waters surrounding the sea ice covering the open ocean in Antarctica.

7.8 Summary of Chapter 7

- The combination of generally high nutrient levels, high dissolved oxygen levels and seasonal light means that the high latitudes have very productive seas when compared with the rest of the world's oceans.

- Within the sea ice is an extremely productive biological system adapted to the low light levels and cold temperatures.

- Both the Arctic and the Antarctic have oceanic food webs focused on key species. In the north this species is often arctic cod, whilst in the south it is krill.

- Polynyas are the oases of the polar seas with open water driving high productivity, which has clear implications for the higher trophic levels and for the management and protection of the polar regions.

8 The management of the polar regions

8.1 Introduction

This chapter brings together the strands and implications of what you have read previously to consider two key questions based on human impact.

- How can one manage the polar regions and the ways in which they are exploited?

- What does the future hold for them?

To answer these questions you will look first at the contrasting ways they are used and then at the effectiveness of current management regimes. Overall, actions with the potential for negative consequences are divided into direct and indirect activities. Direct activities take place in the polar regions, whilst indirect activities take place elsewhere but impact on them.

■ Based on what you have read, give an example of each type of activity.

☐ A good example of a direct activity would be the build-up of waste materials in the Antarctic during the 20th century as a result of human occupation. An example of an indirect activity would be the use of PBDEs leading to their bioaccumulation in ringed seals and polar bears, shown in Figure 6.10.

What is clear is that whereas in the past, protection of a species or regulation of a particular activity might have sufficed, today protection of entire ecosystems is required. Beyond the polar regions, it is humanity's global behaviour that raises an increasing number of issues and indirect impacts.

Today the frozen planet shows the impact of current activities and the legacies of those in the past. Whilst there are many broad-brush similarities, the Arctic and Antarctic are different. Consequently, it makes sense to treat them to some extent separately. This, coupled to the political environment in high latitudes, relates closely to the adequacy of the regimes put in place for their management. You will start with a description of the modern activities and direct impacts within Antarctica, as its geographic isolation, extreme climate and lack of indigenous population has been the overarching control. Then you will consider the same for the Arctic. Finally, you will examine the indirect activities that affect both regions before moving on to the system of international law that has arisen for their management.

8.2 The Antarctic: activities and impacts

Antarctica has often been described as the empty continent, but despite this, several potentially damaging activities still threaten it. The principal one is the relentless rise of greenhouse gases in the atmosphere, resulting from global industrial activity and land clearance, which is driving global temperature increase (Box 8.1).

■ Are greenhouse gases a direct or indirect impact?

You will see in Section 8.4.3 that the ozone hole provides another indirect impact.

☐ They are an indirect impact because they come from regions remote from the areas affected.

Of course there are direct impacts as well, which can be divided into two categories: those happening south of the Antarctic Polar Front in the Southern Ocean, and those on the Antarctic continent. South of the Polar Front there is fishing – both legal and illegal – and scientific whaling. On the continent there is, as Chapter 3 noted, an extensive network of scientific research bases. Combined with tourism, there is both ship and air traffic associated with them.

Box 8.1 Greenhouse gases in the atmosphere

Section 2.3 noted that there are particular atmospheric gases that are so good at trapping heat from the Sun that they are referred to as greenhouse gases.

■ Which greenhouse gases did Chapter 2 name as being important?

☐ Carbon dioxide (CO_2) and methane (CH_4).

Chapter 2 also showed that there is a correlation between atmospheric CO_2 concentrations and global atmospheric temperature (Figure 2.13). Since the Industrial Revolution in the 18th century the atmospheric concentration of CO_2 has increased dramatically as carbon in fossil fuels such as coal has been released into the atmosphere (Figure 8.1).

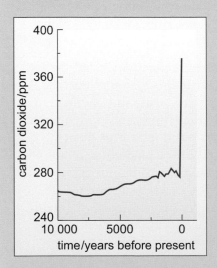

Figure 8.1 Atmospheric concentration of CO_2 for the last 10 000 years.

■ How much higher is the most recent value in Figure 8.1 compared with the last 800 000 years shown in Figure 2.13?

☐ In Figure 2.13 the range of atmospheric CO_2 concentration is ~180–280 ppm, whereas Figure 8.1 shows it to be >360 ppm.

As a result of the increased CO_2, the global mean surface temperature has increased by ~0.9 °C compared with the stable temperatures shown

As this book is published the atmospheric concentration of carbon dioxide is more than 390 ppm.

in the Holocene in Figure 2.19. Both atmospheric CO_2 and global atmospheric temperature will continue to increase.

8.2.1 Whaling in the Southern Ocean

Whaling provides a good example of a direct impact and the role of science in understanding this activity. Chapter 3 noted that whalers and seal hunters were amongst the first humans to work in Antarctic waters and whaling stations were established on South Georgia. Their refuse over the 20th century can still be seen on the Antarctic Peninsula (Figure 8.2).

(a)

(b)

Figure 8.2 The whalers have long gone from Deception Island, on the Antarctic Peninsula, but evidence of their presence is all too visible. (a) Abandoned whaling boats on the shore; (b) barrels whose staves have become separated as the iron bands rusted away.

Commercial whaling in Antarctic waters did not last long but the figures for whales caught during ~1905–1970 are enormous (Table 8.1). The South Georgia whaling stations alone processed 175 250 whales from 1905 to 1964 when they closed. Whilst the lack of remaining whales meant the industry was not commercially viable, a moratorium on commercial whaling issued by the International Whaling Commission (IWC) had to wait until 1986. With sealing, the industry ceased earlier and a ban came into force in 1970. Since then, seal populations have essentially recovered to their pre-industry numbers, but although whaling regulations are reasonably effective, whales have not recovered to the same extent.

A moratorium is a suspension of an activity.

■ Why could whale numbers be rising at only a slow rate?

□ Because they are large animals most whale species have long life cycles and therefore slow reproductive rates (Section 7.5), so it takes many years for populations to increase in size. Also whalers hunted larger individuals, which would most likely be of breeding age.

Table 8.1 Figures for whale catches from just one small area of the Southern Ocean around the South Shetland and South Orkney Islands in a 19 year period at the height of Antarctic whaling. The figures are from a plaque originally on the site of a Norwegian whaling station on Signy Island. Two of the species caught are shown in Figure 8.3.

Whale species	right	blue	fin	sei	humpback	sperm	Total
Number caught	78	61 366	48 023	1796	6742	18	118 159

(a)   (b)

Figure 8.3 Whales in Antarctic waters. (a) A southern right whale. (b) A humpback whale.

Furthermore, despite the moratorium the IWC allows governments to issue permits to kill whales for the purpose of scientific research. On this basis, Japan still (as of 2011) kills ~1000 whales each year within what is termed the Southern Ocean Sanctuary (the Southern Ocean south of 40° S). The aim of their research includes physiological measurements, age determination, an examination of diet and DNA sampling. Once these measurements have been made, the whale meat is sold for human consumption. This activity is controversial and many observers point out that most of the data could be gathered without killing the whales. However, the moratorium is not universally popular and whilst the future for the IWC is probably secure, the total commercial whaling suspension could yet be overturned.

Activity 8.1 Whale monitoring
The estimated time for this activity is 45 minutes.

To set limits on exploiting any natural resource, one needs to know how much there is to begin with. Unfortunately this is usually difficult. In this activity you will watch a video clip on monitoring whale populations in Iceland using acoustic monitors, and you will also investigate the current levels of scientific whaling in both polar regions. The detailed notes for this activity are in the 'Activities' section of the S175 website.

8.2.2 Fishing in the Southern Ocean

Antarctic fishing commenced in the early 1900s and it remains the only current commercial industry. Krill were the first targeted species since seals and whales to be significantly exploited (Figure 7.14), principally by the former Soviet Union, and they have been used as health supplements and food for fish farms.

■ From your knowledge of Antarctic food webs from Chapter 7, what other organisms could be affected by large-scale fishing of krill?

□ Krill are a key species and many animals at higher trophic levels such as whales, seals, penguins and other birds use them as a main food source.

Recognising a potential problem for a key species in the ecosystem, the Convention on Conservation of Antarctic Marine Living Resources (CCAMLR) was established in 1982 as part of the Antarctic Treaty to manage catches and prevent overfishing. However, it was the decline of the Soviet Union and, as with sealing and whaling, the uneconomic nature of the activity that really 'regulated' it. Recently demand for krill as a source of food for fish farms has risen and despite low catch rates, it is an industry being closely monitored. CCAMLR also protect the main fish under threat in Antarctic waters: these are the patagonian toothfish (Figure 8.4) and the mackerel icefish (Figure 5.16e). However, illegal fishing south of the Antarctic Polar Front coupled to a long breeding cycle is driving patagonian toothfish populations into a rapid decline. In addition, the technique for fishing toothfish means that birds such as albatross can be caught and drowned as well, so there is an impact on other wildlife.

Figure 8.4 A patagonian toothfish lives on squid and krill, and is itself prey for sperm whales and elephant seals. It grows slowly, can live as long as 50 years and does not breed until it is at least 10 years old.

Question 8.1

How could overfishing for toothfish affect populations of whales and seals?

8.2.3 Scientific bases and research

Chapter 3 noted that Antarctica is a continent for science and the first bases were established during the Heroic Age (Section 3.1). Permanent stations were established by the UK during World War II in 1944 to mark a presence south of the Falklands, and to deter enemy ships from safe anchorages (Figure 8.5). The first modern research stations were established in the 1950s and currently approximately 30 countries operate ~100 scientific bases employing ~4000 personnel in summer with 30 or so field camps. In the winter the number of personnel falls to less than 1000. Many of these modern bases have involved major civil engineering works such as runway construction, with resultant impacts on the environment. There are also impacts associated with running bases, which come from aircraft and ship activity with their potential for pollution, introduced species and finally human and hydrocarbon wastes. For example, in the 1950s through to the 1970s it was common practice to push waste from the bases

Figure 8.5 Port Lockroy, a permanent research base set up in 1944 now preserved as a historic site. It still contains a post office that is staffed during the summer months.

onto the sea ice where it would sink to the seabed as the ice melted in the summer (Box 8.2).

Box 8.2 The McMurdo bases

There are two permanent bases on the shores of McMurdo Sound, the vast American McMurdo Station with a population of over 1000 (Figure 8.6a) and the New Zealand Scott Base with a population of ~50. Together they illustrate the impact of Antarctic bases on the local area. At one time, waste from the stations was dumped on the shore, covered with petrol and ignited. Other waste was piled on the sea ice in winter to be deposited on the sea floor in the summer. From 1962 to 1972 there was even a nuclear reactor supplying energy until a minor leak led to it being switched off and removed from Antarctica along with much of the surrounding soil. The result of these impacts can be seen in a 2001 survey of the local sea floor which found the following large objects on the seabed: 15 vehicles, 26 shipping containers, 603 fuel drums and some 1000 miscellaneous items dumped on an area of about 0.2 km^2. It was summarised in the following quote:

> 'It's one of the most polluted harbours in the world in terms of oil', says Auckland University zoologist Clive Evans, who studies the fish in McMurdo Sound. 'If you drill a hole, up towards McMurdo, the water that comes up is horribly grey and murky, and when it settles down, there is just a sheen of oil on the surface.'

(Collins, 2004)

Because of environmental laws that you will learn about in Section 8.5.1, the bay has been substantially cleaned up and operational procedures have changed. For example, pumping of raw sewage into McMurdo Sound stopped in 2003 when a treatment plant began operation. Today virtually all Antarctic station waste is separated into specific categories and removed from Antarctica (Figure 8.6b).

8.2.4 Antarctic tourism

Tourists are the other main visitors to Antarctica outnumbering researchers by more than 10 : 1 (over 50 000 tourists to 4000 government personnel in 2008). Typically they spend less time on the land, but their activity tends to be focused around visits to specific penguin and seal colonies, and historic bases (e.g. Figure 8.5). As a consequence, to reduce the potential impact, virtually all operators follow strict codes of practice on wildlife contact, quarantine regulations and waste management, which have been defined by the International Association of Antarctic Tour Operators (IAATO). However, despite IAATO's strict guidelines, accidents have happened and polar-capable ships have foundered, with resulting local pollution (Figure 8.7).

(a)

(b)

Figure 8.6 (a) McMurdo Station is the largest base in Antarctica. Management of the waste from a base such as this is a huge logistical challenge. (b) Old colour-coded fuel drums are used as storage for different types of segregated refuse before its removal from Antarctica.

Figure 8.7 MS *Explorer*, a ship that carried expedition cruises to Antarctica. Although strengthened to withstand sea ice, she sank in 2007 a few hours after striking ice near the South Shetland Islands.

Activity 8.2 Footsteps in the snow

The estimated time for this activity is 45 minutes.

Many Antarctic bases from the Heroic Age are still maintained as monuments. In this activity you will watch a video clip describing Captain Scott's march from Cape Evans on Ross Island to the South Pole. This will be contrasted with the experiences of a modern polar explorer.

The detailed notes for this activity are in the 'Activities' section of the S175 website.

Chapter 2 noted that Svalbard sends millions of tons of coal to Europe.

8.3 The Arctic: activities and impacts

As noted in Chapter 3, just like in the Antarctic, the Arctic was exploited by whalers and sealers in the 18th and 19th centuries. However, whereas in the south this period of exploitation has largely passed, the Arctic has 'progressed' to modern extractive industries in the form of oil, gas and mineral mining. These resources are within Greenland, Northern Canada and Arctic Norway and these areas have an indigenous population of approximately 4 million people. This affects both their direct and indirect impacts.

8.3.1 Shipping

The Arctic is often used as a shipping route rather than being a final destination, with intra-Arctic (i.e. within the region) and trans-Arctic (a route to somewhere beyond) travel. Most Arctic shipping is currently intra-Arctic and a recent climate impact assessment stated: 'reduced sea ice will very likely increase marine transport and access to resources'.

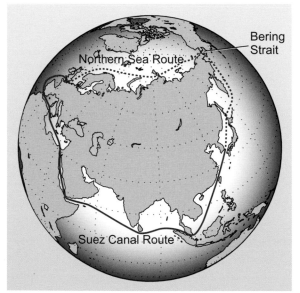

Figure 8.8 A potential Arctic sea route compared with a route via the Suez Canal.

■ Take a moment to think about what environmental impacts may result through increased Arctic shipping.

☐ Ships could be responsible for accidents resulting in pollution (e.g. Figure 8.7), disturbance to marine life, and the normal passage of ships through the water might also produce pollution.

The most famous trans-Arctic routes are the North-West Passage (Section 3.3.1, Figure 3.6) and the Northern Sea Route to the North of Russia (Figure 8.8).

■ Why would the Northern Sea Route from London to Singapore be preferable to that via the Suez Canal Route?

☐ It would be shorter, quicker, and potentially cheaper and it would be remote from many areas with current global conflicts.

A Northern Sea Route could save as much as 6000 km for each journey from Europe to the Far East. Furthermore, as a consequence of the accelerated melt of Arctic sea ice (Figure 4.14a), an even shorter route straight across the Central Arctic Ocean via the North Pole may soon be possible. Regardless of route, all trans-Arctic marine shipping must pass through the narrow Bering Strait and as a result this narrow channel could yet come to global prominence.

8.3.2 Fishing and whaling

As in the Southern Ocean, fishing raises many environmental issues. The ability of fish stocks to recover is threatened not only by overfishing of particular species but also by the so-called 'by-catch', where unwanted fish, birds and marine mammals are also caught and killed. Fishing is usually well managed within 200 nautical miles of a nation's own coast in what is called an Exclusive Economic Zone. In this region a nation may exploit, conserve and manage the natural resources of their waters. Unfortunately, outside this limit are the so-called 'high seas' where there is no jurisdiction and no great incentive for states to act collectively. As a result, Arctic-wide overfishing cannot currently be prevented. Finally, as in the Southern Ocean, despite an IWC moratorium on commercial whaling, Norway, Iceland, Greenland and the Faroe Islands continue to catch whales, arguing that it is a traditional activity with low sustainable numbers being taken. Indigenous people also hunt whales for food although catch limits are relatively small, totalling some 300 animals.

8.3.3 Military activity

During the Cold War, the Arctic was a place of major strategic importance because two adversaries – the USA and the former Soviet Union – were only separated by the Arctic Ocean. Had there been any conflict, a missile strike would have been likely across the Arctic as it is the shortest straight-line distance between them. To detect such a launch, the US built and staffed a long chain of 63 radar stations from Alaska in the west to Baffin Island in the east. The Soviet Union acted similarly and military installations proliferated. As a result, the Russian Kola Peninsula and Severodvinsk regions are thought to have the highest concentration of active and derelict nuclear reactors in the world. Here there are ~115 reactors on active submarines, 101 on inactive submarines and 4 on military surface ships – a total of ~18% of the world's total nuclear reactors. Management of this material is vital as any release could cause untold damage, given the slow rate at which the Arctic is able to recover.

The Cold War is the name given to the political conflict between the former Soviet Union and the west including the USA and UK from ~1946–1991.

- How might the release of radioactive material from the Russian Arctic have indirect impacts?

- The Arctic's air, water and ice would provide very efficient ways to move contaminants over vast distances not only within the Arctic, but beyond, leading to global indirect impacts.

Today, melting ice and the resultant shipping activity is again elevating the strategic importance of this region. Resources are becoming available and consequently military interest is again increasing.

8.3.4 Arctic tourism

In comparison with the Antarctic, which is relatively isolated, Arctic tourism, with its proximity to large populations is a relative giant. Obviously the appeal of seeing a charismatic animal such as the polar bear in the wild is a huge draw and ~1 million tourists each year undertake both land- and water-based activities. With such large numbers, the key issues are wildlife disturbance, pollution and the potential for introduced species. However, there is no Arctic equivalent to IAATO leading the way (Section 8.2.4). Small organisations exist but they work within a framework of national law.

Managing impacts across such a large area and against a background of increasing desire to exploit the region appears to be a Herculean task.

8.4 Climate change

Ironically, despite the harm that humans have historically caused to marine mammals directly (i.e. the impacts associated with activities such as mining, military activity, shipping, tourism and scientific activity), perhaps some of the biggest impacts and ongoing threats to the polar region are trans-boundary in nature. Chapter 2 discussed the climate history of the planet over very long time periods. Over shorter periods, two main factors influence the mean temperature of the Earth: distance from the Sun and the composition of the atmosphere.

■   What would happen to the amount of energy from the Sun on the surface of the Earth if it were further away than it is now?

☐   The amount of energy would be lower.

If there was no atmosphere, the incoming energy from the Sun would reach the Earth and warm it. But all things give off heat in the form of infrared radiation at a rate that depends on their temperature. So the Earth, in turn, would radiate energy back into space. Its surface temperature would rise until the rate at which energy was received was balanced by the rate at which energy was radiated out to space (Figure 8.9a). Over time, if the output from the Sun was constant, the mean surface temperature would stabilise and with no atmosphere the Earth's surface temperature would be approximately −18 °C. But the mean global temperature of the Earth is actually about +15 °C (although it has been getting warmer recently).

■   How much warmer is the mean global temperature of the Earth compared with the temperature it would have if there was no atmosphere?

☐   15 °C − (−18 °C) = +33 °C, so the Earth is +33 °C warmer than if there was no atmosphere.

This entirely natural warming is the difference the atmosphere makes and it is known as the greenhouse effect. As stated in Section 2.3, the Earth's atmosphere is made up almost entirely of three gases: nitrogen (78%), oxygen (21%), with minor inert gases (mostly argon) making up most of the remainder. These three gases do not interact significantly with heat radiation from the Sun or the Earth, but three naturally occurring greenhouse gases are water vapour, carbon dioxide and methane. They are normally present only in small amounts, but their impact is very significant. Greenhouse gases in the atmosphere are largely transparent to incoming solar radiation, but they intercept the outgoing cooler infrared radiation from the Earth by absorbing it and then emitting it again in all directions. As Figure 8.9b illustrates, most of the energy radiating from the Earth's surface no longer escapes directly to space. Instead it is absorbed and re-radiated several times within the atmosphere. Some energy is sent back to the Earth's surface and some to the lower layers of the atmosphere and both are warmed. The radiation that

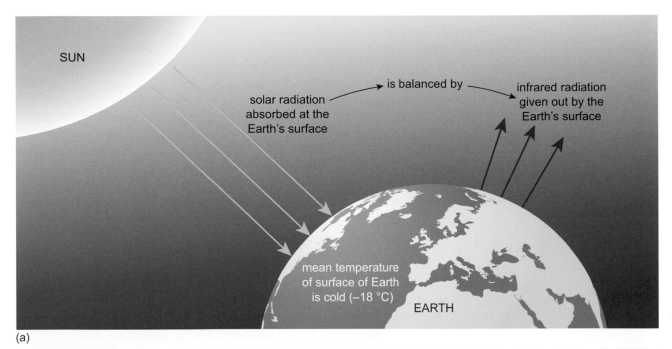

(a)

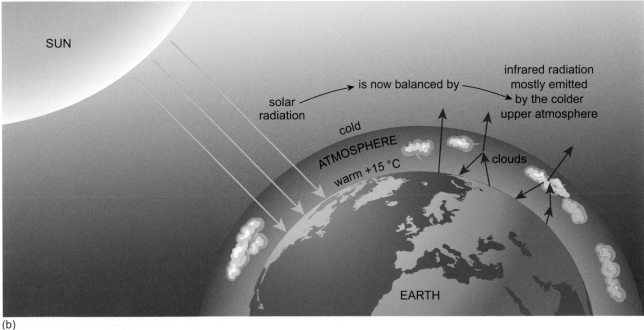

(b)

Figure 8.9 (a) The energy balance at the Earth's surface, without an atmosphere. Solar radiation input balanced by infrared radiation from the Earth would lead to a surface temperature of −18 °C. (b) The 'natural' greenhouse effect of the Earth's atmosphere. The energy balance is maintained, but the surface of the Earth is now at approximately 15 °C and the lower levels of the atmosphere are warmed.

escapes to space mostly comes from high up in the atmosphere, where the temperature is much lower than at the surface. The Earth still radiates at an average temperature of −18 °C, so the theoretical balance still holds, but now the Earth is much warmer at the surface. The overall effect is for the atmosphere to act like the panes of glass in a greenhouse, keeping the Earth's surface much warmer than it would otherwise be.

> The atmospheric greenhouse gases are a natural and vital component of the Earth's climate system.

Unfortunately, as Box 8.1 and Figure 8.1 show, since the Industrial Revolution in the 18th century, humans have contributed large quantities of CO_2 to the atmosphere and a graph for methane shows a similar rise. The proportion of greenhouse gases in the atmosphere is, in the case of CO_2, more than 35% higher than it has been for at least the last million years. The result is the planet is warming, and due to the circulation of the oceans and atmosphere described in Chapter 4, the warming is amplified in the polar regions.

8.4.1 Current changes in Antarctica

As can be seen in plots such as Figure 2.10, the formation of the great Antarctic ice sheets more than 30 million years ago changed the climate of the planet and as the ice sheet grew, sea level fell. As the planet is now warming, the reverse is happening and the sea level is on the rise. The rising surface temperatures have meant that ice shelves on the edge of the Antarctic Peninsula have already began to break up (Box 8.3). The EAIS is at the moment thought to be reasonably stable, but the WAIS is more vulnerable due to its marine nature. Together the latest measurements suggest that $\sim$250 Gt y^{-1} of land ice is melting from the continent. Compared with the $\sim$25 $\times$ 10^6 Gt of ice stored in the ice sheets of Antarctica, this is a relatively small loss – but it is a loss – and the latest measurements suggest that the rate of loss is increasing. There has been no change in extent of sea ice in the Antarctic (Figure 4.12a), although there are not enough measurements to comment on any potential changes in the thickness of the sea ice.

The unit Gt y^{-1} is 10^9 tonnes of ice per year and it is equal to 1 km^3 of ice.

Habitat loss for animals and plants is also occurring. Species of grasses able to cope with warmer temperatures are moving southwards along the Antarctic Peninsula and in the same region gentoo penguins able to cope with warmer temperatures are increasing in number, whilst Adélie penguins – which prefer colder temperatures – are decreasing. There are many factors that influence the populations of plants and animals, but combined with the information about how the climate is changing, the evidence is presenting a coherent and compelling story.

Box 8.3 Break-up of an ice shelf

The largest ice shelf break-up observed so far was the collapse of the Larsen B ice shelf in 2002. The collapse started in January and by the time this satellite image was taken on 7 March (Figure 8.10), 3250 km^2 of the ice shelf had shattered. The collapse of Larsen B has been directly linked to a rise in mean atmospheric surface temperature along the Antarctic Peninsula of $\sim$3 °C since 1940. The result is that the thousands of icebergs formed by the break-up can be seen floating out into the Weddell Sea. Whilst the destruction of an already floating great ice shelf such as Larsen B does not affect sea level, once gone the buttressing effect of the ice is removed. The glaciers that fed the ice shelf on the left of the image have increased their flow rate towards the sea since its decay and so ice, once on the land, is now flowing into the ocean. As a result, the decay of Larsen B is directly increasing the rate of global sea-level rise.

Figure 8.10 A satellite image of the disintegration of part of the Larsen B ice shelf in March 2002.

8.4.2 Current changes in the Arctic

Climate change impacts in the Arctic are a combination of the effects of rising temperatures together with Arctic-specific 'feedback loops' relating to the amount of ice on the surface of the Arctic Ocean and the melting of the vast areas of permafrost that exist in the high latitudes. Overall this has led to three main adverse environmental impacts:

1 The extent of sea ice in summer is decreasing (Figure 4.14a) along with its thickness and as a result the Arctic Ocean is warming.

2 The amount of ground that is currently permafrost is declining and methane – a powerful greenhouse gas – is being released.

3 The Greenland Ice Sheet is melting, just like the Antarctic ice sheets, at a rate of ~250 Gt y^{-1}. However, the total mass of ice in the Greenland Ice Sheet is ~3 × 10^6 Gt so proportionally it is melting at a greater rate than the Antarctic.

■   Is the addition of methane to the atmosphere a positive or negative feedback?

□   It is a positive feedback because increased methane will increase temperatures and so lead to more permafrost melting and so more methane being released.

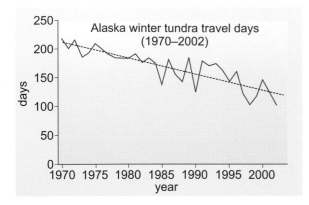

Figure 8.11   The annual duration of tundra travel allowed for oil exploration activities set by the Alaska Department of Natural Resources.

You saw in Section 8.3.1 that increased temperatures are making the Arctic more accessible to ships. On land the reverse is happening – the increased temperatures are making travel more difficult as boggy lands are left by the retreating permafrost. In fact, travel across the tundra is now heavily restricted and it will be more so in the future as the difficulty in land travel increases (Figure 8.11).

In recent decades, average annual temperatures in Alaska and the western Canadian Arctic have increased by more than 3 °C. Such warming is having impacts on animals, such as polar bears; a recent study by a University of Toronto scientist predicts that the thinning ice on Hudson Bay will lead to the demise of Canada's southernmost population of polar bears within just 40 years. You will read more about polar bears in Section 8.5.4.

8.4.3   The polar ozone holes

Ozone (chemical symbol O_3) is an atmospheric gas. In the lower atmosphere it is a pollutant and, for example, there is evidence that it can stunt plant growth and harm humans. However, in the upper atmosphere ozone plays a crucial role in filtering out ultraviolet radiation which is damaging to humans and other animals. Unfortunately, in 1985 scientists at the British Antarctic Survey discovered an enormous ozone 'hole' in the upper atmosphere in spring over Antarctica (Figure 8.12). It was caused by the extremely low spring temperatures and ultraviolet light in the air above Antarctica allowing the formation of chlorine from chlorofluorocarbons (CFCs). CFCs were invented in the 1920s for use as a refrigerant and more recently they were used as a propellant in aerosols and as a cleaning solvent. At high altitude where temperatures are low enough, when exposed to ultraviolet light, CFCs break down, releasing chlorine atoms. Each one of these chlorine atoms is able to break down tens of thousands of ozone molecules to create an apparent hole during the Antarctic spring. When Antarctic summer arrives the weather systems change and the 'hole' disappears. Unfortunately, to fill the region of lower ozone concentration created by the CFCs, the global ozone level decreases. The international community rapidly responded and adopted what became known as the Montreal Protocol to protect the ozone layer. The manufacture of CFCs has been banned, but unfortunately these chemicals persist for decades in the atmosphere, so it will take at least another 50 years for the ozone levels to recover.

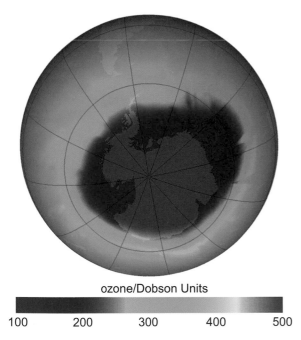

Figure 8.12   The thickness of the layer of ozone at high altitude on 1 October 2010. The units are Dobson Units (DU) and typically the mean thickness of the ozone layer is ~300 DU. Within the Antarctic ozone hole, thickness is as little as 100 DU.

For every 1% decrease in atmospheric ozone, the amount of solar ultraviolet radiation reaching the ground increases by 2% and currently the amount of ozone in the atmosphere has decreased by 4% per decade since 1980.

■ What might be the direct consequences to humans of increased ultraviolet radiation?

☐ Although suntan lotion and sunglasses can provide limited protection, increased ultraviolet radiation could lead to an increase in skin cancer rates and eye damage.

It has been estimated that since 1980, the increase in solar ultraviolet radiation could increase future skin cancer cases by more than 20% each year. Luckily the hole in Figure 8.12 is not over any large population centres, but other organisms will be affected as well. For example, the ultraviolet radiation can adversely affect oceanic plankton at the base of the polar marine food chain. There is also an Arctic ozone hole which forms occasionally in the Northern Hemisphere spring – but ozone levels are typically twice as high there as those in the Antarctic hole.

Question 8.2

Ozone in the upper atmosphere not only absorbs short wavelength ultraviolet radiation coming from the Sun, but it also absorbs long wavelength infrared radiation coming from the ground. What might be the consequence of this for the climate?

Question 8.3

In a paper published in *Geophysical Research Letters* in March 2011, a team from National Aeronautics and Space Administration (NASA) reported on ice loss from the Greenland and the Antarctic ice sheets (Rignot et al., 2011). Based on their findings, they predicted a greater rise in sea levels over the rest of this century, than previously thought. From your study of earlier chapters, plus general knowledge, explain why the sea level will rise as the global mean surface temperature increases.

Activity 8.3 Industrial activity in the Arctic

The estimated time for this activity is 40 minutes.

This activity contains video relating to different facets of industrial activity in the Arctic. You will investigate the issues and concepts raised as well as the future potential hazards.

The detailed notes for this activity are in the 'Activities' section of the S175 website.

8.5 Laws and protocols – managing the threats to the polar regions

In the previous sections you have considered some of the many threats to the polar regions and their ecosystems. Managing these threats has been attempted through a range of laws and standards to control activities and their resulting impacts. This section investigates some of the key agreements and legal frameworks that have evolved. The key difference between the two regions is that at the beginning of the 20th century, with no indigenous human life, no nation laid claim to Antarctica; as a result, a very successful legal framework has come about based on open discussion and consensus. In the Arctic on the other hand, driven by the presence of nations and indigenous populations, there are no such controls and the difference is stark.

8.5.1 The Antarctic – laws and regulations

In the early 20th century, seven Antarctic territorial claims were lodged, principally by those nations with either a legacy of polar exploration in the Heroic Age (Britain, France and Norway), or geographical 'proximity' to Antarctica (Australia, New Zealand, Chile and Argentina). However, these claims were largely irrelevant as by the mid-1950s only a few permanent scientific bases existed around the edge of Antarctica (Figure 8.13a). But in 1957–58 a major international scientific research programme called the International Geophysical Year (IGY) spread the distribution of bases over the whole continent (Figure 8.13b).

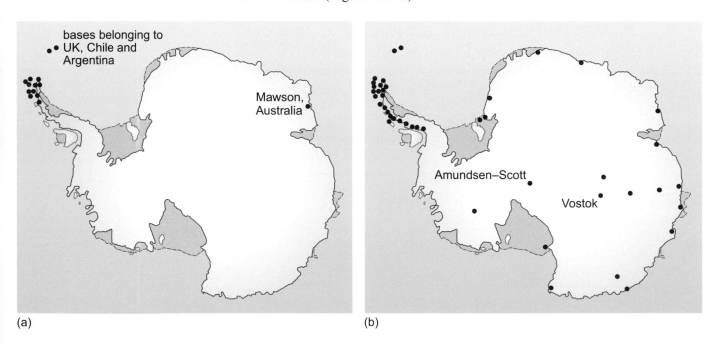

(a)   (b)

Figure 8.13 The expansion in the number of Antarctic research stations during the IGY. (a) The locations of Antarctic research stations before the IGY. (b) The locations of Antarctic research stations during the IGY (1957–58). Amundsen–Scott base is at the South Pole. Vostok is where some of the ice core data discussed in Chapter 2 was collected.

Based in part on the resounding success of the IGY, it was agreed that peaceful scientific cooperation in the Antarctic should continue indefinitely and any political differences should not interfere with ongoing research. To cement this thinking, the negotiation of a unique agreement – the Antarctic Treaty – began, and by 1961 it came into force. The Treaty applied to the area south of 60° S and it recognised Antarctica as a unique scientific and planetary resource for the whole of humanity.

■ How does the latitude of 60° S compare with the definition of Antarctica presented in Chapter 1?

☐ Figure 1.16 shows that latitude 60° S is much further south than most of the Antarctic Polar Front. As a consequence, this definition does not cover the entire Antarctic.

The Treaty itself is rather short – it consists of only 14 articles and some of these were deliberately imprecise and open to problems with interpretation. The key statement, called Article IV (Box 8.4), states that disputes of territorial sovereignty are insoluble and so should be put aside. Various authors have interpreted it as being either a step towards co-ownership of Antarctica, or renunciation. The reality is that it puts all sovereignty claims into abeyance until a later and unspecified date. The Treaty itself has no expiry date and so will remain in force indefinitely; it also states that new decisions about international regulation south of 60° S must be made by 'unanimous agreement'; that is, by consensus. But is a treaty signed by 12 nations a fair and practical way to determine the fate of a huge global resource?

An article is a legal statement, and an example is in Box 8.4.

Box 8.4 Article IV of the Antarctic Treaty

1 Nothing contained in the present Treaty shall be interpreted as:

(i) a renunciation by any Contracting Party of previously asserted rights of or claims to territorial sovereignty in Antarctica;

(ii) a renunciation or diminution by any Contracting Party of any basis of claim to territorial sovereignty in Antarctica which it may have whether as a result of its activities or those of its nationals in Antarctica, or otherwise;

(iii) prejudicing the position of any Contracting Party as regards its recognition or non-recognition of any other State's rights of, or claim, or basis of claim to territorial sovereignty in Antarctica.

2 No acts or activities taking place while the present Treaty is in force shall constitute a basis for asserting, supporting or denying a claim to territorial sovereignty in Antarctica or create any rights of sovereignty in Antarctica. No new claim or enlargement of an existing claim, to

territorial sovereignty in Antarctica shall be asserted while the present Treaty is in force.

Article IX of the Treaty allows other countries to become so-called Consultative Parties (CPs), if they engage in 'substantial scientific research activity' – but what does 'substantial' mean? Any country that signs the Treaty at this level can vote on future agreements. In addition, a second, lower level of membership was instigated for nations who, whilst not engaged in substantial research, agree to abide by the principles of the Treaty (called Non-Consultative Parties, NCPs). Overall, in May 2011 there were 28 CPs, and a further 20 NCPs, with the CPs meeting annually to discuss a wide range of issues including scientific cooperation, logistical issues and environmental protection. With all decisions being reached by consensus, the management regime is now known as the Antarctic Treaty System (ATS).

The final link in the protection of Antarctica is the 1998 Protocol on Environmental Protection which is a very tough international agreement. In it, Antarctica was designated a 'natural reserve devoted to science'. All 'mineral resource activity' except bona fide scientific research is banned, along with all non-indigenous life such as husky dogs. Rubbish in specified categories has to be removed, and discharge of waste materials into the sea is not allowed. Today an Environmental Impact Assessment (EIA) is required for any activity in Antarctica, and things can only proceed if there is sufficient information to determine that their impact is acceptable. Essentially this EIA requirement is the gatekeeper of Antarctica. Any activity that has an impact considered more than minor must undergo a so-called Comprehensive Environmental Evaluation (CEE), which is then reviewed under the ATS. It is a tough system that affects all Antarctic activities from tourism to science. But it is the real reason that, for example, bases such as McMurdo (Box 8.2) are now clean and managed with environmental impacts as a prime consideration.

8.5.2 How the Antarctic Treaty System protects wildlife

The original Antarctic Treaty now has a number of agreements that sit beneath it. One excellent example is an international agreement for wildlife protection – the 1972 Convention for the Conservation of Antarctic Seals (CCAS). The impact of sealers was profound and although the industry declined and ceased, there was a belief in the 1960s that it might return. As a result, CCAS was developed to regulate commercial sealing should it ever recommence. Although at present this is unlikely, the Convention protects some species such as fur seals (Figure 5.7a) and elephant seals (Figure 5.13), whilst establishing modest catch limits for others. Overall the goal is sustainable exploitation rather than complete protection.

■ Why do the regulations fully protect some species, but not all?

☐ Populations of some species are more vulnerable to hunting than others or are too small for hunting.

Seals are part of a wider ecosystem and are towards the top of the food chain. A second convention in the ATS is the previously mentioned CCAMLR (Section 8.2.2) with the aim of sustainably managing the marine ecosystem. CCAMLR uses a so-called ecosystem approach based on the relationship between all the different components in the food web of an ecosystem south of the Antarctic Polar Front. To set a limit on the catch of any particular species, one needs to understand all the ways that the different organisms in the ecosystem rely on that species, and then a catch limit is based on not disturbing this natural state. An ecosystem-wide approach makes sense because unless the lower ends of the food web are conserved, the species at higher trophic levels will not survive.

8.5.3 The Arctic – laws and regulations

All Arctic land falls under the sovereignty of one of the eight Arctic states of Canada, Denmark/Greenland, Finland, Iceland, Sweden, Norway, Russia and the United States. The domestic laws of these sovereign nations are the legal controls on the ~4 million people who live there. International law states that in the Arctic Ocean the national boundaries of these states only extend 200 nautical miles from the coast (Section 8.3.2). The Arctic is therefore like a complex inverse of the Antarctic – an ocean bordered by the land of sovereign states rather than an unoccupied continent surrounded by an ocean. An additional complication has arisen because there is little doubt that the Arctic Ocean contains potentially vast oil and gas reserves (Figure 8.14), as well as the previously noted shipping routes (Figure 8.8). This complex resource-rich geography has defined the nature of the legal framework for managing the Arctic and it consists of so-called 'hard' and 'soft' law (Box 8.5).

Box 8.5 Hard and soft law

Hard and soft law are terms that have arisen in international law. So-called 'hard law' is something that is actually legally binding. For example, in Alaska if one travelled on the tundra for 250 days in a year then, from Figure 8.11, a law will have been broken and there will be a defined penalty – perhaps a fine or even imprisonment. 'Soft law' describes agreements between nations that embody principles, hopes and intentions, but they are not binding like enforceable 'hard' laws. The agreements reached under the consultative process within the Antarctic Treaty System are non-binding soft law. They depend on the signatory governments preparing binding 'hard' domestic laws to support the 'soft' law. For example, the UK signed the 1972 CCAS – but it was a soft law until domestic laws with penalties were approved in the UK Parliament.

The overarching 'hard' law governing the Arctic beyond the boundaries of sovereign states relates to the sea and is the United Nations Convention on the Law of the Sea (UNCLOS). It is this act that defines the 200-mile limit of the Exclusive Economic Zone in which a nation has exclusive resource rights. To

The US has not ratified the UNCLOS and so to them it is 'soft law'.

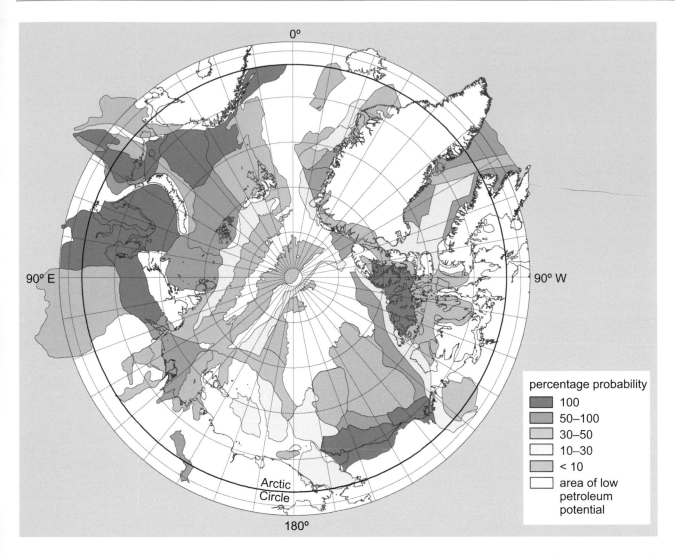

Figure 8.14 A survey of potential oil and gas resources by the US Geological Survey published in 2008 shows significant untapped mineral wealth. The key gives the likelihood in % probability that oil and gas resources are likely to exist. Note this figure is upside down compared with most presentations shown in this book.

claim an area larger than this limit, a nation must submit a case to the United Nations.

■ Based on what you have read about the differences between the Arctic and Antarctic, what factors have prevented the introduction of a treaty governing the entire Arctic region rather than just the sea?

☐ Countries that have people living in the Arctic are unwilling to adopt an Arctic-wide treaty, whereas in Antarctica there have never been resident human populations.

The five states with Arctic coastline broadly abide by the UNCLOS, but recently Russia has presented several cases to the United Nations based on a claim that their continental shelf includes the North Pole! Continental shelf usually means seabed adjacent to the coast, but Russia is arguing that the Lomonosov Ridge which extends to the North Pole is part of their continental

You can see the location of the Lomonosov Ridge on the online map.

shelf. Based on this argument they are laying claim to a sector of the Arctic Ocean from the North Pole to points of longitude in the extreme east and west of their country – this would turn a vast area of what is now jurisdiction-free 'high seas' into Russian territory.

■   Why might Russia want to claim the North Pole and such a wide area of the seabed?

☐   Figure 8.14 shows that there are potentially large amounts of oil and gas resources in this part of the Arctic Ocean.

Given this obvious positioning of the coastal states to try to benefit from the Arctic whilst excluding other nations, organisations such as the European Union have become involved in suggesting the development of an Arctic Policy similar to the Antarctic Treaty. The organisation with which these various actors liaise is called the Arctic Council.

Established in 1996 by the eight Arctic states, the Arctic Council is a means of 'governing' the Arctic, but because it is not a treaty-based organisation it has no legal authority. The Council includes observer states and indigenous groups although they cannot vote on issues such as the Council's six priorities for action. These are persistent organic pollutants, oil pollution, heavy metal pollution, noise, radioactivity and ocean acidification. Box 3.1 noted the existence of the Inuit Circumpolar Council (which too is based around soft law), and this indigenous group offers a unique viewpoint to the Arctic Council based on Traditional Ecological Knowledge (TEK). TEK is a formal recognition that the Inuit and other Arctic peoples have a deep knowledge about their own lands and environment to have successfully survived for thousands of years. Non-voting participation is also open to non-Arctic states (which includes the UK), and non-governmental organisations (NGOs) such as environmental lobby groups like the World Wildlife Fund.

An 'actor' in this context is an organisation which has an interest in the Arctic Policy e.g, the European Union.

■   What sorts of issues are the focus of the Arctic Council?

☐   The six priorities all relate to indirect impacts and cross-border issues.

The Arctic Council recognised that there are other wider environmental issues such as climate change and ozone depletion, but decided that they were already being addressed through other international systems.

Activity 8.4 Traditional Ecological Knowledge (TEK) and polar tourism

The estimated time for this activity is 75 minutes.

In this activity you will discover how scientists are learning from the Traditional Ecological Knowledge (TEK) of Inuit people in the Arctic and about polar tourism. TEK relates to the knowledge about the environment held by members of a largely native or indigenous community, and especially the elders who are often accorded particular respect as the 'living libraries'. Finally you will investigate the motivations and controls on polar tourism.

The detailed notes for this activity are in the 'Activities' section of the S175 website.

8.5.4 How the Arctic wildlife is protected

As you might expect, the Arctic Council cannot protect wildlife. The UNCLOS covers conservation of marine life but nowhere near as comprehensively as that provided by, for example, CCAMLR. The animal perhaps most associated with the Arctic is the polar bear, which is protected by a 1973 Agreement on the Conservation of Polar Bears. Originally this was established to protect the bears against hunting for a five-year period, but discussions about the agreement's future did not formally begin until 2009. There is currently a Polar Bear Specialist Group assessing the global population status and potential for future legislation. However, action on conservation is an urgent need. The total number of polar bears is estimated to be only 20 000–25 000 animals and although not yet on the list of endangered species, many specialists believe it should be. With such a wide-ranging polar animal (e.g. see Figure 3.19b) it is clear that the bear's future is dependent on the continuing accord between Arctic nations, who are not bound together by formal treaty.

Question 8.4

Using information from earlier in the book and from general knowledge, suggest how the number and location of polar bear populations might be monitored.

A summary of polar management

The fundamental geographic differences have defined the management frameworks of both polar regions. These are in turn being tested by indirect impacts associated with human trans-boundary activities, including elevated levels of greenhouse gases, persistent organic pollutants and ozone depletion.

Antarctica has become a model in international law for a purely environmentally focused management regime, with development of its unique legal system made possible by the fact that it is a single continent with no indigenous human population or land-based industry. Consequently, there has never been a tension in balancing science, conservation and economic development like there has been in the Arctic. The result is that since coming into force on 23 June 1961, the Antarctic Treaty has been recognised as one of the most successful international agreements.

In complete contrast, the Arctic is dominated by soft law based on existing national legal systems of the eight Arctic states. These legal systems cover not only Arctic lands but marine territories within the 200 nautical mile Exclusive Economic Zone. Without a formal treaty, the Arctic council is attempting to address indirect impacts but overall –

perhaps necessarily so – the management is not as thorough as in the Antarctic.

8.6 The polar regions and the issues ahead

This final section is an opportunity to look forward to the issues that lie ahead, bearing in mind that the future is not just about bad news.

8.6.1 The Antarctic

Other than the very obvious success of the Antarctic Treaty System (ATS), challenges remain. Although whaling regulations are reasonably effective, as noted earlier (Section 8.2.1), whale populations have not recovered to anywhere near their pre-industry levels. Blue whales, for example are currently at only 1% of pre-industry levels – but given that over 61 000 were taken in just a short period in one area, this is hardly surprising (Table 8.1). In terms of fisheries, CCAMLR is doing a good job. Demand for krill is rising and despite current low catches the industry requires close monitoring. The issue is with the significant illegal, unregulated or unreported fishing, which undermines management efforts not just because of the impact on species such as the patagonian toothfish, but because of fishing techniques that damage habitats and kill non-target species. The local pollution issues are being addressed, but some Antarctic bases have a significant historic legacy (e.g. Box 8.2). Despite relatively low numbers, tourism is a concern, given its coastal focus around penguin and seal colonies. The industry has responded by providing its own voluntary guidelines for managing tourism, and companies are subject to the legally binding requirements under the ATS. However, tourist industry accidents such as the sinking of the MS *Explorer* in 2007 highlight how easily a serious environmental incident could occur. On this basis, close regulation is certain.

8.6.2 The Arctic

Regardless of the positive aspects of the Arctic's regulatory system, many gaps exist within the collection of sovereign laws, the Arctic Council's soft law approach, the UNCLOS (and the various competing claims of its members) and the overall adequacy of international laws in general. The UNCLOS is effective at regulating activity in the Arctic Ocean, but tensions are arising as wider and sometimes overlapping territorial claims are being made by all coastal parties with a view to future resource extraction. The Arctic Council cannot help here as it suffers from agreements that are not legally binding and there is fundamentally no decision-making power. Furthermore, unlike the ATS it has no jurisdiction over military or strategic matters.

The opportunity to increase environmental protection via the laws of the individual Arctic countries is unfortunately not being realised. Russia and Canada, for example, still have large amounts of radioactive material situated in the Arctic. The USA has not ratified international treaties on climate change and has opened up the Arctic National Wildlife Refuge to oil and gas drilling.

Ratification is when an international agreement comes into legal force.

213

Canada is looking to do the same in parts of the currently pristine Mackenzie River Delta. In terms of wildlife protection the story is mixed. Migratory birds are quite well protected but polar bears are threatened, and Arctic sealing and whaling continues – although by mainly indigenous peoples and for cultural reasons.

Regardless of the environmental standards in place to guide the way, very significant environmental risks remain. The extent to which the Arctic is likely to become free of ice in the future, thus offering up new transport routes, combined with the potential for exploitation of mineral resources, means there is likely to be increasing international interest.

8.7 Conclusions

The regimes of both polar regions are fundamentally different in scope, having developed in response to very different circumstances. The Arctic has needed to cater for the interests of its many different interested parties including sovereign nations, indigenous peoples and the broader global community. The ATS is suited to a continent free of many of these conflicting pressures. It is reasonable to suggest that the Arctic requires a more coordinated management approach, both in the scope of agreements, and in that they carry the weight of international 'hard' law.

However, both of these management regimes are at the mercy of indirect factors such as climate change, ozone depletion, trans-boundary pollution and the adequacy of international laws to regulate them. Ultimately our success in managing these global issues will be demonstrated within the frozen planet.

The futures of both poles are inextricably linked to global weather and climate patterns that will determine the future regional climates, the extent of the frozen planet and the wildlife that survives there. The irony is that by not controlling the atmospheric emissions that threaten the ice sheets, the effects of their melting will be felt by us all through sea-level rise and altered global weather patterns.

Climate change and the spectre of positive feedback loops arising from sea ice and permafrost retreat and ice sheet melt will test the adequacy of the management regimes laid out here to the limit. These issues, the measures required to manage them, and our own personal role in the future of the polar regions form the focus of the final chapter of this module.

8.8 Summary of Chapter 8
- Activities are divided into direct and indirect. Direct activities take place within the polar regions, whereas indirect activities take place elsewhere but their impact is still felt in the polar regions.
- Both the Arctic and the Antarctic are widely considered global 'commons' in the sense that nobody owns them and that they are central to life on the planet.
- In the Antarctic, an international framework called the Antarctic Treaty System, backed up by conventions such as CCAS and CCAMLR and

supported with 'hard' law, provides a very effective regional management system.

- The situation is more complicated in the Arctic, and less successfully resolved because of availability of resources, competing national interests, and the necessary approach of the 'soft' law provided by the Arctic Council.

- Climate change is impacting on the polar regions. In the Arctic, sea ice and the Greenland Ice Sheet are melting and permafrost is in retreat. In the Antarctic, ice shelves have collapsed and the continent is melting, albeit slowly. Changes occurring in these regions will affect the rest of the planet.

9 The future for the frozen planet

9.1 Introduction

Throughout this module you have studied the polar regions from the viewpoint of a scientist, considering the different areas of science that are regionally important. You also looked wider, at the way in which natural processes in the polar regions influence – and to a certain extent control – the climate in the rest of the globe. Unsurprisingly, the reverse situation is also true. From the discussion in the previous chapter about indirect activities and from evidence of trans-boundary pollution in, for example, Figure 6.10, it is clear that what happens in the rest of the planet as a result of human activity has a direct impact on the poles. You have investigated some of the science behind the frozen planet and compared processes in the Arctic and Antarctic. Always in the background is, as the previous chapter showed, a complex mix of hard and soft law that governs activities. This final chapter considers the future of the polar regions. Given the many timescales addressed in Chapter 2, that is a somewhat broad remit. After all, in only 150 Ma years or so in the future, Australia will have collided with what is now Antarctica through continental drift! This chapter will focus on the human timescales of the next 100 years or so.

■ What is the most significant threat that the polar regions face over this timescale?

□ The most significant threat to the polar regions is climate change, both in terms of its global consequences – in particular, sea-level rise and potential for ocean current disruption – and the fact that such climate change is an enabler for other potentially damaging activities and industries.

There are, of course, other threats to the polar regions, but here you will concentrate on climate change, an area where scientific studies are making a major contribution to understanding and modelling.

9.2 The climate of the next 100 years

The previous chapter discussed the physics of what is termed the greenhouse effect (Section 8.4), and noted from Figure 8.1 that the atmospheric concentration of greenhouse gases such as CO_2 has increased by a vast amount since the Industrial Revolution. There is no doubting the fact that the global climate of our planet is warming – but one would be hard-pressed to find a scientist who would point the finger anywhere other than at humans as being responsible. In 2008, David King, the UK Chief Scientist at that time, said:

In 2010 Roger Harrabin, a leading British journalist, repeatedly publicly asked and failed to find any active scientist who was willing to speak against human-driven climate change.

> Human activity is to blame for the rise in temperature over recent decades, and will be responsible for more changes in the future. There are plenty of areas for debate in the global warming story but this is not one of them. If

anybody tells you differently they either have a vested interest in ignoring the scientific arguments or they are fools.

(Walker and King, 2008)

It is a very strong quote and a harsh judgement, but it largely represents the view of virtually all governments around the world. One can argue about policy response to human-driven climate change, but not the overarching science. With the fact of global temperature rise (Figure 9.1), there is an urgent need for predictions about the impact of these changes in the near future.

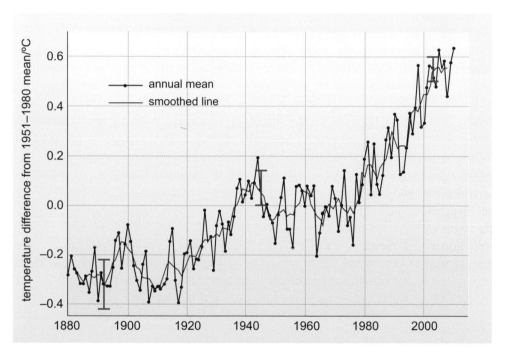

Figure 9.1 The global annual mean atmospheric surface temperature change from 1880 to 2010. 0 °C on the vertical axis is the mean global atmospheric surface temperature minus the mean global temperature from 1951 to 1980. The black line is the annual mean and the solid red line is a smoothed line through the annual mean. The blue bars show uncertainty estimates.

The Intergovernmental Panel on Climate Change (IPCC) was set up in 1988 as a response to the temperature rise, with a remit for 'reviewing and assessing the most recent scientific, technical and socio-economic information produced worldwide relevant to the understanding of climate science'. Its most recent comprehensive report, called the *Fourth Assessment*, was published in 2007 and it predicted that temperatures will continue to rise even more steeply than already measured in Figure 9.1, because of the continued increases in atmospheric concentrations of global greenhouse gases (Box 8.1). To make these predictions, the IPCC uses computer models of the climate and changes the composition of greenhouse gases within the atmosphere represented in the model, based on scenarios of what may happen in the future. One scenario is called 'business-as-usual' and it imagines a world where emissions of greenhouse gases into the atmosphere are at current rates

The Fifth IPCC Assessment will be published in 2013/4.

through the 21st century. However, if everyone were to aggressively replace their use of fossil fuels with renewable energy in the next few decades, then the rate of greenhouse gas increase (and consequently the rate of temperature increase) would slow. Regardless of the scenario, all estimates of the change in global temperatures in 2090–2099 compared with that from 1980–1999 have increased compared with previous predictions. But even compared with the data in Figure 9.1, the values are staggering, with the lower ranges of global temperature rise in 2090–2099 predicted to be from 3 °C to 4 °C through to a maximum of 5.8 °C to 6.4 °C!

> On the basis of their remit to review and assess the most recent scientific work, the IPCC predicts global temperature rise in 2090–2099 of 3.0–6.4 °C warmer than the mean global temperature from 1980–1999.

Despite such predictions, a decisive global agreement on means of countering the factors giving rise to greenhouse gas increases has so far failed to materialise, due to disagreements about how and to what extent different countries should shoulder the burden. For example, why should UK greenhouse gases emissions per person be reduced when US emissions per person are already more than twice as high? Obviously there is much room for discussion and many United Nations conferences will continue to address the issue. Add to this the fact that based on human activities to date, greenhouse gas levels will remain elevated for centuries, it is clear that the climate will change regardless of our current actions. The key unknown is only the extent of changes that might occur, and the magnitude of their impacts on the polar regions.

The average winter temperatures in Alaska, Western Canada and Eastern Russia have increased by as much as 4 °C in the past 50 years, and based on different emissions scenarios the mean annual Arctic surface temperatures north of 60° N are predicted to rise by a further 2–4 °C by the mid-century and to be 4–7 °C higher than now towards the end of the 21st century. You may have noticed straight away that these values are much higher than those shown in Figure 9.1 and higher than that predicted by the IPCC – however, both Figure 9.1 and IPCC values relate to global temperatures as opposed to regional values. The feedback processes noted in Chapters 1, 4 and 8 increase the magnitude of temperature rises in the polar regions in a process called polar amplification caused by for example the ice-albedo feedback loop. Rain and snowfall is also projected to increase by about 8% by the mid-century and by about 20% towards the end of the 21st century. Chapter 8 discussed the ozone hole over Antarctica and noted that it will most likely recover in the next 50 years or so; however, its effects will still be felt until then.

Based on such predictions, there are likely to be three main climate-related impacts on the Arctic:

- Arctic Ocean sea ice melt and associated positive feedback loops arising from ocean warming, including less ice cover resulting in more warming and more ice melt. Associated oceanic current disruption and related knock-on effects include those related to a more ice-free ocean.

- Permafrost melt resulting in structural issues in relation to buildings and other infrastructure and the addition of more greenhouse gases to the atmosphere.

- Increased melting of land-based ice from ice sheets such as the GIS resulting in contributions to sea-level rise and potential for disruption of oceanic currents such as the thermohaline circulation.

Question 9.1

What are likely to be the main climate-related impacts on the Antarctic?

9.3 The future of Arctic ice over the next 100 years

Just as the IPCC did for the whole planet, regional Arctic science experts came together to collate the most up-to-date picture of the future for the northern regions. The result was published in 2005 in a 1000-page book called the *Arctic Climate Impact Assessment* (ACIA). Figure 9.2 shows a prediction from the assessment of the future winter Arctic temperatures.

■ Is the predicted warming in the Arctic shown in Figure 9.2 uniform across the Northern Hemisphere?

□ No. Whilst all regions show warming, clearly some are predicted to experience a greater temperature rise than others.

Question 9.2

On the basis of Figure 9.2, would you expect to observe sea ice in winter at the North Pole in 2090?

Based on projections such as Figure 9.2, the extent of Arctic winter sea ice is predicted to fall by at least 50% by 2070–2090 with the possibility of a totally ice-free Arctic Ocean in the summer. The average thickness of the sea ice has already decreased from ~3 m in the 1950s to ~1.6 m at the end of the 20th century. As for land ice, Chapter 8 quoted an ice-mass loss rate from the Greenland Ice Sheet of ~250 Gt y^{-1}, but this rate of melting is predicted by the ACIA to accelerate and the Greenland Ice Sheet will have contributed ~6 mm to sea-level rise by 2100. Although this may not sound much, Greenland is only one component of the cryosphere. Satellite images illustrate the retreat of glaciers (Figure 9.3) and the formation of large Arctic icebergs (Figure 9.4). It is certain that there will be more. In addition, the extent of snow cover in the Northern Hemisphere, and the area of the tundra is predicted to decrease.

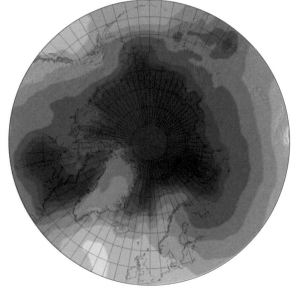

temperature change/°C

0   2   4   6   8   10   12

Figure 9.2 The projected Arctic winter (December to February) atmospheric surface temperature change in 2090 relative to 1990 from the ACIA.

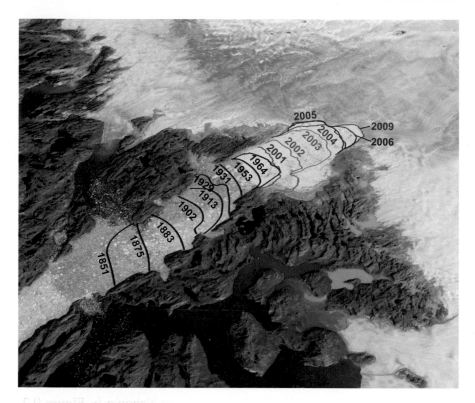

Figure 9.3 The ice front of the Jakobshavn Isbrae glacier on the west coast of Greenland has retreated by more than 40 km between 1850 and 2009.

Figure 9.4 A 260 km² iceberg broke away from the Petermann Glacier in northern Greenland in August 2010. It was over 180 m thick, and was the largest slab to break off the Arctic ice since 1962.

Question 9.3

What are the implications of the opening up of the North-West Passage to shipping as a result of climate change?

9.4 The future of Antarctic ice over the next 100 years

As you read in earlier chapters, Antarctica has two distinct ice sheets: the West (WAIS) and East Antarctic Ice Sheets (EAIS).

■ What are the principal differences between the two ice sheets?

☐ The EAIS is much larger than the WAIS and it rests on land entirely above sea level. The WAIS is smaller and a so-called marine ice sheet that rests on a base generally below sea level.

As Section 8.4.1 noted, significant thinning in some areas of the WAIS is already occurring. The loss of ice shelves such as the Larsen B along the Antarctic Peninsula (Box 8.3) is primarily a result of regional atmospheric warming caused by an intensification of the westerly winds as a result of the ozone hole. The same effect has driven the retreat of almost 90% of glaciers across the Antarctic Peninsula over recent decades. Just as for the Arctic, Antarctic researchers collaborated to produce a book in 2009 called *Antarctic Climate Change and the Environment* (ACCE) (Turner et al., 2009). Figure 9.5 shows the projected Antarctic winter atmospheric surface temperature change up to 2090 based on their work.

The ACIA, IPPC reports and the ACCE are all available online for free.

Just as for the Arctic, Figure 9.5 shows Antarctica has a non-uniform pattern of warming.

■ Where in Antarctica is the greatest warming predicted to occur?

☐ The greatest warming will happen over the oceans close to the continent.

Question 9.4

Using Figures 4.20b and 9.5, do you think it is likely that the extent and thickness of sea ice will change by the end of the 21st century?

Loss of ice mainly from the WAIS is likely to contribute significantly to global sea-level rise, but given the isolation and currently generally cold temperatures, the main difference will be that the outline of the continent will to a certain extent change as smaller ice shelves collapse and glaciers continue to retreat.

9.5 Global sea-level rise over the next 100 years

The melting ice from the poles along with expansion of water caused by temperature increase means that sea level will rise by most likely ~120 cm by 2100 (Figure 9.6). The prediction changes depending exactly on which IPCC climate scenario is used – but it could be greater than 160 cm. It is worth pausing for a moment and putting that into a height you can visualise. Think,

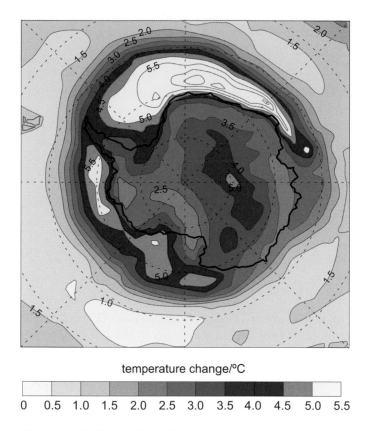

temperature change/°C

0 0.5 1.0 1.5 2.0 2.5 3.0 3.5 4.0 4.5 5.0 5.5

Figure 9.5 The projected Antarctic winter atmospheric surface temperature change over the 21st century from the ACCE.

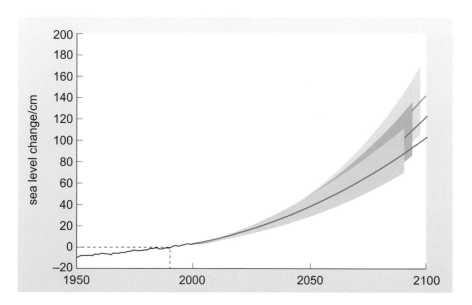

Figure 9.6 Projection of sea-level rise from 1990 to 2100 based on IPCC climate projections for three different emissions scenarios. Each colour reflects a particular scenario and the shaded region around each line represents the possible range of values expected. The line in red is the observations-based annual global sea-level data.

for example, of standing on a beach at high tide, and then imagine the sea level being increased by about the height of a 7-year-old child.

A sea-level increase of this magnitude has the potential to cause major global impacts including inundation of low-lying areas and increased damage due to storm surges and tides. Furthermore, there would be impacts on the quality of water in coastal aquifers via saline intrusion; that is, when the seawater floods over into land and contaminates the ground water. Globally, extensive low-lying coastal areas will be vulnerable. For example, approximately 22 000 km^2 of Bangladesh would be inundated by sea-level rise of 1.5 m – but large areas are already flooded there in storm surges. These events will become more frequent if no action is taken. In addition, the flooding of aquifers has the potential to affect thousands of water wells which supply freshwater to approximately 17 million people.

9.6 Thermohaline disruption

Section 4.4 described the thermohaline circulation of the oceans (Figure 4.18). In this schematic, large amounts of heat and salt are moved around the global oceans with the result that, for example, northern Europe has a moderate climate. But what will happen when the sea ice has retreated somewhat and large amounts of freshwater from the ice sheets has changed the density of the surface waters? Box 2.4 discussed the impact of just such a circulation change ~12 000 years ago in what was called the Younger Dryas. Large areas of the planet cooled at this time as ocean circulation – and the heat it moves around the planet – changed. It is not clear, but such an effect may yet moderate the predicted warming shown in Figures 9.2 and 9.5.

9.7 The future of polar wildlife

In the Antarctic, the immediate consequences of loss of sea ice west of the Antarctic Peninsula will be reductions in algal growth and thus in the stocks of krill that rely on this as a food source. The amount of krill in the Southern Ocean has already significantly declined and presumably this decline will continue. Some whale species may not continue their recovery from whaling if the krill population remains at a low level. The distribution of Adélie penguins has also changed, with many populations on the northern Antarctic Peninsula declining due to reduced sea ice and food – although just as in the irregular warming shown in Figure 9.5, it is not possible to make general statements about the entire continent. In the Ross Sea and East Antarctica, for example, Adélie populations are generally stable or increasing.

In the Arctic, reductions in sea ice will shrink habitats for some seal species, sea birds and the polar bear, which use the ice as a platform for hunting. Polar bears hunt where the ice is thinnest, catching seals as they access holes in the ice to breathe. As the pack ice retreats north in the summer, the bears must travel between ice floes to continue hunting. Summer ice is currently receding much further than just a few decades ago and the bears must swim longer distances. The tundra and taiga ecosystems will also change. In previous periods Arctic plants, animals and microbes adapted to changing climates primarily by relocation. It is likely that their main response to future changes will be the same. The treeline may advance northwards, displacing tundra vegetation and with a resulting impact on grazing animals and migrating species such as reindeer. Unfortunately, in many parts of the Arctic, relocation possibilities are likely to be limited by regional and geographical barriers. Some species – especially those that are adapted to the cold Arctic environment such as mosses, lichens, and some herbivores and their predators – are particularly at risk of loss. Finally, species that currently live in temperate latitudes now will most likely advance northwards and spread into the Arctic. This could displace existing species and bring new diseases to animal and human populations.

Activity 9.1 Changes in the frozen planet
The estimated time for this activity is 60 minutes.

You have read about some of the environmental changes occurring in the polar regions and their potential impacts. In this final activity you will watch video clips which highlight the current issues of greatest concern.

The detailed notes for this activity are in the 'Activities' section of the S175 website.

9.8 Preserving the 'frozen planet'

The polar regions have always been in a state of change, and they will continue on this path. Now that you have followed this account of the Arctic and Antarctic, you are in a position to make reasonable predictions about some of the changes that will be seen during this century. Not all of them will be negative, but the overriding threat to the present polar environments is the change to global mean surface temperature that is a consequence of human influences on climate.

■ What are the three key influences that humans have on the regions?

□ Apart from climate changes, mentioned above, there are three other key influences. Firstly, there is the exploitation of wildlife with the consequential effects on ecosystems. This includes hunting and trapping as well as the future whaling and fishing industries. Secondly, there is the exploitation of the resources of the regions in all its forms. Finally, there is the issue of trans-boundary pollution.

There would be little need to discuss the future of the polar regions if the evolutionary trajectory of humans had been different. Now it will be shaped as much by human activities as by natural processes and many of those influential activities are a consequence not so much of the existence of humans, as of the propensity of the species to expand, explore and exploit. Arguably, no other single species has followed an evolutionary pathway that enabled them to change the climate of the planet over such short timescales. By releasing carbon into the atmosphere at an ever-increasing rate, the polar regions will reduce in extent. Given these human-centred influences on the poles, can individuals contribute to their preservation?

Our personal influence is limited, but with an understanding of science and evidence one can question elected representatives and lobby for changes. Generating smaller amounts of greenhouse gases is something that everyone can contribute to, although sometimes it is difficult to work out exactly how much individual savings are. But, many people saving small amounts will add up. The big, and really influential changes required, however, are in industry, power generation and transport. It is arguable that nothing short of a complete overhaul of our society can turn us from fossil fuel energy consumers to carbon-neutral renewable energy ones. Meanwhile, the more we understand of the frozen planet and our influence on it – and the wider that we spread that knowledge – then the greater the chance that the societal changes that are needed will become acceptable.

It has been said that people only get interested in conserving habitats when they can visit them. With the increase in polar tourism, more people are experiencing the Arctic and Antarctic habitats for themselves. As you have read in this book, tourism is not without its drawbacks. But they are special areas. If you choose to visit, then follow the advice that BBC presenter and President of the Galápagos Conservation Trust Andrew Marr gave to visitors to another part of the world at risk – the Galápagos archipelago. Marr said people should visit but it should be a once-in-a-lifetime event: 'I'm never going back,' he says. 'It's great to go once, but go responsibly.'

Running throughout this book has been the science theme: science providing explanations for the formation of the polar regions and the risk to their integrity from global warming; science as the driver for exploration; and now science as the major Antarctic activity. As a fitting end to this journey around the frozen planet, let's return to scientists in the Antarctic and their personal experiences. Two of the authors of this book stood together on the deck of an expedition ship off James Ross Island on the Antarctic Peninsula. The ship was sailing into Whisky Bay (Figure 9.7) and using its echo-sounder to map the sea floor, as no charts existed. They were on the first ship to enter that bay since exploration of the area started in 1903 with a visit by the Swedish explorer Otto Nordenskjöld and his expedition. Other humans had visited but the break-up of the small Prince Gustav Ice Shelf meant that Whisky Bay was ice-free for the first time. Most likely nobody had even visited since the 1970s when a geological survey of the land around the bay had been undertaken from one of the bases. This experience provided a dramatic example of the effects of the rising temperatures, but it also showed how there is still much to explore in these remote and fascinating lands.

Figure 9.7 Whisky Bay, a small cove on the Antarctic Peninsula, is now accessible by ship because of the break-up of the Prince Gustav Ice Shelf.

9.9 Summary of Chapter 9

- The most significant threat to the polar regions comes from climate change engendered by human activities. The result is that the global mean surface temperature of the Earth is predicted to rise by 3–6 °C by the end of the century.

- Polar amplification will increase warming at high latitudes although the warming will not be spread evenly.

- The major predicted impacts of climate change on the Arctic are melting of the ice sheets, sea ice and permafrost, and changes in ocean currents.

- The major predicted impacts of climate change on the Antarctic are melting of land-based ice and ice shelves, warming of the Southern Ocean and increased ultraviolet radiation from the hole in the ozone layer, although this is likely to decrease later in the century.

- Global sea levels are predicted to rise by more than 1 m as a consequence of land-based ice melting. The large amounts of freshwater that result may alter the thermohaline circulation pattern.

- Wildlife is already being affected by global warming in the polar regions; ranges of animals and plants will change and new species will be able to survive.

Answers and comments

Answers to questions

Question 1.1

If the minimum average surface temperature for London is ~7 °C in January and the maximum average surface temperature is ~22 °C in August:

range = (maximum − minimum)

= 22 °C − 7 °C

= 15 °C

So the range of temperature in London is 15 °C. This is much smaller than the range at the polar regions. At Alert the temperature range between summer and winter (Figure 1.2) is 35 °C, whilst at the South Pole it is ~30 °C.

Question 1.2

From Figure 1.4 the locations are:

(A) Cairo: 30° N, 30° E

(B) London: ~50° N, 0° E

(C) Rio de Janeiro: ~20° S, 45° W

It is harder to estimate the latitude and longitude of London and Rio de Janeiro using the widely spaced scales of Figure 1.4, but higher resolution maps will usually have a smaller scale grid.

Question 1.3

If the same amount of energy reaches a desert and a conifer forest in summer, the amount of energy available to heat up the material will be the same for both. Table 1.1 shows you that a desert has an albedo of 40%, so the proportion of energy available to heat up the sand will be:

proportion of energy = 100% − 40% = 60%

so, 60% of the incoming energy will be available to heat up the sand.

For the conifer forest in summer, Table 1.1 shows that a conifer forest has an albedo of 9%, so the proportion of energy available to heat up the forest will be:

proportion of energy = 100% − 9% = 91%

If snow falls on the conifer forest, then its albedo will increase from 9% to 80–90% and so the proportion of energy available to heat up the conifer forest will be:

proportion of energy = 100% − 80% = 20%

So only 20% of the incoming energy is now available to heat up the forest, and almost all of the incident energy is reflected away. Clearly the albedo is extremely important for the polar regions.

Question 1.4

The completed paragraph is:

It gets so cold in the polar regions because energy from the Sun has to pass through more of the *atmosphere* and so proportionally more is *absorbed* than at *lower* latitudes. Where ice-covered, the polar regions have a high *albedo* and so much of the energy is *reflected* straight back out into space. The angle of the Earth's *axis* is not vertical which means that at different times of the year, the solar energy is greatly reduced, or at latitudes higher than *66.6°* completely absent for part of the year. This also explains the divergence in the two lines seen in Figure 1.2 where when it is summer in the Northern Hemisphere it is *winter* in the Southern Hemisphere and vice versa. Finally, the reason there is such a huge difference between summer and winter conditions in Figure 1.2 is because both locations are at high *latitudes* and so experience the polar *night*.

Question 1.5

Both Cape Farewell and the Shetland Islands are the same distance from the Equator at ~60° N (Figure 1.7a). Because they are both in the Northern Hemisphere and both at the same latitude, over the course of a year (from Figure 1.11), they could be expected to receive a similar amount of solar energy.

Question 1.6

In North America, Canada and Siberia, along the coasts, the lines are close together. The only significant divergence is in Russia between the longitudes ~40° E and 90° E where the treeline is much further south than the 10 °C July isotherm. Both the treeline and the 10 °C isotherm are generally south of the Arctic Circle in the Western Hemisphere and north of the Arctic Circle in the Eastern Hemisphere.

Question 2.1

The plates are moving apart at 1 cm each year, so in 100 years, they will have moved 100 cm, which is 1 metre. To move 1 km, they will need 1000 times as long, since there are 1000 m in 1 km.

So, to move 1 km, will take 1000×100 years, which is 100 000 years.

To move 1300 km, they will need 1300 times longer, so that is $1300 \times 100\ 000$ years, which is 130 000 000 years, or 130 million years.

So if the plates are moving apart at 1 cm each year then the current distance between Greenland and Norway suggests that the coastlines have been moving apart for 130 million years.

Question 2.2

(a) The ammonite should be placed at around 250 Ma; (b) the continents as shown in Figure 2.5b were around 65 Ma; (c) coal was formed around 300 Ma; and (d) the human species first appeared around 7 Ma.

Question 2.3

(a) The ammonite should be placed between the Permian and Triassic; (b) the continents as shown in Figure 2.5b should be at the end of the Cretaceous Period; (c) coal was formed at the start of the Carboniferous Period; and (d) the human species first appeared during the Pliocene.

- Coal formed in a relatively warm period but when the planet was clearly cooling.
- The ammonite existed in a warming period.
- The time period of Figure 2.5b is almost the warmest point on the record, and finally the human species appeared when the climate was cooling.

Question 2.4

According to Figure 2.9 there have been three cool periods in the earliest 4 billion years of the Earth's history. There is one relatively short and only slightly cool period at ~2.5 billion years ago, a longer duration and slightly colder period approximately 2 billion years ago and a much longer duration and colder period from approximately 850 to 600 million years ago. This last longer duration event is the Cryogenian.

Question 2.5

A typical cycle starts with a temperature about 2 °C above the present temperature followed by an irregular temperature fall to the minimum temperature which is ~10 °C below current temperature. This fall of a total of 12 °C takes place over most of the 100 000 year cycle, which is ~9000 years. There is then a relatively much shorter period, of maybe 10 000 years, when the temperature rises very quickly back to the warmest part of the cycle. Your values may not be exactly the same as shown here but the description should be similar.

The shape of this pattern of temperature change is sometimes called a saw-tooth pattern because of the shape of the temperature profile against time (Figure 2.21).

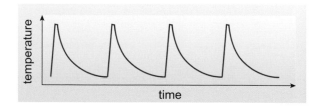

Figure 2.21 Answer to Question 2.5. A schematic of the saw-tooth pattern of slow cooling of the Earth and rapid warming.

Question 2.6

Based on Figure 2.13, 150 000 years ago, the world was in a cold period, so I would expect the Arctic area to have been a great deal larger than it is now. Then there was a sudden warming to about 4 °C above current temperatures, so I would expect significant melting of the ice, so that the Arctic was much smaller, and possibly there would have been no ice at all. By about 120 000 years ago, the temperature was falling rapidly, and so the

Arctic would have been growing again, reaching its maximum size about 20 000 years ago, when the average temperature was about 10 °C colder than it is now. Since then, the Arctic will have been slowly shrinking again, till the present day, as the temperature warmed up to its present value.

Question 3.1

At the LGM, Figure 2.18a shows that a large part of the Siberian and Alaskan coastline would have been ice-free. Whilst ice-free, they would probably have been snow-covered for part of the year, but there would have been access to the Arctic Ocean for the hunters.

Question 3.2

There was not an equivalent to the Arctic land bridge between the continents. South America and Antarctica have been separated by the wide and deep Drake Passage (Figure 2.5c) for at least 35 million years, and Australia and Antarctica have been separated for even longer. Therefore Antarctica was never populated by humans and so remained isolated until the Heroic Age of exploration.

Question 3.3

The sealers and whalers would undertake secret voyages to stop others finding out where they had been and so be able to keep the profits for themselves.

Question 3.4

The island of South Georgia is south of the Polar Front (Figure 1.16) and so it is surrounded by polar waters. It would probably have been this way since the Drake Passage opened about 30 million years ago and the great ice sheets began to form in Antarctica (Figure 2.10).

Question 3.5

The photograph in Figure 1.12 was taken after the summer solstice in Antarctica and so the days will be decreasing in length. As the Sun rises in the morning it will skim the horizon through the day and then descend. As a result, the sunlight is passing through more atmosphere than when it is overhead (Figure 1.9b). This means there are intense colours all day. The Sun only descends a little each day and so in a couple of days' time, a similar effect would be expected.

Question 3.6

Given that there is a lot of maintenance, you could expect there to be:

* 2 engineers
* 2 general mechanics
* 2 general builders
* 1 doctor

- 1 computer/communications person
- 1 cook
- 2 electricians
- 2 carpenters
- 1 communications specialist

Perhaps 14–15 support staff, so there could be 15 or so scientists.

Question 4.1

Typical albedos can be extracted from Table 1.1. At 30° N in North America it would be reasonable to expect that there were grassy fields and so a typical albedo would be 25%. At the same latitude in the Pacific Ocean there would only be water and so the albedo would only be typically ~3%. As described in Activity 1.5, the Pacific Ocean has a much higher specific heat capacity than the land.

Question 4.2

If a wind is blowing at a speed of 20 m s^{-1} over the surface of the ocean, and the speed of the wind-driven ocean current is typically 3% of this, then the ocean current is:

20 m s^{-1} × 0.03 = 0.6 m s^{-1}, or 60 cm s^{-1}.

You may be unfamiliar with these units of wind and ocean speed, so to make it more understandable it can be converted to a unit you may be more familiar with, km per hour (km h^{-1}).

Now, 1 m s^{-1} is equivalent to 3.6 km h^{-1}.

So the wind is blowing at 20 × 3.6 = 72 km h^{-1} – obviously this is a very strong wind!

However the corresponding surface current would only be ~2 km h^{-1}.

Question 4.3

Close to the North Pole, Figure 4.8 shows that sea surface temperatures are apparently below zero degrees. Far from the pole where the red-coloured values indicate temperatures above 22 °C (which are at lower latitudes), the picture shown for the Antarctic also seems to generally hold true for the Arctic and temperatures do seem to increase with distance from the pole. However, in the temperature ranges between 0 °C and ~14 °C the picture for the Arctic is very different. The isotherms – particularly in the Atlantic Ocean – do not match up well with the lines of latitude.

Question 4.4

The first stage of ice formation is frazil ice and it is made up of loose floating crystals. The second stage is pancake ice which is a rounded amalgamation of frazil crystals with raised edges. Finally there is pack ice which is made of an amalgamation of pancakes. However pancake ice can grow directly into pack ice under calm conditions.

Ordering the ice types by age you would have a picture which looked like Figure 4.27.

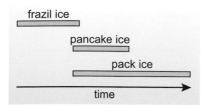

Figure 4.27 Stages of sea ice formation.

Question 4.5

If the area of Antarctica is approximately 14 million km^2 and in winter, as Figure 4.11b shows, more than 14 million km^2 of sea ice has grown, then the ice-covered part of the Antarctic has more than doubled in size.

Question 4.6

In the Antarctic the sea ice area cycles between ~3 and ~16 million km^2 (Figure 4.12), and in the Arctic the sea ice area cycles between ~6 and ~14 million km^2 (Figure 4.14). Therefore there is a much greater seasonal cycle of ice growth and decay in the Southern Hemisphere.

Question 4.7

The minimum area of sea ice in September 2010 at ~3 million km^2 is actually off the bottom of the scale of the plot shown in Figure 4.14a. It is clear that the minimum of sea ice area has continued to decrease since the end date of this plot.

Question 4.8

The west coast of Norway is only approximately −5 °C in winter, whereas the east coast of Greenland is below −15 °C. In addition, the isotherms are closer together in east Greenland. The reason for the difference is the heat from the warm water flowing northwards past Europe as shown in Figure 4.19.

Question 4.9

Figure 4.13 shows that the west coast of Svalbard remains free of sea ice in both summer and in winter as a result of the heat transported to the north.

Question 5.1

(a) Figure 4.25b shows the annual cycle of atmospheric temperature in Svalbard. In winter (December to March) the atmospheric temperatures are below −10 °C, reaching almost −15 °C. From April to June there is a rapid increase in temperature from −10 °C to +5 °C before it again cools down to winter temperatures. Therefore an animal or plant in Svalbard will have to endure conditions from −15 °C to 15 °C.

(b) On the Antarctic Peninsula, from Section 4.5.1 and Figure 4.20 you can see that in the southern summer, temperatures are approximately 0 °C; whilst in winter the temperatures near the coast are in the range ~−4 °C to −8 °C depending on latitude. Therefore, animals and plants on the Antarctic Peninsula would have to endure apparently less difficult conditions than in Svalbard – although it does not appear to get above 0 °C like Svalbard.

Question 5.2

The average surface temperature of the polar bear from Figure 5.5 is approximately 3–4 °C. The bear is losing most heat from its nose which has a surface temperature of ~20 °C, and also its paws which have a surface temperature of ~10 °C.

Question 5.3

(a) Figure 5.9 shows the coldest part of the husky is its paws, which are shown as having a temperature of 0 °C.

(b) The core temperature is 37 °C, so the paws are 37 °C − 0 °C = 37 °C colder than the core.

(c) The temperature of the surrounding air is given as −30 °C, so the paws are:

0 °C − (−30 °C) = 0 °C + 30 °C = +30 °C warmer than the surrounding air.

Clearly the countercurrent system is very effective at reducing the heat carried to the skin.

Question 5.4

The three main adaptations exhibited by polar endotherms are as follows: the first is that they have extremely efficient insulation systems consisting of some mechanism of trapping air (either through fur or feathers) with body fat beneath the skin. They can vary and control the amount of heat lost through blood flow to the body surface, by means of countercurrent heat exchange systems. Finally, they have evolved a shape that maximises the body volume in relation to the surface area.

Question 5.5

Antarctica has been isolated for over 30 million years (Figure 2.10) and successive ice ages would have covered virtually the entire Antarctic continent with ice like in Figure 2.18b. These ice ages would have wiped out plant life. Only two species have colonised the continent since the LGM and currently, as your answer to Question 5.1 shows, the Antarctic Peninsula has a temperature range ~0 °C to ~−5 °C. Presumably these must be marginal conditions for plants compared to the relatively warm +5 °C summers of Arctic lands such as Svalbard.

Question 6.1

A habitat is the place where an organism lives. A biological community is the group of organisms in one or more habitats. An ecosystem is the community and associated non-living components in one or more habitats, and a niche is the place that a particular species has within a community.

Question 6.2

Arctic willow, purple saxifrage and grass and sedge are occupying the same ecological niche of primary producers.

Question 6.3

For photosynthesis, light is required and the ice sheets would be dark for part of the year. There would need to be water (Equation 5.1a) but as it is below 0 °C there will be no free water. Clearly this is not an easy environment for most forms of life you will be familiar with.

Question 6.4

From Figure 4.25, in Svalbard the temperatures are above 0 °C for part of May, June, July and August – so the growing season for the particular plant is approximately 100 days.

Question 6.5

Reptiles and amphibians are ectotherms and so they need external sources of heat energy to regulate their own body temperature. They would do well in the warm summers but would find it difficult to survive the cold winters and short summers.

Question 6.6

There are eight organisms in the ecological niche of the highest trophic level in Figure 6.13. They are: owl, lynx, fox, hawk, human, wolf, weasel and marten.

Question 6.7

The Arctic peoples mostly live in the tundra.

Question 7.1

(a) From Figure 4.8, the surface temperatures of the water are in the range 26–28 °C. This means that the maximum amount of oxygen that can be dissolved in the water will be ~200–205 µmol kg^{-1}.

(b) The saturation curve shows data below 0 °C because at typical seawater salinities it does not freeze until ~−1.8 °C.

Question 7.2

Neglecting the distortion caused by the map projection in Figure 7.3 and taking note of the non-linear scale, with the exception of a line along the Equator, clearly the chlorophyll concentration in the tropical seas is much less than that in the polar seas. Some of the highest values are clearly in the seasonally ice-covered waters of the north and south.

Question 7.3

At higher latitudes above 66.6° N and 66.6° S seasonally there will be a lack of light which is a component in Equation 5.1a. In addition, there will be a further lack of light caused by winter sea ice growing on the surface of the ocean.

Question 7.4

Whilst a detailed comparison between Figures 7.9 and 7.3 is difficult because of the colour scale used in the latter, what is apparent straight away is that there are generally much higher than average chlorophyll concentrations with higher nutrient levels. For example, around the Antarctic the elevated nutrients match well with the increased averaged chlorophyll. In the Arctic, as you have seen, there is elevated averaged chlorophyll and whilst the absolute nutrient values are generally lower – they are still higher than the tropical seas.

Question 7.5

Figure 7.15a shows data collected by satellite. This sensor presumably cannot detect the relatively high concentration of chlorophyll that may exist within the sea ice cover.

Question 8.1

Toothfish are a prey item for some whales and seals. If they were removed from the ecosystem in large numbers it could cause starvation at these higher trophic levels.

Question 8.2

Ozone in the upper atmosphere absorbs long wavelength infrared radiation coming from the ground, warming the upper atmosphere which re-radiates an increased quantity of long wavelength radiation to the ground. So, ozone acts as a greenhouse gas like carbon dioxide and could contribute to global warming. However, the effect would be much less than from carbon dioxide, and ozone is being depleted from the upper atmosphere.

Question 8.3

Ice that is floating does not raise sea levels when it melts. However, when ice sheets that rest on land melt, the water flows into the sea and raises the level. As Box 8.3 stated, when ice shelves decay, glaciers increase their flow rate and feed more water into the oceans. In addition, as water gets warmer its volume increases.

The prediction in the journal article was that the average sea level will rise by 15 cm by 2050 and 56 cm by 2100 *solely* from the melting of the polar ice sheets. Melt from glaciers and thermal expansion of water is predicted to add a similar amount.

Question 8.4

In Section 3.7.2 you read about radio tracking of animals. These methods are being used to track polar bears, providing information about survival rates of cubs, habitat use, movements and population boundaries. In addition, the amount of time spent in water can be determined, giving a proxy measure of ice melt.

Question 9.1

From what you have read about the Antarctic in Chapter 8 and the analysis of the Arctic impacts of climate change, you have probably identified the following as the main climate-related impacts likely to affect Antarctica into the future:

- The ongoing presence of an ozone hole with increased ultraviolet radiation levels and their impacts on all forms of life.
- Continued climate warming on the Antarctic Peninsula.
- Melting of land-based ice and ice shelves due to a combination of greenhouse gas-related climate change and ozone hole influences.
- Warming of the Southern Ocean.
- Potential future decrease in extent and thickness of Antarctic sea ice.

Question 9.2

Figure 4.24b shows the temperature in the central Arctic Ocean and winter temperatures are approximately −30 °C. Figure 9.2 shows a prediction that the central Arctic Ocean will warm up by approximately 8–10 °C. If the prediction is true, the winter temperature in the central Arctic Ocean will be ~−20 °C to −22 °C and there will still be sea ice in winter.

Question 9.3

The opening up of the North-West Passage to shipping as a result of it becoming ice-free in the summer would increase the risks of pollution and the introduction of new marine species, as well as opening up the area to industrialisation and exploitation.

Question 9.4

Figure 4.20b shows that the areas of ocean where there is maximum warming should still be cold enough for sea ice in winter. However, the general warming will mean that it is likely there will be a reduced sea ice extent around the continent as the coldest isotherms will be pushed closer to the land.

Comments on activities

Activity 1.1

The set of answers shown below is from one of the module team who asked a family member with no experience of the frozen planet. Here are her answers:

(a) Images for the Arctic: cold; polar bear; igloo. For the Antarctic: penguin; whale; ice.

(b) Words for the Arctic: polar bear; the Titanic; Eskimo. For the Antarctic: the windiest and coldest place on earth; heroic exploration; remote.

(c) For the Arctic: a news story about the continued shrinking of the sea ice. For the Antarctic: a news story about a giant iceberg the size of Wales breaking away and drifting northwards.

(d) For the Arctic: it is owned by Russia, Canada, Norway and America. For the Antarctic: the United Kingdom, Argentina and perhaps the United States or Russia?

You should keep in mind that these answers are most likely not definitive.

It would be surprising if in your answers to Activity 1.1 there was not at least some mention of ice and the cold. Personally, I was surprised to see no mention of the dark and the incredible beauty, but that is just my view. What is clear is that the cold and climate of both regions are highlighted along with the wildlife. There were media stories about how the regions are changing and finally there appear to be some interesting questions around the subject of ownership. Ownership relates to the management of, and ultimately who could live in the polar regions.

Activity 1.3

You were asked to draw two large shapes so that you can see the distortion. Depending on where you put your cuts it is unlikely that your shapes will be exactly as you originally drew them. In the jump from three dimensions to two dimensions the shape has become distorted. The way this distortion is avoided is by using a map projection.

Activity 1.5

When you think about it, metal heats up very quickly, so you most likely recognised that the 1 kg of iron would be the hottest. It does not take very much heat energy to change the temperature of the iron because it has a low specific heat capacity. The other two items are harder to place, but the cork will be cooler than the iron and finally the coldest will be the water, which has the highest specific heat capacity of the three.

Water has an extremely high specific heat capacity and it takes a vast amount of energy to heat it. This fact is often used to our advantage. For example, virtually all car engines use water in their cooling systems to stop the engine overheating.

Activity 4.1

(a) When the ice is first put into the glass, the water level will change, but as the ice melted the water level in the glass should not have changed at all. This is the situation with sea ice decay and the sea level does not change as it grows or melts. You did add the ice initially but you could repeat the experiment by putting a polystyrene cup of water with a tea towel wrapped around its sides into a freezer and on top of a newspaper for 30 or so minutes until a skin of ice forms on the surface. The polystyrene, tea towel and newspaper insulate the sides and bottom and so force the ice to grow from the surface just as it would in nature. Then take the cup out of the freezer and repeat the melting experiment. You should get the same result.

(b) If you add snow (which is not very dense) to the top of the ice cube then you are adding water to the system and the water level in the cup will go up. Ultimately the water level will be higher than when the ice first started to melt. This is just like adding snow on top of the sea ice like you can see in Figure 4.10c. When the sea ice and snow melt, the sea level is higher because adding snow is just like adding water to the glass.

(c) Again, just like in (b) the level of water in the glass will go up – although it will be higher than when adding the lower density snowflakes. This is analogous to when glaciers drop icebergs into the sea. The ice is being added to the sea so sea level rises.

Activity 6.1

The first example was a set of key words, which does not show the relationships between the terms used. The second example illustrates the linear relationship between trophic levels, showing what eats what; that is, a food chain. The third example shows the food chain in the context of links with other organisms; that is, a food web. It is visually appealing and perhaps easy to remember. However, such a picture can soon get cluttered.

References

Cherry-Garrard, A. (1922) *The Worst Journey in the World, Antarctic 1910–1913*, London, Constable and Co., Ltd.

Collins, S. (2004) 'Frozen continent: time to clean up the ice', *New Zealand Herald*, January. Available from: http://www.nzherald.co.nz/nz/news/article.cfm?c_id=1&objectid=3542263 (Accessed August 2011).

Hough, R. (1994) *Captain James Cook*, London, Hodder and Stoughton.

Kunzig, R. (1999) *The Restless Sea*, New York, W.W. Norton and Company.

McGhee, R. (2005) *The Arctic Voyages of Martin Frobisher: An Elizabethan Adventure*, Montreal and Kingston, McGill-Queen's University Press.

Richardson, J. (1844) *The Zoology of the Voyage of the H.M.S. Erebus & Terror, Under the Command of Captain Sir James Clark Ross, during the years 1839 to 1843*, By authority of the Lords Commissioners of the Admiralty, London, E. W. Janson.

Rignot, E., Velicogna, I., van den Broeke, M. R., Monaghan, A. and Lenaerts, J. (2011) 'Acceleration of the contribution of the Greenland and Antarctic ice sheets to sea level rise', *Geophysical Research Letters*, 38(5).

Scoresby, W. (1820) *An Account of the Arctic Regions, with a History and Description of The Northern Whale-Fishery*, Edinburgh.

Shackleton, E.H. (1909) *The Heart of the Antarctic*, London, Heinemann.

Solomon, S. (2001) *The Coldest March: Scott's Fatal Antarctic Expedition*, Yale University Press.

The Times (1818) 'Red snow from the Arctic regions', 4 December, p. 2.

The Times (1854) 'The Arctic Expedition', Issue no. 21879, p. 7.

Turner, J. et al. (eds) (2009) *Antarctic Climate Change and the Environment 2007–2008*, A Contribution to the International Polar Year, Cambridge, Scientific Committee on Antarctic Research.

Walker, G. and King, D. (2008) *The Hot Topic: What Can We Do about Global Warming*, Orlando, FL, Harcourt, Inc.

Acknowledgements

Chapter 1

Figures 1.1, 1.2, 1.3, 1.6. 1.7, 1.8, 1.12, 1.13 and 1.16: Copyright © Mark Brandon; Figure 1.14: Copyright © National Snow and Ice Data Center; Figure 1.15: Copyright © Arctic Council Secretariat.

Chapter 2

Figure 2.1a: From www.wikimedia.org Attribution Halvard. Licensed under the terms of GNU Free Documentation Licence; Figure 2.1b: From www.wikimedia.org Attribution Chris73. Licensed under the terms of the GNU Free Documentation Licence; Figure 2.2: Copyright © Manul Vaquero Lefanso. Licensed under Creative Commons Attribution Share-Alike 2.0 Generic Licence; Figure 2.4: Adapted from Fowler, C.M.R. (1990) *The Solid Earth: An Introduction to Global Geophysics*, Cambridge University Press; Figure 2.5: Scotese, C.R. (2001) *Atlas of Earth History,* vol. 1, *Paleogeography*, PALEOMAP Project, Arlington, Texas, USA; Figure 2.8: Copyright © Woods Hole Oceanographic Institution; Figure 2.9: Kump, L., Kasting, J.F. and Crane, R.G. (2004) *The Earth System*, Pearson Education; Figure 2.10: Archer, D. and Ramstorf, S. (2010) *The Climate Crisis*, Cambridge University Press; Figure 2.11: Reprinted by permission from Macmillan Publishers Ltd. Raymo, M.E. and Huybers, P. (2008) 'Unlocking the mysteries of the ice ages', *Nature*, vol. 451, no. 7176. Copyright © 2008; Figures 2.12, 2.16, 2.17 and 2.19: Copyright © Mark Brandon; Figure 2.13: Reprinted by permission from Macmillan Publishers Ltd. Lothi, D. et al. (2008) 'High-dioxide concentration record 650 000 and 800 000 years before present', *Nature*, vol. 453, no. 7193. Copyright © 2008; Figure 2.14a: Copyright © Walter Siegmund. Licensed under the terms of the GNU Free Documentation Licence; Figure 2.14b: Copyright © Les Hasbargen; Figure 2.14c: Copyright © Walter Hunt; Figure 2.15: Copyright © IPCC; Figure 2.18: Copyright © Hannes Grobe/AWI Licensed under Creative Commons Attribution 3 licence; Figure 2.20: Copyright © Opiola Jerzy. Licensed under the terms of the GNU Free Documentation Licence.

Chapter 3

Figures 3.2, 3.13, 3.14, 3.15 and 3.20a: Copyright © Mark Brandon; Figure 3.4: Copyright © AKG-Images; Figures 3.6: and 3.18: Copyright © NASA; Figure 3.8: Copyright © Dean Ayres; Figure 3.11: by permission of The British Library; Figure 3.12a: Copyright © William M Connolley. Licensed under the terms of GNU Free Documentation Licence; Figure 3.16: Copyright © ESA-AOES Medialab; Figure 3.17: *The Cryosphere Today* Copyright © The Polar Research Group, University of Illinois at Urbana-Champaign; Figure 3.19a: Copyright © George Durner, US Geological Survey; Figure 3.19b: Wiig, O. et al. (2003) 'Movement of female polar bears (*Ursus maritimus*) in the East Greenland ice pack', *Polar Biology*, vol. 26, August 2003, Julius Springer Verlag GmbH & co Kg; Figure 3.20b: Croxall,

J.P. et al. (2005) 'Global circumnavigations: tracking year-round ranges of non-breeding albatrosses', *Science*, vol. 307, no. 5707, American Association for the Advancement of Science; Figure 3.21: Charrassin, J-B et al. (2008) 'Southern Ocean frontal structure and sea-ice formation rates revealed by elephant seals', *Proceedings of the National Academy of Sciences*, vol. 105, no. 33 Copyright © (2008) National Academy of Sciences, USA.

Chapter 4

Figure 4.1: Copyright © Richard P. Hoblitt/US Geological Survey; Figure 4.3: Copyright © NASA; Figure 4.5: Perry, A.H and Walker, J.M. (1977) *The Ocean-Atmosphere System*, Pearson Education; Figure 4.6: Licensed under the terms of GNU Free Documentation Licence; Figures 4.9 and 4.10: Copyright © Mark Brandon; Figures 4.11 and 4.13: National Snow and Ice Data Center; Figures 4.12 and 4.14: Comiso, J.C. and Nishio, F. (2008) 'Trends in the sea ice cover using enhanced and compatible AMSR-E, SSM/1 and SMMR data', *Journal of Geophysical Research*, vol. 113, American Geophysical Union; Figures 4.15 and 4.16: Schlilzer, R. (2000) *Electronic Atlas of WOCE Hydrographic and Tracer Data*, Alfred Wegener Institute for Polar and Marine Research, www.ewoce.org; Figure 4.20: adapted from Walton, D.W.H. (1987) *Antarctic Science*, Cambridge University Press; Figure 4.22: Soloman, S. (2001) *The Coldest March*, Yale University Press; Figures 4.23, 4.24 and 4.25: Serreze, M.C. and Barry, R.G. (2005) *The Arctic Climate System*, Cambridge University Press; Figure 4.26: Yang, D. et al. (2002) 'Siberian Lena river hydrologic regime and recent change', *Journal of Geophysical Research*, vol. 107, American Geophysical Union.

Chapter 5

Figure 5.2a: adapted from Clutton-Brock, J. (2002) *Mammals*, Dorling Kindersley Ltd, a Penguin Company; Figure 5.2b: adapted from Willmer, P. et al. (2000) *Environmental Physiology of Animals*, Blackwell Publishing Ltd; Figure 5.3: Pough, F.H., Heiser, J.B. and McFarland, W.N. (1996) *Vertebrate Life*, 4th edition, Pearson Education; Figures 5.4, 5.7a, 5.8, 5.13, 5.17b and 5.20: Copyright © Mark Brandon; Figure 5.5: Copyright © Malcolm A. Ramsay; Figure 5.6: Copyright © Caroline Pond; Figure 5.7b: Copyright © NOAA; Figure 5.9: Copyright © Bunji Tagawa. By permission of the Executrix of the Estate of Bunji Tagawa; Figures 5.11 and 5.19b: Copyright © Audrey Brown; Figure 5.14: Copyright © Frederique Oliver; Figure 5.17a: Copyright © Opiola Jerzy. Licensed under the terms of the GNU Free Documentation Licence.

Chapter 6

Figure 6.2: Copyright © Imatics Inc and Canadian Museum of Nature; Figure 6.4: Copyright © Sten Porse. Licensed under the terms of GNU Free Documentation Licence; Figure 6.5: Copyright © Stephen Hudson. Licensed under the terms of GNU Free Documentation Licence; Figure 6.6: Copyright © Peter Rejcek, US Antarctic Program; Figure 6.7: Copyright © Mark Brandon; Figure 6.8: Copyright © US Fish & Wildlife Service; Figure 6.9: Copyright © Hanne Grobe/AWI. Licensed under the Creative Commons

Module team

Chair
Mark Brandon

Authors
Mark Brandon
David Robinson

Critical Readers
David Robinson
Jeff Thomas

Curriculum Manager
Kat Garrow

Consultant Authors
Audrey Brown
Lizzie Hawker
Tim Jarvis

External Module Assessor
Dr John Shears

Production Team
Jenny Barden (*Media Project Manager*)
Martin Chiverton (*Producer*)
Corinne Cole (*Media Assistant*)
Roger Courthold (*Media Developer*)
Nicky Farmer (*Module Assistant*)
Tot Foster (*Producer*)
Michael Francis (*Media Developer*)
Chris Hough (*Media Developer*)
Jenny Hudson (*Module Team Assistant*)
Martin Keeling (*Media Assistant, Rights*)
Margaret McManus (*Media Assistant, Rights*)
Bina Sharma (*Media Developer*)

Index

Pages in *italics* refer to entries mainly, or wholly, in figures or tables.

8.2 ka event 60
10 °C July isotherm 25, *26, 27,* 63, 115, 230
41 000-year world 49, 56
100 000-year world 49, 56, 231

A

abiotic factors 153
active layer 158
adaptations 123, 124, 126
    evolutionary 174
    fish 139–41
    physiological and behavioural 133, 136–7, *138,* 140
    phytoplankton 182
    plants 141–5
    polar endotherms 137–8, 235
    tiny animals 145
    in the tundra 158, 159
Adélie penguins *129,* 130, *189,* 224
Adventure, HMS 69
Agreement on the Conservation of Polar Bears (1973) 212
air pressure *94*
albatross 86, *87*
albedo 16–18, 229–30
    and latitude 93, 233
Alert, Canada, research station *5, 7,* 71
Alfred Wegener Institute for Polar and Marine Research (AWI) 79, *80*
algae 144–5, 156
    exponential increase 171–2
    photosynthesis 168–9
    see also phytoplankton
Altaic family *27*
ammonites *33,* 39, 43, 231
amphibians 164, 236

amphipods *183*
Amundsen, Roald 71, 77, 114–15
Amundsen–Scott base *206*
animals
    Antarctic Treaty protection 208–9
    Arctic protection 212, 213–14
    benthic 110
    ectothermic 124, 138–41, 236
    endothermic 124, 126–38, 235
    in a food chain 148–9
    in a food web 149, *150,* 151
    migration 159
    in ocean measurements 86, 88
    polar, future of 224–5
    polar coastlines 123
    in the taiga 163–4
    tiny, adaptations 145
    tracking 86, *87,* 160, 238
    trophic interactions *152*
    in the tundra 158–9
    see also individual animals
anoxia 141
Antarctic *3*
    activities and impacts 191–7
    climate 111–15, 137
    climate change 202–3
    climate-related impacts 220, 238
    coastal polynyas *188,* 189
    commercial whaling and sealing 68, 232
    definition 24, 28, *29*
    formation 46
    fossils 32, *33*
    ice measurements 85
    laws and regulations 206–9
    Mercator projection 12–13
    plants 141
    scientific bases and research 195–6, *197, 206*
    sea ice, next 100 years 222, 238
    temperature *5, 7,* 8

    tourism 196–7, 213
    tundra 160
    winter temperatures 112–13, 155, *223*
    see also East Antarctic Ice Sheet (EAIS); South Pole; Southern Hemisphere; Southern Ocean; West Antarctic Ice Sheet (WAIS)
Antarctic Bottom Water (AABW) 107, *108*
Antarctic Circle 22, *29*
Antarctic Circumpolar Current (ACC) 28, *29,* 46, 51, 95–7, 113, 178, *180*
Antarctic Climate Change and the Environment (ACCE) 222
Antarctic field trip 80–4
Antarctic Peninsula *193*
    climate 91
    mean atmospheric temperature 124, 234–5
Antarctic Treaty 207–9, 212
Antarctic Treaty System (ATS) 208, 209
antifreeze 139
Archaean Period *44*
Arctic *3*
    activities and impacts 198–200
    climate 115–19, 234
    climate change 203–4
    climate-related impacts 219–20
    definition 23–8
    European contact with 66–72
    habitats 25–8, 162, 165
    ice measurements 84–5, *86*
    industrial activity in 205
    last glacial maximum 63
    laws and regulations 209–12
    Mercator projection 12–13
    sea ice *102,* 103–4, 220–2, 234, 238

Arctic *contd*
  size 51, 231–2
  temperatures *5, 7, 8*, 25–8, 230
  tourism 199–200
  winter temperatures 115, 116–19,
    219, *220*, 234
  see also Arctic Ocean; Canada;
    Greenland; North Pole;
    Svalbard; taiga; tundra
Arctic Circle 22, 24
  indigenous peoples *27*, 63, 64–6,
    236
  map *26, 27*
Arctic Climate Impact Assessment
  (ACIA) 220
arctic cod *139*, 182, *183*
Arctic Council 211, 212, 213
arctic fox 126–7, *128, 130*
  in a food web 149, *150*
arctic hare 130, *150*
Arctic National Wildlife Refuge
  213
Arctic Ocean 64, 232
  chlorophyll levels 182
  fishing and whaling 198–9
  food web 182, *183*
  mean monthly temperature 116,
    117
  nutrient values 178, *179*, 237
arctic tern 159
arteries 132, *133*, 134
Article IV, Antarctic Treaty 207–8
Atlantic Ocean
  circulation pattern *108*
  salinity *106*
  temperature section *105*, 106
  see also North Atlantic
atmosphere 39, 45
  see also greenhouse effect;
    greenhouse gases; mean
    atmospheric surface
    temperature; ozone
atmospheric circulation 92–3, *94*,
  233
atomic mass 177
atoms 14, 41
Australian Antarctic Division
  (AAD) 79–80
autotrophs 148
autumn equinox 20, *21*

axes, graphical 5
axis of rotation 19–20, *21, 22*, 23,
  230

B

bacteria 169
Bagshawe, Thomas 77
Barents, Willem 67
Barrow, Sir John 70
BCE (before the common era) 31
beavers *128*, 129
behavioural adaptations 133, 136–
  7, *138*
benthic animals 110
Bering Strait 64, *65*, 198
bioaccumulation 160–1
biological community 147
biological diversity 153, 158
biological interactions 148–9
biological production, and sea ice
  181–2
biomes 153–65
biotic factors 153
birds 129
  migratory 158–9, 164
  see also penguins
Blood Falls *155*
blood flow
  ectotherms 140–1
  endotherms 132–4, 235
blubber 131–2, 134
body size and shape 134–8
body temperature control 124
  insulation 126–32, 235
  by varying blood flow 132–4,
    235
Bowers, Henry 76
BP (before present) 37
British Antarctic Survey (BAS) 79,
  80, 81, 204
British Antarctic Territory 78
British Arctic Air Route Expedition
  (1930–31) 77
British Graham Land Expedition
  (BGLE 1934–37) 77

C

calcium 177
Cambrian Period 37

Canada
  Alert research station *5, 7*, 71
  Resolute Bay *117*, 118, 158
Cape Farewell, Greenland 24, 230
capillaries 140
carbohydrates 142–3, 150
carbon dioxide *49*, 50
  greenhouse gas 45, 192–3, 202
  in the ocean 169, 181
  in photosynthesis 142–3
  in respiration 151
  in the tundra 159–60
Carboniferous Period 231
caribou 159
carnivores 148, 149
carotenoid 145, 156
Cassini projection *96*
Cenozoic Era 38, 46–8
Central England Temperature
  (CET) data set 51
cetaceans 131, 133
chemical compounds 14, 15
chemical elements 14–15
chemical formula 15
chemical symbols 14, 15
chemosynthesis 155–6
Cherry-Garrard, Apsley 76, 77
chlorine 204
chlorofluorocarbons (CFCs) 204
chlorophyll 142, 144–5
  Arctic Ocean 182
  in the Earth's oceans 169, *170*
  and nutrient concentrations 178,
    237
  in the polar seas 170, 172, 236
  Southern Ocean 180–1, 182, 237
  Southern Ocean, November–
    April levels 184, *185*
Chukotko–Kamchatkan family *27*
climate
  Antarctic 111–15, 137
  Antarctic Peninsula 91
  Arctic 115–19, 234
  Earth's, through history 39–57
  vs weather 51
  see also temperature
climate change 200–5
  next 100 years 217–20, 238
climate proxy 41–4
coal 32–3, 39, 43, 231

coastal ocean, light penetration *174*
coastal polynyas 186, *187,* 188, 189
Cold War 199
colours, spectrum *173,* 174
community 147
Comprehensive Environmental Evaluation (CEE) 208
conifer forest 163, 164–5
  albedo *16,* 17, 229–30
Consultative Parties (CPs) 208
consumers 148, 149, 151, 158, 184
continental drift 34, 35
continental shelf 210
convection currents 92
Convention for the Conservation of Antarctic Seals (CCAS) (1972) 208, 209
Convention on Conservation of Antarctic Marine Living Resources (CCAMLR) 195, 209, 212, 213
Convergence 97
Cook, Captain James 69
cool currents *95*
coreless winter 112–13, 115, 155
Coriolis effect 93
countercurrent heat exchange 132, 133, 134, 235
Cretaceous Period *36,* 37, 38, 46, 231
cryoconite hole 156
Cryogenian 45–6, 231
CryoSat mission 85
cryosphere 157
Cynognathus 34

D

day length 19–20, 22, 81–2, 123
Debenham, Frank 75
deep time 31–9
degrees of latitude 8, *9,* 10, 74, 229
degrees of longitude *9,* 10, 229
δ^{18}O 41–4, *48,* 49
density 98–9, 105, 106, 107, 109, 187
depth of ocean
  Atlantic Ocean 105–6
  and light intensity *171,* 172, *173*

and light penetration *174*
and nutrient concentrations 178, *180*
oxygen in seawater *168,* 169
and temperature profile 175, *176*
vertical migration 185–6
desert sand
  albedo *16,* 17, 229
  see also polar desert
detritivores 149
detritus 149, *150*
diatoms *169*
diel (diurnal) migration 185
dipole magnet *73,* 74, 75
direct activities 191
direct impacts 191, 192, 193, 198
distortion in maps 11–13, 239
Dobson Units (DU) *204*
dormancy 126, 144
Drake Passage *204*
dwarf hamsters 136

E

Earth
  age of 31, 37
  albedo of typical features *16*
  axis of rotation *see* axis of rotation
  climate history 39–57
  global atmospheric circulation 92–3, *94,* 233
  global sea-surface nutrient concentrations 178, *179*
  global terrestrial biomes *154*
  Lambert equal-area azimuthal projection 11, *12*
  land configuration over time *36,* 37
  magnetic field *73*
  mean global temperature 200, *201, 218,* 219
  Mercator projection 12–13
  orbit round the Sun 20, *21,* 53, *54, 55*
earthquakes 35
East Antarctic Ice Sheet (EAIS) 46–7, 101, 115, 154, 155, 202, 222
eccentricity 53, *54, 55,* 56

ecological niche 147–8, 149, 151, 164, 236
ecosystems 147–53
  boundaries 152–3
  definition 148
  large-scale 153
ectothermic animals 124, 138–41, 236
eider duck 129
elephant seals *88, 136,* 208
ellipse 53, *55*
emperor penguins 76–7, 84, 126, 137–8
endothermic animals 124, 126–38, 235
energy
  definition 15–16
  and food webs 149–52
  renewable energy 219, 226
  see also solar energy
energy balance 14–18
environment 147
environmental impact
  climate change 203–4
  shipping 198
  waste 196, *197*
Environmental Impact Assessment (EIA) 208
Eocene Period 43, 46
Equator
  day length 19
  latitude 8, *9*
  longitude 10
  solar energy 18, 21–2
equinoxes 20, *21,* 22
Erebus, HMS 70, 74
Erebus, Mount 74
erector muscles *127,* 128
Eskimo–Aleut family *27,* 63
Eskimos 65
  see also Inuit
European Project for Ice Coring in Antarctica (EPICA) *49,* 53, *55, 56, 59*
European Space Agency (ESA) CryoSat mission 85
evaporation 141, 142
Exclusive Economic Zone 199, 209
Explorer, MS *197*
exponential decay 171, 172, 174

exponential increase 171–2

F

fat
    blubber 131–2, 134
    PBDEs 160, *161*
    subcutaneous 129–30
fathom 69
feathers 129, 130, 131
feedback loops 45–6, 50, 203, 204, 214, 219
fish
    adaptations 139–41
    in food chains *183*
    light perception *174*
    see also arctic cod; icefish; krill; patagonian toothfish
fishing
    Arctic Ocean 199
    Southern Ocean 195, 213
flippers *133,* 134
food chains 148–9, *152*
    oceanic 182–6
    in the tundra 158
food webs 148
    Arctic Ocean 182, *183*
    and energy 149–52
    marine-based 170
    in the taiga *164*
foraminifera 42–3
forestry 165
fossil fuels 219, 226
    see also coal; oil and gas resources
fossils 34, 37, 75
    ammonites *33, 39,* 43, 231
    Antarctic 32, *33*
Fourth Assessment (IPCC) 218
Fram 75
Franklin, Sir John 70–1, 75
frazil ice *98,* 99, 233
Frobisher, Martin 66–7
frozen seas *see* Arctic Ocean; Southern Ocean
fur 126–9, 130, 131
fur seals 131, 208
furious fifties 95

G

geological time 37–9, 231
glacial buttercup 142, *143,* 158
glacial erratic *52*
glacial–interglacial cycling 53–7
glacial periods *see* ice ages
glacial scouring *52*
glaciers 24, 48, 51
    retreat of 220, *221,* 222
global *see* Earth
Global Positioning System (GPS) 10
Glossopteris 34
glucose 150–1
graphs 5–7
grassy fields, albedo *16,* 233
greenhouse effect 200, *201,* 202
greenhouse gases 45, 49, 192–3, 200–202
    future emissions 218–19
    see also carbon dioxide
Greenland
    Cape Farewell 24, 230
Greenland Ice Sheet (GIS) 47, 115, 154, 203
    ice-mass loss 220
    mean monthly temperature 116, *117*
guard cells *142*
guard hairs 131

H

habitats
    in an ecosystem 153
    Antarctic, loss of 202
    Arctic 25–8, 162
    definition 147
    in ice sheets 156
haemoglobin 140
hair 126–9, 131
hard law 209
herbivores 148, 149, 163, 164, 184
Heroic Age 63, 75, 76–7, 114–15, 195
heterotrophs 148
hibernation 126
high latitudes 8, 18, *19,* 22
high-nutrient low-chlorophyll (HNLC) 180

Holocene Period 59
hominins 64
Homo sapiens 64
human impact
    Antarctic 191–7
    Arctic 198–200
    climate change 217–19
    on the taiga 165
    on the tundra 160
humans 31, 39, 43, 231
hunter-gatherers 64, 65, 66
husky dog *132,* 133, 235
hydrogen atoms 41, 177

I

ice, density 98–9
    see also sea ice
ice ages 43, 51–2, 231
    Cryogenian 45–6
    EPICA ice core temperatures *56*
    see also last glacial maximum
ice cores
    dating 92
    EPICA 49, *53, 55, 56, 59*
ice crystals, nucleation *139*
ice sheets
    biomes 153, 154–6, 236
    formation 46, *47,* 48, 52, 99, 233–4
    in the last glacial maximum 57–8
    and Milanković cycles 57
    and sea levels 42, 47, 52, 58, 100, 205, 220, 237, 240
    see also East Antarctic Ice Sheet (EAIS); Greenland Ice Sheet (GIS); sea ice; West Antarctic Ice Sheet (WAIS)
ice shelves, break-up 202–3, 226, *227*
icebergs 28
    formation of 220, *221*
icefish 74–5, *140,* 195
inclination 53–4
indigenous peoples
    Arctic Circle *27,* 63, 64–6
    lack of sovereignty 68
    whaling 199
    see also Inuit

indirect activities 191
indirect impacts 191–2, 198, 211
Indo–European family *27*
infrared radiation 200, *201,* 205,
237
and ocean depth *173,* 175
infrared thermography *130*
insolation 54–6, *59*
insulation 126–32, 235
Inter-Tropical Convergence Zone
(ITCZ) *93, 94*
Intergovernmental Panel on Climate
Change (IPCC) 218, 219, *223*
International Association of
Antarctic Tour Operators (IAATO)
196
International Geophysical Year
(IGY) 206–7
International Strait 72
International Whaling Commission
(IWC) 193, 194
intra-Arctic routes 198
Inuit 65, 67, 189
Inuit Circumpolar Council 68, 211
Investigator, HMS 71
iron limitation hypothesis 180–1
iron pyrite 67
isotherms 97, 109, 111, *112,* 233
10 ºC July isotherm 25, *26, 27,*
63, 115, 230
Arctic 115–16, 234
isotopes 42
Cenozoic temperature
reconstruction *47*
δ^{18}O 41–4, *48, 49*

J

James Clark Ross, RRS 81, *82*
Japan, whaling 194

K

ka (thousands of years) 37
kinetic energy 16
krill 184, *185,* 186, 189
fishing 195, 213
future populations 224

L

Lambert equal-area azimuthal
projection 11, *12*
land bridges 64, 232
language families, Arctic Circle *27*
Larsen B ice shelf 202, *203,* 222
last glacial maximum (LGM) 57–8,
63, 64, *65,* 232
latitude
Antarctic 28, *29*
Arctic Circle 24
and day length 20
degrees of 8, *9,* 10, 229
lines of 8, *9,* 10, 12–13
and solar energy 18, *19,* 24, 230
laws
Antarctic 206–9
Arctic 209–12
hard and soft 209
Lena River discharge 118, *119,* 124
Lester, Charles 77
lichens *157*
light
and biological production 182
and oceanic vertical migration
185
and primary production 171–4,
179
and productivity 237
light intensity, and ocean depth
171, 172, *173*
lines of latitude 8, *9,* 10, 12–13
lines of longitude 8, *9,* 10, *12*
Lomonosov Ridge 210
longitude
degrees of *9,* 10, 229
lines of 8, *9,* 10, *12*
low latitudes 8, 18
Lystrosaurus 34

M

Ma (millions of years) 37
McMurdo bases 196, *197*
magnetic field 73
magnetic North Pole 72–3
magnetic South Pole 74
magnetic variation 73
map projection 11, *12,* 239

maps 10–14
global terrestrial biomes *154*
Lambert equal-area azimuthal
projection 11, *12*
Mercator projection 12–13
stereographic projection *13,* 25
marine ectotherms 138–41
marine life
food chains 182, *183*
photosynthesis 168–9
visibility of 173
see also algae; fish; penguins;
phytoplankton
mean atmospheric surface
temperature 4, *5,* 6, 25, 200, 229
Antarctic Peninsula 124, 234–5
Arctic 116, *117,* 118, 219, *220*
global 200, *201, 218,* 219
South Pole *113*
Southern Hemisphere 111, *112*
Svalbard *117,* 118, 124, 234
mean value 7
median 182
melanin 123
Mercator projection 12–13
Mesosaurus 34
Mesozoic Era 38
methane 203, 204
microbes 155, 156
microclimate 142
micromols 177–8
midnight Sun 22
migration 158–9, 164
oceanic vertical 185–6
Milanković cycle 53, 56, 57
military activity 199
millimols 177–8
minor gases 39
minutes, latitude 74
mixed layer 175, *176,* 179
mixing, and ocean stratification
175, *176*
mole 167, 177
molecules 15
monochromatic light 174
Montreal Protocol 204
moulting 131
Muscovy Company 68
myoglobin 140

N

Na–Dene family *27*
Nansen, Fridtjof 75, 77
natural resources, European
discovery of 66–70
natural selection 136, 145
nautilus *33*
navigation, polar 72–3
negative correlation 41
Nelson, Edward 76
net primary production 170
neutrons 41–2
niche 147–8, 149, 151, 164, 236
nitrate 175, 177, 178, *179*
nomogram 124, *125*
Non-Consultative Parties (NCPs)
208
non-governmental organisations
(NGOs) 211
North Atlantic, sea surface
temperature 109
North Atlantic Deep Water
(NADW) 107, *108,* 110
North Atlantic Drift 95
North Pole
day length 22
latitude 8, *9*
longitude 10
magnetic North Pole 72–3
sea surface temperature 97, 233
stereographic projection *13*
see also Arctic; polar regions
North-West Passage 70–2, 73, *117,*
158
expedition 144–5
shipping 198, 222, 238
Northern Hemisphere
last glacial maximum *58*
sea ice extent and concentration
102, 103, 234
seasons
wind direction *93*
see also Arctic; Arctic Ocean;
North Pole
Northern Sea Route 198
nucleation 92, *139*
nucleus 41
nutrients, and primary production
175, 177–81, 237

O

ocean currents 93, 95–6, 233
see also Antarctic Circumpolar
Current (ACC)
ocean measurements 86, 88
ocean surface
albedo *16, 17, 18,* 233
wind speed across 93, 95–6, 233
oceans
chlorophyll concentration in 169,
170
food chain 182–6
light penetration *174*
sea ice effect on 105–11
sea-surface concentration of
nutrients 178, *179*
stratification 175, *176*
see also Arctic Ocean; Atlantic
Ocean; depth of ocean;
Southern Ocean
oil and gas resources *210,* 211, 213
omnivores 148, 163
Ordovician Period 38
overfishing 195, 199, 213
overheating 130, 133–4
oxygen
atoms 41
concentration units 167
$\delta^{18}O$ 41–4, *48,* 49
dissolved, in seawater 110, 140–
1, 167, *168,* 169, 236
in photosynthesis 143
ozone 204, 205, 237
ozone holes 204–5

P

pack ice *98, 99,* 233–4
polynyas 186–9
see also sea ice
Palaeozoic Era 38
pancake ice *98, 99,* 105, 233, 234
Pangaea *36, 37*
parts per million (ppm) 49
patagonian toothfish *195,* 213, 237
paws *130,* 235
PBDEs (polybrominated diphenyl
ethers) 160, *161*
Peace of Westphalia 68

penguins 24
adaptations 126, 133
colony size *189*
eggs 76–7, 84, 137
feathers *129,* 130, 131
future populations 224
size 136–8
tracking 86
visibility in the sea 173
Permian Period *36,* 37, 38
persistent organic pollutants (POPs)
160–1
phosphate 175, 177, 178, *179*
photic zone 174, 178, 179
photosynthesis 142–3, 148, 150–1,
159, 236
and light 174
marine life 168–9
physiological adaptations 132–3,
136–7, 140
phytoplankton 168, *169,* 170, *174,*
183
adaptations 182
consumers of 184
nutrients required 175, 177, 178–
81
see also algae
pigment 128, 129, 145, 156
pinnipeds 130, *131,* 133
piscivorous fish *183*
plants
adaptations 141–5
Antarctic 141
in a food chain 148–9
in a food web *150,* 151
in the taiga 163, *164*
tropic interactions *152*
in the tundra 158, *159,* 236
Pliocene Period 231
polar amplification 219
Polar Bear Specialist Group 212
polar bears
adaptations 126
average surface temperature 130,
235
body fats 160, *161*
climate change, impact on 204
future populations 224
heat emission *130*
insulation 127, *128,* 129

protection 212
size 136
tracking 86, *87*, 212, 238
polar desert 113, 118
biomes 153, 154, 157
polar exploration
Antarctic field trip 80–4
earliest European 66–7
Heroic Age 63, 75, 76–7, 114–15
North-West Passage 70–2, 144–5
science as motivation 72–8
Polar Front 28, *29*, 97, 184, *185*, 232
polar management 212–13
polar ozone holes 204–5, 222
polar regions
climate of the next 100 years 217–20
human impact 225
solar energy 18, 23
temperature 4–10, 23, 230
see also Antarctic; Arctic; North Pole; South Pole
polar research stations
Alert, Canada *5*, 7, 71
Antarctic 195–6, *197, 206*
Rothera Station 82, *83*, 84, 232–3
setting-up 79
polar seas 97–104
chlorophyll concentration in 170, 172, 236
productivity 170, 237
see also Arctic Ocean; Southern Ocean
pollution 160–1
polybrominated diphenyl ethers (PBDEs) 160, *161*
polynyas 186–9
Port Lockroy *195*
positive correlation 40
positive feedback 45, 204, 214, 219
pre-Cambrian Era 37, *44*
precession 54, *55*
primary consumers 148, 149, 151, 158
primary producers 148, 149, 151, 158, 168, 236

primary production
coastal polynyas *188*, 189
and light 171–4, 179
and mixing 175, *176*
net 170
and nutrients 175, 177–81, 237
Southern Ocean *188*, 189
productivity
polar seas 170, 237
primary productivity 153, 154, 155, 236
Proterozoic Period 43, *44*, 45
Protocol on Environmental Protection (1998) 208
protons 41, 42
proxy data 40–1
climate proxy 41–4
psychrophiles 155
ptarmigan 130

Q–R

Quaternary Period 49
rabbits 127, 128
radioactive material 199, 213
see also isotopes
Rae, John 71
red blood cells 75, 140–1
red snow 144–5, 156
regulations *see* laws
reindeer 165
renewable energy 219, 226
reptiles 164, 236
research stations *see* polar research stations
Resolute Bay, Canada *117*, 118, 158
Resolution, HMS 69
respiration 143, 151, 169
ringed seals 160, *161*
rivers, in the taiga *163*
roaring forties 95, 96
rockhopper, crested penguin 136
Ross, James Clark 74
Ross, Captain Sir John 144
Ross Island 74, 197
Ross Sea 111
Rothera Station 82, *83*, 84, 232–3
Russia
Arctic territory claims 210–11

Lena River discharge 118, *119*, 124

S

saline intrusion 224
salinity 106–7, 187
salt rejection 105, 106, 107, 187
satellites
ice measurement 85, *86*
tracking animals 86, *87*, 160, 238
saturation curve 167, *168*, 236
saw-tooth pattern, temperature change *231*
scientific research
Antarctic 80–4, 195–6
modern era 78–80
pre-modern era 72–8
remote-based 84–8
see also polar research stations
Scoresby, William 72, 75
Scott, Captain Robert Falcon 75, 76, 77, 114–15, 197
sea floor depth *see* depth of ocean
sea ice
albedo *16, 17*
Antarctic, next 100 years 222, 238
Arctic *102*, 103–4, 220–2, 234, 238
and atmospheric temperature 112
and biological production 181–2
measurements 84–6
oceans, effect on 105–11
permanent extent *26*
Southern Ocean 100–4, *185*, 234
Svalbard 118, 234
see also ice sheets; pack ice
sea levels
global rise, next 100 years 222, *223*, 224
and ice sheets 42, 47, 52, 58, 100, 205, 220, 237, 240
sea smoke *98*
sea surface temperature (SST) 96–7, 109, 233
sealing 68–9, 70, 78, 232
seals
body temperature control 134

seals *contd*
  insulation 131
  in ocean measurements 86, 88
  PBDEs in 160, *161*
  protection of 208
  size 136
seasonal cycle
  prevailing winds *94*
  sea ice extent 100, *101, 102,*
    103–4
  taiga *162,* 163
seasons 19–23
seawater
  density 105, 106, 107, 109
  dissolved oxygen in 110, 140–1,
    167, *168,* 169, 236
sebaceous glands *127,* 128
secondary consumers 148, 149, 158
seeds 142, 144
Shackleton, Ernest 32, 77
Shetland Islands 24, 230
shipping 198, 222, 238
shivering 126
silicate 175, 177, 178, *179*
Simpson, George 76
skin cancer 205
snow
  albedo *16, 17,* 18, 229–30
  red snow 144–5, 152, 156
snowball Earth 45–6
snowy owls 130
sodium 177
soft law 209
solar energy 16, 18–23, 200, *201*
  and elliptical orbits 53, *55*
  and latitude 18, *19,* 24, 230
  and photosynthesis 142–3, 150–1
solar radiation *see* solar energy
Solar System, age of 31
South Georgia 24, 28, 69, *88,* 97,
  232
  whaling stations 193
South Pole
  day length 22
  latitude 8, *9*
  longitude 10
  magnetic South Pole 74
  mean atmospheric surface
    temperature *113*
  research station *5,* 7

stereographic projection *13*
  see also Antarctic; polar regions
Southern Hemisphere
  last glacial maximum *58*
  mean atmospheric surface
    temperatures 111, *112*
  sea ice
    area of *102*
    extent and concentration *101,*
      234
  sea surface temperature 96–7
  seasons, passage of *21*
  solar energy 24
  wind direction *93*
  see also Antarctic; South Pole;
    Southern Ocean
Southern Ocean
  chlorophyll levels 180–1, 182,
    184, *185,* 237
  fishing 195, 213
  food chains 184
  nutrient values 178, *179,* 237
  primary production *188,* 189
  sea ice 100–4, *185,* 234
  temperature measurements *88*
  whaling in the 193–4, 213
Southern Ocean Sanctuary 194
sovereignty 68, 77, 78, 207
space programs 80
specific heat capacity 17–18, 93,
  233, 239
spectrum, colours of *173,* 174
spring equinox 20, *21*
stereographic projection *13,* 25
stomata 141, *142*
stratification, oceans 175, *176*
stress
  climatic 159
  physical 123–4, 130
subcutaneous fat 129–30
subduction zones 35
summer solstice 20, *21,* 22
summer temperatures 7
  Antarctic 111–12
  Arctic 115–19
  tundra 157
supercooled fish 139
surface area to volume ratio 134–6,
  142
Svalbard 78

coal mines 32–3
mean atmospheric temperature
  117, 118, 124, 234
reindeer 165
sea ice 118, 234

T

taiga *154,* 162–5
tectonic plates 35, 37, 230
temperature
  Atlantic Ocean water *105,* 106
  Earth's
    last 3 million years 48–51,
      231
    through history 39, 43, *44,*
      231
  and energy 15–16
  EPICA ice core *56, 59*
  global cooling in the Cenozoic
    46–7
  and greenhouse gases 192
  and habitats in the Arctic 25–8,
    230
  and oxygen in seawater 167,
    168, 169, 236
  polar regions 4–10, 23, 230
  range 7, 229
  sea surface temperature 96–7,
    109, 233
  Southern Ocean *88*
  taiga *162*
  and wind chill 124–5
  Younger Dryas 60
  see also body temperature
    control; climate; climate
    change; ice ages; mean
    atmospheric surface
    temperature; summer
    temperatures; winter
    temperatures
temperature profiles 175, *176*
temperature section, Atlantic Ocean
  105, 106
Terra Nova expedition 76–7
Terror, HMS 70, 74
tertiary consumers 148, 149
thermocline 175, *176*
thermohaline circulation *108,* 109
thermohaline disruption 224

tilt 53–4, *55, 56*
time, deep time 31–9
timeline *38, 39,* 43, *44,* 231
tourism 226
    Antarctic 196–7, 213
    Arctic 199–200
    and traditional ecological
      knowledge 211
Traditional Ecological Knowledge
  (TEK) 211
Trans-Antarctic Mountains 75
trans-Arctic routes 198
treeline 25, *26,* 28, 163, 230
Triassic *34,* 231
trophic levels 149, *150, 152,* 164,
  183, 236
Tropic of Cancer 20, *21*
Tropic of Capricorn 20, *21*
tundra 25, *154,* 157–62, 236
  travel restrictions *204*
turbulent mixing 175, *176*

U

U-shaped valley *52*
Ukraine, scientific expeditions 78
ultraviolet radiation 204, 205, 237
United Nations Convention on the
  Law of the Sea (UNCLOS) 209,
  210, 212, 213
units, graphical *6*
Universe, age of 31
Uralic family *27,* 63

V

variables 40, 41
veins 132, *133,* 134
ventifacts *157*
vertical profiles *180*
Viking settlements 66
viscosity, blood 140
visibility, marine life 173
volcanic ash 92
voles 164
Vostok *206*

W

walruses 131
warm currents *95*
warm water polynyas *187*

waste, environmental impact 196,
  197
water
    chemical formula 15, 41
    density 98–9, 187
    molecule 177
    in photosynthesis 142–3
    specific heat capacity 239
    vital function of 123
    see also seawater
water flow, plants 141–2
water mass 107, *108,* 110
waves 91–7, 233
  and turbulent mixing 175, *176*
weasel 128
weather 51
Weddell, James 69
Weddell Sea 111
Wegener, Alfred 34, 35
West Antarctic Ice Sheet (WAIS)
  47, 101, 154, 202, 222
West Wind Drift 96
wet fur *128,* 129, 131
whales 131, *194*
whaling 68–9, 70, 78, 232
    Arctic Ocean 199
    monitoring 194
    in the Southern Ocean 193–4,
      213
Whisky Bay 226, *227*
white dryas *60, 141*
wildfires 164–5
wildlife *see* animals
Wilson, Edward 76–7
wind chill 124–5
winds 91–7, 233
    coastal polynya formation *187,*
      188
    and turbulent mixing 175, *176*
winter mixing *176*
winter solstice 20, *21*
winter temperatures 7, 91
    Antarctic 112–13, 155, *223*
    Arctic 115, 116–19, 219, *220,*
      234
    Scott and Amundsens'
      expeditions 114–15

Y–Z

Younger Dryas 59, 60, 224
zooplankton *183,* 184, 186